1993

THE HOUSE OF SI ABD ALLAH

The House of Si Abd Allah

The Oral History of a Moroccan Family

Recorded, Translated, and Edited by

Henry Munson, Jr.

Yale University Press
New Haven and London

Published with assistance from
the Louis Stern Memorial Fund.

Designed by James J. Johnson
and set in Caledonia Roman type.
Printed in the United States of America by
Vail-Ballou Press, Binghamton, N.Y.

Library of Congress Cataloging in Publication Data

Muhammad, al-Hajj.
  The house of Si Abd Allah.

  Narrations of: al-Hajj Muhammad and Fatima Zohra.
  Bibliography: p.
  Includes index.
    1. Si 'Abd Allāh family.   2. Morocco—Genealogy.
3. Morocco—history—20th century.   4. Islam—Morocco.
I. Munson, Henry, 1946– . II. Fatima Zohra.
III. Title.
CS1749.S52   1984   964'.04'0922 [B]   83–19837
ISBN 0–300–03084–3 (cloth)
        0–300–05029–1 (pbk.)

10 9 8 7 6 5 4 3 2

TO MY WIFE

Contents

Illustrations

Photographs following page 142

Preface

This is an oral history of a Moroccan family composed primarily of a peasant named Si Abd Allah (1870–1932), his eight children (five of whom were still alive in 1977), and his thirty-one grandchildren (most of whom were married with children of their own in 1977). The history of this family is at the same time a miniature social and cultural history of northwestern Morocco from the late nineteenth to the late twentieth century.

The book is constructed from the life histories of the members of "The House of Si Abd Allah" as narrated and interpreted by two of Si Abd Allah's grandchildren: al-Hajj Muhammad, a Muslim "fundamentalist" peddler of Tangier, and Fatima Zohra, a "westernized" young woman who is a part-time university student in the United States, where she lives with her husband and children. In recording the way al-Hajj Muhammad and Fatima Zohra describe the people and events in their lives and the lives of their relatives, I have tried to convey some idea of how everyday life and history are interpreted by a "traditional" Muslim man and a "modern" Muslim woman. (The cultural dichotomy represented by al-Hajj Muhammad and Fatima Zohra is discussed in the Introduction.)

Most of al-Hajj Muhammad's narrative and roughly half of Fatima Zohra's were recorded in northwestern Morocco from June

1976 through December 1977, when I was engaged in research related to my dissertation, "Islam and Inequality in Northwest Morocco" (University of Chicago, 1980). During this period, my wife and children and I lived for three months in the Jbalan highland village where Si Abd Allah and his eight children were born and raised, and where some of his children and grandchildren still live. (This village is referred to as "the village of the streams" in this book.) We also lived for fifteen months in the city of Tangier, where most of Si Abd Allah's surviving children and grandchildren now live. (We lived on the outskirts of the popular quarter here referred to as "the cobblestone quarter.")

About half of Fatima Zohra's narrative was recorded in the United States from 1978 through 1980. And she also helped, during this period in the United States, to fill in a number of lacunae in al-Hajj Muhammad's narrative by telling me how he typically spoke of certain people.

Oral history inevitably reflects the social situation in which it is recorded (Crapanzano 1980: ix, 8; Ives 1983), and this one is no exception. However, in the event of a conflict between the obligation to reveal all the dimensions of this social situation and the obligation to avoid endangering those whose history has been recorded, the latter takes precedence. Moreover, Fatima Zohra has specifically requested that this subject not be discussed. So it is not.

But I should emphasize that the narratives of both al-Hajj Muhammad and, to a lesser degree, Fatima Zohra were "recorded" in various contexts by various methods. I taped almost all of al-Hajj Muhammad's description of his own life and fragments of the rest of his narrative as a whole. But I have incorporated into this narrative, not only statements attributed to al-Hajj Muhammad by Fatima Zohra, but also statements I overheard him make on a variety of "everyday" and festive occasions during the year and a half we were in Morocco. This is significant for the obvious reason that people sitting in a room with a "foreigner" and a tape recorder do not speak the same way they do with their friends and relatives in everyday life. As for Fatima Zohra's narrative, none of it was taped. I wrote it down as she narrated it, both in Morocco and in the United States. Roughly 10 percent of it consists of statements I overheard her make while speaking to her relatives in Morocco. She has helped me edit both narratives. And she has checked the accuracy of my translation of them from Moroccan Arabic to English. She has also checked the accuracy of my translation of the Quranic verses frequently quoted by al-Hajj Muhammad (cited here by chapter and verse according to the standard Egyptian enumeration.)

I have done my best to protect the anonymity of the family. Pseudonyms have been used to refer to some individuals as well as to communities that play a central role in the family history. And surnames have generally been replaced by single letters (not necessarily initials).

I have altered several passages to avoid "second-person" references to myself.

Most of the dates in the genealogical outline and the genealogical diagrams are approximate, because exact dates of birth and death are not considered significant in Moroccan popular culture and are not generally known.

References to money refer to the rate of exchange in 1977, when 4.50 Dirhams equaled one American dollar. Money is usually referred to in terms of "francs" (450 francs to a dollar) or "riyals" (one riyal equals fifty francs *in northern Morocco*).

There are no footnotes to the text. The Introduction places the family history in its broader social and cultural context; the meaning of Arabic words is provided parenthetically, as needed, and there is a glossary at the end of the book. The genealogical outline and the individual diagrams preceding the seven sections should enable the reader to keep track of the dramatis personae despite the fact that different kinsmen share such common names as Muhammad, Abd Allah, and Rahma.

With respect to names, it should be noted that a few which appear to be virtually identical are in fact distinct. Thus Muhammad and Mhammad are different names, as are Fatna, Fatma, and Fatima.

A small number of honorific titles frequently precede names. The honorific *Si*, as in Si Abd Allah, is in principle used only before the names of *tulba*, men who have memorized the Quran. But it is in fact also used to address and refer to men to whom respect is owed for other reasons, usually wealth, power, or a secular education. Thus, Si Muhammad Qasim merits the title *Si* because he is the wealthiest peasant in his village. *Tulba* condemn this usage but generally conform to it nevertheless, at least in address if not reference. The honorific titles *Sidi* and *La* (short for *Lalla*) precede the names of men and women who are believed to be patrilineal descendants of the Prophet Muhammad. The term *Sidi* can also be used as a respectful secular form of *address*, as in the phrase *Naam ya Sidi*, which means "Yes, sir." But *Sidi* is not used as a form of *reference* in this secular sense. The honorific titles *al-Hajj* and *al-Hajja* precede the names of men and women who have made the pilgrimage to Mecca.

Al is the definite article "the." In spoken Moroccan Arabic, the *l* of *al* assimilates to following dental, alveolar, and alveopalatal consonants. Thus before nouns beginning in *t, d, r, s, z, sh, j,* and *n, al* becomes *at, ad,* etc.

With respect to transliteration, I have had to use an extremely simplified version of the standard system employed by the *International Journal of Middle East Studies*. The *'ayn*, or voiced pharyngeal fricative, and vowel length are not indicated at all, nor are the emphatic consonants distinguished by diacritics. Readers who know Arabic will generally know where the missing symbols would occur in a more precise transliteration. And readers who do not know Arabic will find the simplified transliteration easier to read, thanks to the absence of diacritics representing sounds with which they are not familiar. Generally speaking, the letters that do occur in the transliteration represent essentially the same sounds as in English, with the following exceptions. *Kh* represents the *ch* of *Bach* (a voiceless velar fricative). *Gh* represents a sound similar to the uvular or "rolled" *r* of French, as in *Maurice*. Both *kh* and *gh* involve vibration of the uvula at the back of the mouth. But the vocal cords vibrate when *gh* is pronounced whereas they do not when *kh* is pronounced. *Q* is like a *k*, but is articulated farther back on the soft palate of the roof of the mouth. A single quotation mark within a word, as in *a'ila* ("family"), represents the glottal stop, a quick closure of the vocal cords so that air cannot pass through them, followed by the opening of the vocal cords so that air does pass through them. This consonant frequently replaces *t* in both American and British English, as in the Cockney pronunciation of *bottle*. When said in isolation, English words beginning with a vowel usually actually have a glottal stop before this vowel, as in *apple*. Our transliteration does not indicate the glottal stop when it occurs at the beginning of a word. (This is true of most transliterations of Arabic.)

Arabic names that are well known in their anglicized or gallicized forms, such as *Quran, Tangier,* and *Zohra,* are given in these forms rather than in transliteration.

A number of institutions and individuals have contributed to the creation of this book. My fieldwork in Morocco was made possible by fellowships from the Social Science Research Council and the Fulbright-Hays program of the Office of Education. And it was greatly facilitated by the Moroccan Ministry of Housing and Urbanism. I would also like to thank the University of Maine at Orono for a Faculty Summer Research Award that enabled me to complete the final version of the introduction.

Rose Mucci, of the Department of Anthropology at the University of California at Santa Barbara, and Lillian Shirley, of the Department of Anthropology at the University of Maine at Orono, typed the final manuscript. Steve Bicknell, also of the Department of Anthropology at the University of Maine at Orono, drew the genealogical diagrams. Paul Heuston, of the Department of Anthropology at the University of California at Santa Barbara, drew the map.

For various forms of assistance and advice, I am grateful to the following people: Janet Abu-Lughod, James Acheson, Richard T.

PREFACE

Antoun, Daniel Blaise, Donald E. Brown, Vincent Crapanzano, Dale Eickelman, Ernest Gellner, Alex and Julie Grab, David Hart, Elvin Hatch, Edward Ives, George Joffe, Roger and Terri Joseph, Jack LeCamus, Mattison Mines, Jim Paul, Deborah Rogers, David Sanger, David Seddon, Raymond T. Smith, Jean-Claude Vatin, Jacques Vignet-Zunz, Barbara Voorhies, John Waterbury, and Steven Youra. I would also like to thank Mary Douglas, Richard Feinberg, and Michael Meeker for their comments on a preliminary version of my paper "Geertzian Interpretive Anthropology and the Analysis of Islam in Morocco." I have taken some of their suggestions into consideration in writing the introduction of this book. I am also grateful to Ellen Graham and Barbara Folsom of Yale University Press for their suggestions concerning the introduction and the editing of the book as a whole.

The photographs were taken by R. Bernikho, Daniel Blaise, George Joffe, and Jacques Vignet-Zunz. The people whose faces appear in photographs are not members of the House of Si Abd Allah.

My most obvious debt is to al-Hajj Muhammad and Fatima Zohra, especially Fatima Zohra, who participated in virtually every phase of the gestation of this oral history. She has expressed the hope that by making people aware of what it means to be poor in Morocco, and what it means to be a woman there, this book will encourage the present and future governments of that country to alter many of the conditions depicted in this history of the House of Si Abd Allah. I share that hope.

Finally, I would like to thank my wife and children for their patience and support—and everything else.

Henry Munson, Jr.

Orono, Maine
July 1983

Genealogical Outline of the House of Si Abd Allah

(All dates approximate)

SI ABD ALLAH   and his wife   FATNA
1870–1932   1900–1954

CHILDREN OF SI ABD ALLAH	CHILDREN'S SPOUSES, GRANDCHILDREN AND SPOUSES, AND NUMBER OF GREAT-GRANDCHILDREN IN 1977
1. **Fatma** (1914–1930)	*Husband*: Abd as-Slam B., shoemaker. *Children*: none.
2. **Si Muhammad** (1917–1943), peasant and reciter of the Quran in the village of the streams	*Wife*: Khadduj A. *Children*: one. **Rahma** (1938–). First married to and divorced by her mother's sister's son, a peasant and charcoalmaker. Then married her present husband, Mustafa, son of Shama (her father's sister's son), a waiter in an ice cream parlor in Tangier. Four children.
3. **Shama** (1918–1960)	*First husband*: rich government official in Casablanca. *Children*: none. *Second husband*: Abd as-Slam B., the shoemaker who married Shama after his first wife, Shama's older sister Fatma, died in childbirth. *Children*: four.

al-Hajj Muhammad (1932–). Peddler in Tangier. Married nine times to eight women (one remarriage). All but the latest marriage to Rahma, daughter of the *fqih* Muhammad A., ended in divorce. Claims that the daughter of one of his wives is his child.

Ahmad (1934–). Factory worker in Belgium and landlord in Tangier. First married and divorced his father's sister's daughter. Then married his present wife Fatma, who came to Tangier from the Ghmaran highlands. Five children.

Mustafa (1935–). Waiter in an ice-cream parlor in Tangier. First married and divorced woman from the Ghmaran highlands. Then married his present wife Rahma, daughter of Si Muhammad (his mother's brother's daughter). Four children.

Fatima (1939–). Wife of Mshish, a flower vender in Gibraltar. They live in Tangier. Eight children.

Third husband: Si Muhammad A., peasant, charcoalmaker and former bandit, whom she divorced after a few years.

Children: two.

Habiba (1943–). Cleaning woman in Belgium and landlady in Tangier. Married and divorced twice. Now living with factory worker in Brussels.

Zohra (1947–). First husband died. Now married to Chino, a laborer in Tangier, originally from the Ghmaran highlands. Three children.

4. **Amina**
(1919–)

Husband: Si Muhammad Qasim, the wealthiest peasant in the village of the streams.

Children: six.

Muhammad (1937–). Peasant and charcoalmaker in the village of the streams. Married

to Slama from the village of the weavers.
Nine children.

al-Ayyashi (1940–). Miller, peasant, and
charcoalmaker in the village of the streams.
Married to Zohra daughter of *at-Talib*
Muhammad B. of the village of the streams.
One child.

Khdiuwij (1942–). Wife of peasant and charcoalmaker in the village of the two springs.
Four children.

Hmidu (1945–). Peasant and charcoalmaker
in the village of the streams. Married to
Zohra, daughter of Si Abd as-Slam al-M.,
from Bni Yidir.

Abd as-Slam (1950–). Peasant and charcoalmaker in the village of the streams. Married
to Malika B. from the village of the shoemakers. One child.

Hamman (1953–). Ladies' man and loafer in
the village of the streams.

5. **Suudiyya**
(1920–)

First husband: Si Ahmad Bu H., *fqih* (teacher
of the Quran) in the village of the two springs.
Children: two.

Si Muhammad (1939–). Peasant, charcoalmaker, and reciter of the Quran in the village of the two springs. Married to Rahma
from the village of al-Hsakra in the *qbila* of
Bni Yidir. Five children.

Abd as-Slam (1940–). Fruit and vegetable
transporter in Tangier. Married to La Slama,
daughter of La Ftuma. Seven children.

Second husband: Ahmad al-M., night watchman in Tangier.
Children: two.

Muhammad (1949–). Shoemaker in Tangier.
Married to Zohra from the *qbila* of Bni
Yidir. Three children.

Malika (1954–). Wife of Abd as-Slam Q.,

sales clerk in a bazaar in Tangier. One child.

6. **Hmid** (1923–), laborer in Tangier

First wife: Aysha (his father's brother's daughter). Divorced her after two and a half months.

Second wife: Zohra, sister of the *fqih* of the village of the streams.

Children: five.

> **Abd al-Aziz** (1955–). Housepainter in Tangier.
>
> **Fatma** (1959–). Seamstress in a "lingerie factory" in Tangier.
>
> **Halima** (1960–). Seamstress in a "lingerie factory" in Tangier.
>
> **Latifa** (1966–). Student in Tangier.
>
> **Abd al-Latif** (1969–). Student in Tangier.

7. **Mhammad** (1925–), peasant in the village of the streams (car "watchman" in Tangier as of November 1980)

First wife: Fatma B. from the village of al-Hrisha. Divorced her after many years of marriage.

Children: four.

> **Muhammad** (1948–). Housepainter and smuggler in Tangier. Married to Najjat. One child.

Second wife: Aysha d Sfiyya, sister of *at-Talib* Muhammad, from the village of the streams. Nicknamed *at-Tirrum* (the "Butt").

> **Rahma** (1954–). Wife of factory worker in Tangier. One child.
>
> **Abd Allah** (1958–). Housepainter in Tangier. Divorced first wife from village of the spring of as-Snad. Now married to second wife from the village of Hammadish.
>
> **Abd as-Slam** (1962–). Goatherd in the village of the streams. Married to Ftuma (his mother's sister's daughter). Factory worker in Tangier as of November 1980.

8. **al-Hajja Khadduj** (1926–)

Husband: al-Hajj M.B. (1890–1980), merchant in Tangier.

Children: five.

Fatima Zohra (1950–). Part-time university student in the United States. Two children.

Zubida (1952–). Wife of television repairman in Tangier. One child.

Rhimu (1954–). University student in Rabat.

Suad (1960–). Retarded girl in Tangier.

Nufissa (1961–). Graduate of the American School in Tangier.

Introduction

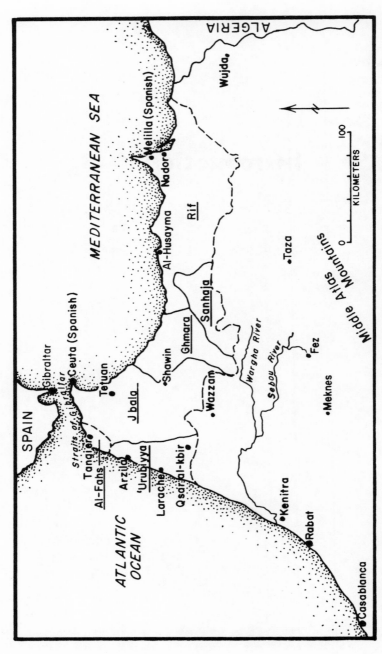

Northern Morocco. The broken line is the boundary of the Spanish Zone, 1912–1956.

ORAL HISTORY, LIKE THE NOVEL, can help us to understand great historical transformations as they are experienced by "ordinary people" during the course of their everyday lives. And it can help us to explain how the semantic structures of religions, cultures, and ideologies interact with economic, social, and political structures to both shape and be shaped by this "everyday" experience of history. *The House of Si Abd Allah,* at any rate, was written in order to contribute to such understanding and explanation.

This history of a Muslim family of Morocco is told in the words of a "fundamentalist" Muslim man and a "westernized" Muslim woman. These two cousins, al-Hajj Muhammad the peddler and Fatima Zohra the housewife and part-time university student, have radically different conceptions of their religion and of the major historical processes that have transformed their family and country over the past century. Among the most conspicuous of these processes are "imperialism" and "nationalism," "dependence" and "modernization," the incipient change in the status of women, and the large-scale transformation of landless peasants into "the urban poor" of Morocco and "the guest workers" of Europe. This oral history is about these processes as they have been experienced by a particular Moroccan family over three generations. It is also more specifically about the role of Islam in shaping the way Moroccan

Muslims interpret such phenomena—and the role of such phenomena in shaping the way Moroccan Muslims interpret Islam.

Oral history is a record not just of events, but of the way events are understood by those who participate in them. And the significance attributed to events by the narrators of oral history can provide considerable insight into the basic structures of belief and value in terms of which they think and act. By contrasting the way al-Hajj Muhammad and Fatima Zohra interpret the same actions and perceive the same people, I have tried to create a portrait of Islam as it is understood by two believers who have spent much of their lives in very different social and cultural environments. And I have particularly tried to convey a sense of the significance of the terms *fundamentalism* and *westernization* in the Islamic context.

Al-Hajj Muhammad's narrative shows how the "ideology" of Islamic fundamentalism is related to the basic world view and ethos of "traditional" Islam. His narrative also demonstrates that Muslim fundamentalists define their socioeconomic and nationalistic grievances in religious terms and generally fuse them with grievances of an irreducibly religious and cultural character. Thus, al-Hajj Muhammad condemns the Moroccan elite for being wealthy while most Moroccans are poor, for not eliminating foreign domination of the Moroccan economy, and for having assimilated the culture of "the Christian" (the westerner) in violation of the laws of God as interpreted from a Muslim fundamentalist perspective. Islamic fundamentalism cannot be reduced to a mere expression of any one or two of these three categories of discontent (socioeconomic, nationalistic, and religious). And if one wishes to explain the political appeal of Islamic fundamentalism in the Islamic world today, it is necessary to understand how these different kinds of discontent are interpreted and fused in the mind of the fundamentalist believer. One of the most valuable aspects of al-Hajj Muhammad's narrative is precisely the insight it provides into these processes of interpretation and fusion.

Fatima Zohra's narrative, on the other hand, demonstrates that, although Islam remains basic to the sense of self and national identity of westernized Muslims, and although they often share many of the socioeconomic and nationalistic grievances of Muslim fundamentalists, they generally conceive of and articulate them in a relatively secular idiom. Among the grievances that pervade Fatima Zohra's narrative are her resentment of foreign domination, which she perceives as affecting virtually every aspect of Moroccan society, and her resentment of the subordinate status of the Moroccan woman. Her reflections on the cultural and psychological effects of colonialism are often reminiscent of the writings of Frantz Fanon and Albert Memmi (Fanon 1952 and Memmi 1972). And her views concerning the status of women in Morocco often resemble those of Arab feminists such as Fadela M'rabet and Nawal El Saadawi (M'rabet 1967 and 1977; El Saadawi 1982). But Fatima Zohra is not of a radical ideological orientation. In fact, she is not committed to any specific ideology at all. Nevertheless, implicit in her general cultural orientation is what would be called a "liberal Democratic" perspective in the United States.

The narratives of both al-Hajj Muhammad and Fatima Zohra are also intended to convey a sense of the specifically religious dimension of Islam as it is experienced in ritual as well as in daily life. Despite the interest generated by the Iranian revolution of 1978–79, very little attention has been paid to "the religious experience" in Islam. Passages such as al-Hajj Muhammad's description of prayer (in III.10) and Fatima Zohra's descriptions of the visitation of saints (in III.3 and VII.2) provide considerable insight into the nature of such experiences "from the believer's point of view."

THE FAMILY

As noted in the Preface, "the house of Si Abd Allah" consists primarily of Si Abd Allah himself, his eight children (five daughters and three sons), and his thirty-one grandchildren. The book is structured in terms of the life histories of these forty people. (The "family" or *a'ila*, also includes a fourth generation of children too young to figure prominently in this history.) The lives of kinsmen particularly significant to al-Hajj Muhammad and/or Fatima Zohra are described in considerable detail, while those of other kinsmen are summarized in a paragraph or two. Generally, each life history is first narrated by al-Hajj Muhammad from his fundamentalist perspective, and then by Fatima Zohra from her relatively westernized one. Some of the life histories, however, are narrated by only one of the two cousins.

Si Abd Allah himself (1870–1932) lived and died in "the village of the streams" in the Jbalan highlands of northwestern Morocco. He was the wealthiest peasant in this village, owning its sole water mill and (according to al-Hajj Muhammad) four hectares of arable valley land. Si Abd Allah's first child, his daughter Fatma (1914–30), was married to a shoemaker and died in childbirth. Si Abd Allah's second child, his son Si Muhammad (1917–43), was a peasant and a *talib* (reciter of the Quran) in the village of the streams. Si Abd Allah's third child, his daughter Shama (1918–60), was first married to a government official in Casablanca. After this husband's death, she married the shoemaker widower of her sister Fatma. And when this husband died, she married a peasant and charcoalmaker who had been a bandit before the imposition of the Spanish Protectorate upon northern Morocco (1912–56). Shama eventually divorced this third husband. She spent much of her adult life in Tangier, where most of her children, including al-Hajj Muhammad, were born. Si Abd Allah's fourth child, his daughter Amina (1919–), is married to a man who is now the wealthiest peasant in the village of the streams and who cheated the children of Si Abd Allah out of most of their father's arable valley land. Si Abd Allah's fifth child, his daughter Suudiyya (1920–), was first married to a *fqih* (teacher of the Quran and leader of congregational prayers) in the village of the two springs, a highland village not far from the village of the streams. When this husband died, she married a peasant and charcoalmaker who eventually migrated to Tangier, where he became a night watchman. Si Abd Allah's sixth child, his son Hmid (1923–), used to be a peasant and charcoalmaker in the village of the streams, but he migrated to Tangier and became a laborer in construction and then a laborer for a tilemaker with a small shop in the cobblestone quarter. Si Abd Allah's seventh child, his son Mhammad (1925–), has been a peasant in the village of the streams most of his life. But he migrated to Tangier and became a "car watchman" in November of 1980, *after* the narratives of this oral history had been recorded. Si Abd Allah's eighth child, his daughter Khadduj (1926–), married a merchant who once owned one of the biggest bazaars in Tangier. But this merchant, Fatima Zohra's father, eventually died penniless. Khadduj has made the pilgrimage to Mecca, so she is called al-Hajja Khadduj. She has lived most of her life in Tangier. But she has also lived for about a year in Belgium and for several years in the United States, with her daughter Fatima Zohra.

Of Si Abd Allah's thirty-one grandchildren, twenty-one live in Tangier, seven remain in the mountains, two work and live eleven months of the year in Belgium (where both al-Hajj Muhammad and Fatima Zohra also used to work), and one (Fatima Zohra) lives in the United States. (One of the grandchildren in Tangier, Abd as-Slam son of Mhammad, migrated to Tangier after this history had been recorded, so the fact that he is now a factory worker in Tangier rather than a goatherd in the village of the streams is not mentioned in his life history. See VI.5.) The seven grandchildren remaining in the mountains are generally peasants and charcoalmakers or the wives of peasants and charcoalmakers. The twenty-one grandchildren in Tangier include twelve women and nine men. Except for two teenage seamstresses in a lingerie factory (a "sweatshop"), none of these twelve women was employed in 1976–77. Most of them are the wives of petty tradesmen (including a flower vendor in Gibraltar), laborers, unskilled factory workers, and other irregularly employed workers who generally earned less than $67 (300.00 DH) a month in 1977. The nine grandsons of Si Abd Allah in Tangier have similar kinds of occupations and incomes (except for Abd al-Latif son of Hmid, who was in school in 1976–77). The two grandchildren of Si Abd Allah in Belgium are a factory worker and a cleaning woman, both of whom have invested their savings in houses and land in Tangier. These two emigrant workers (al-Hajj Muhammad's brother

7

Ahmad and his half-sister Habiba) are financially better off than their kinsmen in Morocco, who generally have an extremely difficult time "making ends meet." Fatima Zohra, the granddaughter of Si Abd Allah who lives in the United States, is also financially better off than most of her relatives in Morocco. But she is by no means wealthy by American standards. She is married to a professor.

Aside from the lives of Fatima Zohra and several of her sisters (who shall be discussed below), the history of the house of Si Abd Allah is a miniature social and cultural history of the transformation of the generally impoverished peasantry of the Jbalan highlands of northwestern Morocco into the "lumpenproletariat" and nascent working class of Tangier, where the workers in Europe own homes and plan to retire. (The "lumpenproletariat" consists of the urban poor without regular incomes.) In this respect, *The House of Si Abd Allah* is analogous to Oscar Lewis's *The Children of Sanchez,* with Europe replacing the United States as the destination of labor emigration from an underdeveloped country with too few jobs for its people.

But Fatima Zohra and her sisters add another social and cultural dimension to *The House of Si Abd Allah.* Fatima Zohra's father, al-Hajj M.B., was once a wealthy merchant in Tangier. He had owned several bazaars that catered to European tourists. But he was reportedly cheated out of his half of his largest bazaar by his partner. He then had several smaller shops and a series of jobs. He worked as a watchman on a boat in the harbor of Tangier, as a supervisor of longshoremen, as a purchaser of food for a hospital, and then as an orderly and watchman in a hospital. He eventually died penniless in 1980. But for most of his life, al-Hajj M.B. was wealthier than anyone in the house of Si Abd Allah. And, although his only education had consisted of the memorization of the Quran, he was keenly aware of the social and economic value of a modern "Christian" (i.e., Western) style education. So he enrolled all of his five daughters in school, except for one who is retarded. (No girls in the house of Si Abd Allah had ever attended school before.) And he

8

even enrolled two of Fatima Zohra's younger sisters, Rhimu and Nufissa, at the American School of Tangier. This scandalized everyone in the house of Si Abd Allah. Al-Hajj Muhammad recalls:

> When al-Hajj M.B. first decided to send his daughters Rhimu and Nufissa to the American School in Tangier, I told him that if he sent his daughters to a Christian school, they would become Christians. He and my aunt Khadduj said no. They said their daughters would meet rich Moroccan men at a Christian school because all rich Moroccans send their children to Christian schools. . . . And just as I warned al-Hajj M.B. many, many years ago, they have become like Christians. What Muslim girl would smoke cigarettes in front of their mother as they do? [VII.3]

Rhimu and Nufissa not only studied at the American School in Tangier, where many of their classmates were American, they also studied for several years at American schools in the United States, where they lived with Fatima Zohra and her husband. They have thus assimilated a great deal of American culture, more so than Fatima Zohra (who never attended the American School in Tangier and did not go to the United States until she was eighteen). Rhimu and Nufissa generally wear blue jeans and sweaters, whereas most of the other women of the house of Si Abd Allah wear *jillabas,* hooded outer garments that descend to the ankles. (The brown woolen *jillabas* worn by Jbalan men reach just below the knee.) Most of the other women of the family also wear the veil, which Rhimu, Nufissa, and Fatima Zohra have never worn. The westernized cultural orientation of these young women is regarded as "Christian" by most of their relatives. And it is condemned.

But Fatima Zohra and her sisters not only represent the westernized dimension of Moroccan culture, they also connect the house of Si Abd Allah to the Moroccan elite. This is primarily true of Fatima Zohra's sister Rhimu, who was a student at Muhammad V University in Rabat when this oral history was recorded. Rhimu is a good-looking young woman who has had a number of "boy friends," two of whom are the scions of prominent families of the Moroccan elite. One of these young men is a professor at Muhammad V University. He asked Rhimu to marry him but insisted that she live with his family. She refused. Commenting on this professor, who is a Marxist, Fatima Zohra notes: "This great revolutionary who wanted to marry my sister wanted her to live with his family so that his mother and sister could treat her as their servant."

Another one of Fatima Zohra's sisters, Zubida, studied at Moroccan public schools. And Fatima Zohra contends that "she could have passed the *baccalauréat* exam but she had to leave high school to come to New York with my parents when I was married in 1971." Zubida did not continue her studies in the United States, where she only stayed for a year. She is of a far more traditional cultural orientation than Fatima Zohra, Rhimu, and Nufissa. Fatima Zohra describes how her two westernized sisters ridiculed Zubida when she sacrificed a chicken at the tomb of the patron saint of Tangier to induce him to cure her husband's cold. Her husband is a successful television repairman.

Fatima Zohra herself is the oldest daughter of al-Hajj M.B. and al-Hajja Khadduj (seven of their twelve children died in infancy). Her mother forced her to stay at home and take care of her younger sisters after she obtained the certificate (*ash-shahada*) at the end of elementary school. Her parents, especially her mother, tried to force her to get married, but she refused. Then, when she was about sixteen years old, Fatima Zohra went to work in Belgium, where her cousins al-Hajj Muhammad, Ahmad, and Habiba already had jobs. After working in Brussels for about two years (as a salesclerk in a department store and a cook in a restaurant), Fatima Zohra persuaded her father to allow her and Rhimu to go to the United States to work and study. Everyone in the family was convinced that Fatima Zohra's father was insane to allow his young daughters to travel to a "Christian" country where they had no relatives.

In New York City, Fatima Zohra attended courses in English and high-school subjects at night while working as a waitress in a Greek restaurant by day. She eventually obtained her high-school equivalency diploma and went on to study at the university level. In

1971, she married a graduate student, who is now a professor at the university where she studies part-time. At the time her narrative was recorded (from 1976 through 1980), she had two children.

Al-Hajj Muhammad's life has been less unusual than Fatima Zohra's. He was born in the cobblestone quarter of Tangier in about 1932. Then his parents, Abd as-Slam the shoemaker and Shama the daughter of Si Abd Allah, returned to his mother's village, the village of the streams. Al-Hajj Muhammad lived in this village from about the ages of seven to fourteen, when his mother brought him and his brothers and sisters back to Tangier. His only education consisted of the traditional memorization of the Quran. He never memorized the entire Quran, but he knows most of it by heart. He can read the modern literary Arabic used in newspapers and books, but not very well. And when he writes letters to his brother in Belgium or to Fatima Zohra in the United States, he transcribes colloquial Moroccan Arabic in the alphabet of the literary language.

Al-Hajj Muhammad returned to Tangier shortly after the end of World War II, which he refers to as "the great war of the Christians."

> I was thirteen or fourteen then. My mother sold bread in the old city. And I worked as an apprentice (*mitallim*) in a Spanish candy factory (*mamal al-halawiyyat*). Then I worked in a Spanish ice cream factory (*mamal al-ladu*). And then I worked for a Jew unloading bags of cement from trucks. [I.2]

During the 1950s, al-Hajj Muhammad participated in the Moroccan nationalist movement led primarily by the Istiqlal, or "Independence" party, which was (and is) of an Islamic reformist orientation (Waterbury 1970). Al-Hajj Muhammad's description of his role in the famous demonstrations and riots of March 30, 1952 conveys quite graphically how most Moroccans perceived the nationalist struggle as a "holy war" (*jihad*):

> God knows how many Muslims the Christian policemen killed that day. They lined up on the rooftops above the market place

11

and mowed us down with machine guns. But all the Muslims who died went straight to heaven because they died fighting the *jihad* against the infidels. [II.2]

Like many Moroccans, al-Hajj Muhammad was bitterly disappointed when independence in 1956 did not result in any improvement in his standard of living. For a while, he sold popsicles from a bicycle pushcart. Then he worked as a laborer. And for many years, he sold "old clothes, kerosene lamps, dishes, radios and other things" in Tangier's *Jutiyya*, or "flea market." He also earned some extra money making magical charms (*hjuba*) to ward off the *jnun* (spirits) and to induce passion in women. But he says that he stopped doing this because "it is forbidden by Islam."

Al-Hajj Muhammad continued to work for the Istiqlal party and for the Moroccan Union of Labor (Union Marocaine de Travail) after independence. But he apparently did so more in the hope of obtaining a passport than because of ideology:

> In 1960, I handed out papers and told people to vote for the Istiqlal candidates in the local elections. I had my stall in the Jutiyya flea market then. I worked hard for the party. But the years passed and still I had no passport. So I started working for the new party, the National Union of the Popular Forces (*al-Ittihad al-Watani li il-Quwat ash-Shabiyya*). [II.2]

The Union Nationale des Forces Populaires (UNFP) was established in 1959 by socialist intellectuals dissatisfied with the conservatism of the leadership of the Istiqlal party (Ben Barka 1968: 48–49; 77–79). (In 1974, the Rabat section of the UNFP seceded from the party and established the Union Socialiste des Forces Populaires, which has since become Morocco's principal socialist party.) Al-Hajj Muhammad claims to have organized the campaign of the UNFP in a popular quarter of Tangier during the 1963 parliamentary elections. He also claims that some of his former associates in the Istiqlal party tried to have him killed because of his involvement with the UNFP. And he was afraid the government would arrest him because eighty-five leaders of the UNFP were arrested and tried in 1963 on charges of plotting to overthrow the regime of the king Hasan II (Waterbury 1970: 293–95). But he survived this crisis. He notes that "after all this trouble, I decided to have nothing to do with politics any more. It is too dangerous."

It should be noted that only one other member of the house of Si Abd Allah has been involved in politics. This is al-Hajj Muhammad's cousin (mother's sister's son) Hmidu, who ran unsuccessfully for a seat on a rural district council (*al-majlis al-qarawi*) in the local elections of November 1976 and almost lost his profitable vegetable garden because he did not support a government-approved candidate in the parliamentary elections of June 1977.

The problems faced by both al-Hajj Muhammad and Hmidu because of their involvement in politics have reinforced the family's view that politics is a dangerous and pointless activity that should be avoided at all cost. Almost everyone in the house of Si Abd Allah would endorse al-Hajj Muhammad's contention that "no man with a brain in his head gets involved in politics in Morocco." But it is also true that the Islamic revolution in Iran has excited the imagination of a great many Moroccans of al-Hajj Muhammad's general religious and cultural orientation.

As already noted, a primary factor in al-Hajj Muhammad's political activities in the early 1960s appears to have been his desire to obtain a passport so that he could go to work in Europe. He states that "all Moroccans dream of getting a passport and working in Europe." Although this may not be true of *all* Moroccans, it is certainly true of all the young men of the house of Si Abd Allah. Labor emigration plays a major role in the Moroccan economy, as it does in other third world countries where economic development has not kept pace with population growth. Between 1960 and 1971, some 230,000 Moroccans left Morocco to work in Europe (Lahbabi 1977: 189). And among them were al-Hajj Muhammad, his brother Ahmad, his sister Habiba, his brother-in-law Mshish (who sells flowers in Gibraltar), and his cousin Fatima Zohra.

After finally obtaining a passport in 1964, al-Hajj Muhammad went to work in a coal mine in France for a few months. He then joined his brother Ahmad in Brussels, where he worked with a pneumatic drill for five years and as a stonecutter for four. He returned to Tangier permanently in 1973. (Almost all labor emigrants in Europe return for at least three weeks every summer.) Since returning, he has peddled everything from transistor radios to used clothing at markets in Tangier and the surrounding countryside. Unlike most labor emigrants, who save and invest their earnings in houses and land, al-Hajj Muhammad has never been able to save money—except for his pilgrimage to Mecca.

Al-Hajj Muhammad is generally considered a failure not only in his "career" but also in his marital life. He has been married nine times and divorced eight. In Morocco, as in most of the Islamic world, it is easy for a man to divorce his wife and not impossible for a woman to divorce her husband (Rosen 1970a). Seventeen of the fifty marriages (34 percent) of the house of Si Abd Allah had ended in divorce by December 1979, a relatively low rate in the Moroccan context (H. Geertz 1979: 391 and Maher 1974: 194). But no other man in the family has been divorced more than once, so that al-Hajj Muhammad's eight divorces are clearly atypical. Fatima Zohra attributes them to his emotional instability and his sterility. (Although al-Hajj Muhammad claims to have a daughter, everyone else in the family says that this girl is the illegitimate child an ex-wife of his had with an Algerian worker in Belgium.)

Al-Hajj Muhammad is both the family buffoon and the family bard. At family gatherings he delights everyone with his jokes and stories, which are often of a Rabelaisian character. He is loved, but he is also viewed as being irresponsible and unstable. He has had several "nervous breakdowns," which his relatives other than Fatima Zohra and her sisters generally explain in terms of possession by the *jnun*. However, despite the fact that al-Hajj Muhammad's *behavior* is often eccentric, the basic world view in terms of which he interprets the history of his family and country is typical of "traditional" and "fundamentalist" Muslim men not just in Morocco but throughout much of the Islamic world. This shall be demonstrated by comparing some of al-Hajj Muhammad's statements with

14

statements made by some of the most influential Muslim fundamentalist theorists of the twentieth century.

Similarly with respect to Fatima Zohra, her views are relatively typical of "modern" and "westernized" young Muslim women—in many respects at any rate. But her *life* has definitely been unusual. Not many Moroccan women forced to leave school at an early age go on to live and study at an American university.

But before examining the religious and cultural orientations of al-Hajj Muhammad and Fatima Zohra, I should briefly summarize the broad outlines of Moroccan history since the late nineteenth century. Without some awareness of this history, the resentment of foreign domination that pervades the narratives of both al-Hajj Muhammad and Fatima Zohra cannot be understood.

MOROCCO SINCE THE LATE NINETEENTH CENTURY

As in most of the rest of the Islamic world, Morocco's independence was gradually eroded in the nineteenth century by a series of military defeats, treaties, and loans (Miège 1961–63). This process eventually culminated in the imposition of French and Spanish Protectorates upon southern and northern Morocco in 1912. The French Protectorate in the South was about nine times as large as the Spanish zone along the Mediterranean Sea. Tangier and its immediate environs became an International Zone in which French influence was paramount (Stuart 1955).

The Spanish Protectorate in northern Morocco included the Arabic-speaking Jbalan highlands in the west and the Berber-speaking Rif in the east (see map, p. 2). The Spanish faced considerable resistance in both of these regions. The early phase of the resistance was intermittently led by the infamous Jbalan bandit-cum-"primitive rebel" Mulay Ahmad ar-Raysuni, who was typical of many such rebels in the late nineteenth and early twentieth centuries (Munson 1980: 146–50). Raysuni (referred to as *Bir-Raysul* by the Jbala and as *Raysuli* in Western sources) had amassed a fortune stealing cattle and kidnapping Europeans in Tangier (Forbes 1924). And he used this fortune and his European hostages to obtain important government positions, including the governorship of most of northwest Morocco (ibid.: 96–99). He was the dominant political figure in the Jbalan highlands for the first quarter of the twentieth century.

Raysuni was revered as a *sharif* (a patrilineal descendant of the prophet Muhammad) and as a descendant of the patrilateral uncle of the patron saint of the Jbalan highlands, Mulay Abd as-Slam bin Mshish (Munson 1980: 146–54). He portrayed himself as a *mujahid*, or fighter of holy war against the Christians who were in the process of subjugating Morocco, but he actually spent as much time helping the Spanish as he did opposing them. That is why al-Hajj Muhammad condemns him as "a traitor who sold the house of Islam to the Christians." The Spanish faced far stiffer resistance in the Berber-speaking Rif from 1921 to 1926 (al-Bu Ayyashi 1976; Hart 1976). (The social history of the Jbalan highlands is analyzed in Munson 1980, 1981, and 1982b.)

After the French and the Spanish had suppressed the last of the highland resistance to their Protectorates, a new nationalist movement emerged in the 1930s, led by the old elite of the city of Fez, known as the Fassis (*Fasiyyin*). The precipitating cause of this movement was a decree issued by the French Protectorate in 1930, which stated that Berber-speaking Moroccans in the highlands would no longer be subject to Islamic law (Brown 1976: 199). This was perceived as a prelude to the conversion of the Berber-speakers to Christianity and as an attempt to "divide and conquer" (ibid.).

The nationalist movement eventually coalesced into the Istiqlal (Independence) party, which led Morocco to independence in 1956. The movement was of an Islamic reformist orientation, demanding not only independence but a return to the pristine Islam of the prophet Muhammad. The Islamic character of the nationalist movement demonstrates quite clearly the central role of Islam in the national identity of most Moroccans.

After independence, Morocco was governed from 1956 to 1961 by King Muhammad V, whose son Hasan II has ruled since then.

Hasan II is an autocratic ruler similar to King Husayn of Jordan and the late shah of Iran (who sought refuge in Morocco in the spring of 1979). Under the rule of Hasan II, Morocco has remained economically dependent upon the United States and France (Lahbabi 1977: 274; Oualalou 1980). Although the king is still revered by many peasants and some of the lumpenproletariat by virtue of his descent from the prophet Muhammad, opposition to his regime has spread to most segments of urban Morocco. He has succeeded in diverting some of this opposition, thanks to the war Morocco has been waging against the Polisario guerrillas of the Sahara since 1976. (Morocco claims the western Sahara as Moroccan territory, whereas the Algerian-backed Polisario wants an independent state.) But this war has exacerbated Morocco's serious economic problems (Oulalou 1980: 166).

In 1979, the government was confronted by a wave of strikes by both "blue" and "white" collar workers demanding wage increases to keep pace with inflation. Hundreds of union activists and striking workers were arrested, although wage increases to minimum-wage workers were granted (ibid.: 195). The government was then confronted by widespread demonstrations on the part of students, teachers, and other Moroccans outraged by the presence of the shah of Iran (Europa 1981: 612). Many of the university students who participated in these demonstrations were of an Islamic fundamentalist orientation. And in the wake of the Islamic revolution in Iran, Islamic fundamentalist organizations in Morocco have attracted more support than ever before (Leveau 1980; Etienne and Tozy 1980; Yassin 1979 (?) and 1981).

The government faced further student strikes and demonstrations in 1980, when it attempted to reduce government expenditures by lowering student scholarships and reducing the number of students who could be admitted to the national universities. These strikes were strongly supported by the Union Socialiste des Forces Populaires (USFP).

But the government's most serious political crisis in recent years occurred in 1981. In 1980–81, drought destroyed much of the year's harvest, causing food prices to rise and exacerbating the already severe problems of rural–urban migration and urban unemployment (Paul 1981). The government was forced to obtain a loan of over a billion dollars from the International Monetary Fund, to which it was already heavily indebted, on the condition that it reduce its subsidies for basic foodstuffs and gas (Legum 1981: B80). Coupled with inflation, the subsidy reductions entailed sharp increases in the prices of the basic necessities of life, which in turn led to widespread strikes, demonstrations, and the worst riots since 1965. The lumpenproletariat of Casablanca went on a rampage in the opulent downtown areas of that city, destroying and looting cars, buses, banks, expensive stores, and government buildings (Jibril 1981: 29). Security police killed hundreds of the rioters, most of whom were unemployed young men from families similar to the house of Si Abd Allah (Paul 1981: 31; Boularès 1981).

The government has blamed much of the unrest of recent years on the socialist party, the USFP, and its affiliated federation of trade unions, the Confédération ·Démocratique du Travail (CDT) (Paul 1981: 31). But the government appears to feel even more threatened by its Islamic opposition than by the Left. The king has always derived much of his legitimacy from Islam—from his patrilineal descent from the prophet Muhammad and his status as "Commander of the Faithful" (Tozy 1980: 221–22). And he has always been able to undermine the socialist Left by portraying its leaders as "apostates" and enemies of Islam (ibid.: 231–33). But now the Islamic fundamentalists are echoing the main themes of the Left (e.g., condemnation of social inequity and foreign domination) and they are articulating these themes in terms of the basic "sacred symbols" of Islam. They are also expressing widespread discontent provoked by the westernized, or "non-Islamic," culture of the Moroccan elite. They can thus appeal to Moroccans such as al-Hajj Muhammad in a way that the westernized socialist intellectual leaders of the USFP cannot. This frightens the USFP as much as it does the king. In the words of one Moroccan intellectual, "Better a Moroccan shah than a Moroccan Khomeini."

FUNDAMENTALIST IDEOLOGY
AND POPULAR ISLAM

In order to explain the potential political significance of Islamic fundamentalism in Morocco and the rest of the Muslim world, it is necessary to understand what it *is* and the nature of its relationship to the basic structures of belief and value in terms of which Muslims interpret their lives. We cannot explain religious movements, or social movements of any kind, without some understanding of how their adherents and potential adherents perceive the world. More generally, we cannot explain what people *do* unless we have some understanding of how they *think*.

The first point to be emphasized with respect to the term *fundamentalism* is that it is derived from the American Protestant tradition rather than from Islam. This does not mean, however, that it must be discarded. Even when attempting to understand religious phenomena from the believer's point of view, it is sometimes useful to employ terms that believers themselves do not use. The term *fundamentalist* is useful because it names a phenomenon for which there is no generally accepted name in Islam. The people generally referred to as Muslim fundamentalists by western analysts simply call themselves "Muslims," the implication being that all those who do not share their views are in effect infidels, even if they have names such as Muhammad, Abd Allah, and Fatima (Mawdudi 1976: 22–23). As for nonfundamentalist Muslims, they too lack any generally accepted name for fundamentalists. So the term *Muslim fundamentalist* is convenient, especially since it has come to be used in virtually all studies of Islam written in the English language.

As generally employed in the United States, the word *fundamentalism* refers to the belief that a specific set of sacred scriptures are the divine and inerrant word of God and that all believers must conform to the literal text of these scriptures in their everyday lives

(Falwell 1981: 219–20). At the core of the fundamentalist ethos is the idea that "the word of God" cannot be forced to adapt to the world of man; it is, rather, the world of man that must be forced to conform to "the word of God." This implies a tendency to reject social and cultural innovations, most of which are perceived as being contrary to the laws of God, as well as the corollary tendency to reaffirm the validity of traditional beliefs and values, most of which are perceived as being in accordance with divine law.

However, if the term *fundamentalism* is to be utilized in the Islamic context, it is necessary to distinguish between the ideological fundamentalism of political activists committed to the goal of establishing a "truly Islamic" state and the fundamentalism that is innate in traditional Islam as it is understood by "the masses" of the Islamic world. Both of these forms of Islamic fundamentalism, the ideological and the innate, are rooted in the same basic world view and ethos, and they are both articulated in terms of the same religious symbols. Thus the fundamentalist ideologist has a tremendous advantage over the advocates of alternative ideologies—for example, Marxism—in that he can articulate popular grievances in the religious idiom in terms of which most Muslims interpret virtually every facet of their lives.

But the fundamentalist ideologist often uses the basic symbols of Islam in a decidedly nontraditional manner. All traditional Muslims—that is, all Muslims who interpret their religion much as did earlier generations—accept the idea that the Quran is the divine and inerrant word of God to which all behavior should conform. However, despite their shared belief in the inerrancy of the text of the Quran, the ideologically fundamentalist Muslim and the innately fundamentalist traditional Muslim interpret this text in different ways. Thus the Quran portrays Satan as the paradigmatic rebel against God (II : 34–36; VII : 11–18). And human beings are said to be obliged to choose between following God (*Allah*), the personification of goodness, or Satan (*Shaytan/Iblis*), the personification of evil (IV : 117–20). In traditional popular Islam, this conflict is perceived primarily as a moral one. But in the ideological fundamentalist literature, the conflict between God and Satan is political as well as moral. The "party of God" (*hizb Allah*) consists of all those Muslims actively striving to enforce the laws of God in all aspects of life, whereas the "party of Satan" (*hizb ash-Shaytan*) consists of all infidels and all westernized Muslims who seek to replace the laws of God by the "satanic" and immoral laws of the infidel (Mawdudi 1976: 108, 120, 184). Moreover, the conflict between God and Satan is also often interpreted to refer to the struggle of "the oppressed" versus "the oppressor." Thus when an Islamic republic was instituted in Iran, the Ayatollah Khomeini declared that "the government of the oppressed—which is the government of God" had replaced the "satanic" regime of the shah (Khomeini 1981: 266). And Khomeini has often referred to the shah and other rulers with close ties to the United States as pawns of "the Great Satan" (ibid.: 301).

So the fundamentalist ideologist interprets the basic symbols of Islam in a somewhat innovative manner. But while this interpretation differs from that which prevails in traditional popular Islam, it does not differ to the point of being unintelligible. Al-Hajj Muhammad, for example, has not been involved in any political activities for over twenty years. He is not actively trying to overthrow the government of Morocco. And he has not read any of the writings of fundamentalist theorists. Yet we find in his narrative as well as in these writings a similar fusion of religious, cultural, and socioeconomic grievances coupled with resentment of foreign domination.

Al-Hajj Muhammad describes his disillusion after Morocco became independent as follows:

> In those days, we thought that once we obtained independence everything would be wonderful. We thought we Muslims would live the way the Christians live, with villas, cars, and servants. But now we are no better off than we were under the Christians. Now the Fassis rule as the Christians used to. *They* have villas, cars, and servants. But those of us who toil for a mouthful of bread have gained nothing since independence.
> And the Fassis and the other rich Moroccans have forgot-

ten their religion. They have become like Christians. Sometimes they speak French among themselves. They send their
children to French schools. They marry French women. And
even their Muslim wives and daughters bare their bodies like
Christian whores. They wear bikinis at the beach and short
skirts and low-cut blouses in the streets. . . .

And even today the Christians still control Morocco. The
biggest villas on Jbil al-Kbir (the Big Mountain) still belong to
Christians. The factories are still controlled by Christians. . . .
[II.2]

(The core of the Moroccan elite consists of Fassis, people whose
families once lived in the city of Fez.)

Al-Hajj Muhammad's description of Moroccan society resem-
bles the following summary of the impact of Western imperialism
upon the Islamic world by Hasan al-Banna, the founder of Egypt's
Muslim Brotherhood:

they [the Europeans] were able to gain the right to penetrate
the economy and flood the countries with their capital, their
banks, and their companies. They were able to control the
economic infrastructure as they wished. And they amassed
fantastic wealth without sharing it with the local population.
After that, they transformed the bases of government, law,
and education and fashioned them in their own manner. And
they brought to these regions their naked women, their
liquors, their theaters, their dance halls . . . and their shame-
lessness. They tolerated crimes in these regions that they
would not have tolerated in their own lands. And they
adorned this clamorous wicked world that reeks of sin and
overflows with debauchery so as to dazzle the eyes of the
naive and gullible among Muslims of wealth, knowledge, high
rank, and power. And as though all of this were not enough,
they established schools and scholarly and cultural institutes
in the heart of the Islamic region to cast doubt and apostasy
into the minds of its sons, and to teach them to think of themselves as inferior, despise their religion and nation, strip them-

selves of their beliefs and traditions, and revere all that which is western. [al-Banna 1965: 221]

Both al-Hajj Muhammad, the innately fundamentalist traditional Muslim, and Hasan al-Banna, the fundamentalist ideologist, articulate and fuse resentment of foreign domination, social inequity, and the violation of the values of Islam. Both men appear to be as outraged by the exposed limbs of "Christian whores" as they are by the economic subjugation of their countries by European powers. And both men perceive the "westernization" of the elites of their lands as the substitution of the decadent values of the infidel for the pure and inerrant laws of God. They thus both perceive westernization much as the Maccabees perceived hellenization over two thousand years ago (Bickerman 1947: 13–21; Lewy 1974: 70–75).

The fact that ideological fundamentalism and traditional popular Islam are rooted in the same world view and ethos is further demonstrated by al-Hajj Muhammad's explanation of the power and wealth of the infidel as opposed to the weakness and poverty of the Muslim:

> Why did God allow the Christians to rule over the house of Islam? Why did God allow the Jews to take Palestine and holy Jerusalem? Why does God allow the Christians to live like sultans in our land while we are like slaves in their land? This is God's punishment. And this is God's test. Muslims have left the path (*kharju min at-triq*) of Islam. [I.1]

This conception of foreign domination as a sign of the wrath of God due to deviation from his laws leads quite logically to al-Hajj Muhammad's view that "until we return to the path of Islam, the Christians will continue to control our stores, our factories, our hotels, our mines and the minds of our young people." This kind of reasoning has often played an important role in fundamentalist movements in all three of the monotheistic religions, which share a common vision of history as the reflection of the will of God. The

Zealots who revolted against Roman rule in ancient Palestine were convinced that only strict conformity to the Torah would induce God to lead them to victory (Lewy 1974: 76–79). And in a book published in 1981, the American Christian fundamentalist Jerry Falwell declared that the only way "to rebuild America to the greatness it once had" was "to call America back to God, back to the Bible, and back to moral sanity" (Falwell 1981: 186).

Al-Hajj Muhammad's interpretation of the subjugation of the Islamic world by the West is a basic theme of Muslim fundamentalist ideology, as is the corollary idea that only a return to strict conformity to the precepts of the Quran will lead to liberation (Haddad 1980: 119; Khomeini 1981: 210, 304; Laroui 1967: 20; Mawdudi 1976: 14–20, 161–62). Modern Muslims like Fatima Zohra dismiss this kind of logic as nonsense. But it is perfectly plausible from the point of view of the traditional Muslim, who believes that God would never allow the infidel to subjugate the believer except to punish the latter for deviating from the laws of Islam.

The fact that the ideology of Islamic fundamentalism is embedded in the basic religious and cultural framework in terms of which traditional Muslims perceive the world and live their lives may seem obvious. But this extremely important fact has been overlooked by many anthropologists who have assumed a radical disjunction between "orthodox" and "popular" Islam, with fundamentalist ideologies emerging from the former. This disjunction has received various labels, for example, the "great" versus the "folk" tradition (Gellner 1981: 80), the "Protestant" versus the "Catholic" syndrome (Gellner 1969: 7–8), and "scripturalism" versus "maraboutism" (Geertz 1968: 65–82).

The orthodox tradition of Islam is said to be a puritanical religion based on strict conformity to the rules of Islam as elaborated in the Quran, the traditions concerning the prophet Muhammad, and Islamic law (ash-sharia) (Gellner 1969: 7). The popular tradition, on the other hand, is viewed as bearing virtually no relationship to the Quran, the traditions of the prophet, and formal Islamic law. Thus the orthodox tradition is portrayed as the religion of urban elites that have access to scripture by virtue of literacy, while popular Islam is portrayed as the religion of the illiterate masses (ibid.: 8).

The orthodox tradition is said to emphasize the unmediated relationship between man and God, whereas the popular one emphasizes the role of saints as mediators in this relationship. The orthodox tradition is characterized as strictly monotheistic, whereas the popular one tends toward "saint worship" (Geertz 1968: 9). The orthodox tradition is said to be egalitarian, whereas the popular one is hierarchical, with the patrilineal descendants of the prophet Muhammad and prominent saints being of much higher status than other believers (Gellner 1969: 7–8). And the orthodox tradition is characterized as being "sober" and "rational," whereas the popular one is prone to "ritual indulgence" associated with the shrines of saints and Sufi mysticism (ibid.).

This orthodox/popular dichotomy definitely does exist, and fundamentalist ideologies *are* quite obviously rooted in the ortho- dox tradition. At the present time in Morocco, the conflict between the fundamentalist ideologists and the king follows the lines of the orthodox/popular dichotomy as characterized above. The funda- mentalists stress the egalitarian ethos of Islam, while the king frequently reminds his subjects of the obedience and reverence they owe him because of his traditional position at the apex of the religious hierarchy of popular Islam (Leveau 1980: 210–11; Tozy 1980: 221–22). The fundamentalists praise Khomeini for having "renounced the goods of this world," while tacitly condemning the king for perpetuating a society in which "the patrimony of humanity is being wasted to satisfy the taste for luxury of the rich to the detriment of the wretched of the earth" (Leveau 1980: 211). The king, on the other hand, reminds the Moroccan people that he is a descendant of the prophet Muhammad and "commander of the faithful obliged to serve as the divine shadow on earth and the bow of God" (Tozy 1980: 222).

But while the orthodox/popular dichotomy exists, both of its components are intertwined in the minds of the overwhelming majority of Muslims throughout the world. Anthropologists have tended to view the dichotomy in terms of its social and behavioral manifestations, rather than in terms of its semantic substance as understood from the believer's point of view. They have thus neglected to note that both the orthodox and popular versions of Islam are rooted in the same basic world view and ethos. This is particularly true, and particularly surprising, in the case of Clifford Geertz, whose book *Islam Observed: Religious Development in Morocco and Indonesia* (1968) has influenced virtually all subsequent anthropological studies of the role of Islam in Moroccan culture (see Crapanzano 1973; Rabinow 1975; Eickelman 1976; Munson 1980 and 1982a).

In both *Islam Observed* and his influential essay "Religion as a Cultural System" (1973: 87–125), Geertz argues that the social and psychological implications of a religion cannot be adequately analyzed without some understanding of what it means from the believer's point of view (1968: 2; 1973: 125). "What a given religion is—its specific content—is embodied in the images and metaphors its adherents use to characterize reality" (1968: 2). But while rejecting the reduction of religion to its social institutions, Geertz notes that religions (like cultures and ideologies) are not autonomous and immutable systems unaffected by social transformations. And he emphasizes the importance of analyzing how religions, as well as cultures and ideologies, are implicated in such changes (1968: 20–21; 1973: 30).

Geertz contends that every religion consists of a set of "sacred symbols" that "formulate an image of the world's construction and a program for human conduct that are mere reflexes of one another" (1968: 97). And the world view and ethos embodied in these "sacred symbols" are primarily fused and reinforced in the mind of the believer during the course of ritual (1968: 100; 1973: 112–13). Thus Geertz argues that rituals, especially the "more elaborate and usually more public ones," represent the point at which the fusion of world view and ethos "can be most readily examined by the detached observer" (1973: 113). But he emphasizes that the analyst should also study how religious symbols are used in everyday life so as to learn how they shape what the believer regards as "common sense" (1968: 95; 1973: 119). And this entails the description of the "sorts of interpretations the members of a society apply to their experience, the constructions they put upon the events through which they live" (1968: 90).

It is probably obvious to many readers that I have recorded, translated, and edited the narratives of al-Hajj Muhammad and Fatima Zohra on the basis of assumptions quite similar to many of the premises of Geertzian "interpretive anthropology." (For a detailed appraisal of this school of thought, see Munson 1982a.) However, the manner in which Geertz implements these theoretical premises leads to precisely the kind of reductionism that he has himself so vigorously condemned.

In *Islam Observed,* Geertz concludes his chapter on "the classical styles" of Islam in Morocco and Indonesia by contrasting the "characteristic conception of what life was all about" in these two countries:

On the Indonesian side, inwardness, imperturbability, patience, poise, sensibility, aestheticism, elitism, and an almost obsessive self-effacement, the radical dissolution of individuality; on the Moroccan side, activism, fervor, impetuosity, nerve, toughness, moralism, populism, and an almost obsessive self-assertion, the radical intensification of individuality. [Geertz 1968: 54]

This passage conveys a good idea of how Moroccan and Indonesian behavior is perceived by an American observer but relatively little about how Islam shapes the conception of life in the two countries. Terms such as *activism, fervor,* and *moralism* could be used to characterize the behavior of "true believers" in religious and political causes all over the world. At best, they may impart some information concerning the values that shape behavior, but none about the world view in which these values have their roots.

27

Geertz discusses the social institutions of Islam in Morocco in considerable detail. Thus he describes the organization of Sufi brotherhoods, the sultanate, the shrines of saints, and the reformist-cum-nationalist movement that led to independence. But despite his theoretical emphasis on the need to study the basic symbols of a religion as they are used in ritual, Geertz does not devote any of *Islam Observed* to the basic rituals of Islam, such as the daily prayers, or to its fundamental "sacred symbols," notably, Allah, the prophet Muhammad, and the day of judgment.

However, by implementing some of Geertz's ideas concerning how religions *ought* to be studied, that is, by examining how religious symbols are used in ritual as well as in everyday life, we can gain a good idea of how Islam is understood from the believer's point of view. And we can see that orthodox and popular Islam are less distinct than many anthropologists have believed.

THE BASIC SYMBOLS OF ISLAM
IN RITUAL AND EVERYDAY LIFE

There are five basic ritual obligations in Islam: (1) the attestation of faith (*ash-shahada*); (2) prayer (*as-sala*); (3) almsgiving (*az-zakat*); (4) fasting during the month of Ramadan (*as-sawm*); and (5) the pilgrimage to Mecca (*al-hajj*), if one is physically and financially able to undertake it (al-Faruqi 1979: 19–34). Muslims such as al-Hajj Muhammad tend to fulfill these obligations "religiously" (at least when they grow old), whereas westernized Muslims such as Fatima Zohra do not. All of these "five pillars" are mentioned in the text of this book, but the five daily prayers, fasting during Ramadan, and the pilgrimage to Mecca are particularly important.

The attestation of faith states: "I attest that there is no god but God (*Allah*) and I attest that Muhammad is his messenger." According to Islamic law, one need.only say this phrase with genuine faith in order to convert to Islam. This attestation occurs repeatedly in the call to prayer that Muslims hear five times a day, as well as in the daily prayers themselves (Kamal 1978: 24). And it is supposed to be the last phrase spoken by a Muslim before death so that he or she may die as a good Muslim and thus be assured of admittance to heaven. Al-Hajj Muhammad was saying the most important part of the attestation of faith—"there is no god but God"—when he was beaten unconscious by five European policemen during the riots of March 30, 1952.

The attestation of faith illustrates the fundamental significance of God (*Allah*) and Muhammad the messenger of God in the religion of Islam. The word *Islam* means "submission"—that is, submission to the will of God as revealed to Muhammad—and a *Muslim* ("Moslem") is literally "one who submits." The word *Allah* is the Arabic cognate of the Hebrew *Elohim*. And both Christian and Muslim Arabs use this term to refer to God.

Muslims believe that God revealed the basic precepts of Islam to a series of prophets—notably Noah, Abraham, Moses, Jesus, and Muhammad. The sacred scriptures of Judaism and Christianity are regarded as garbled versions of God's revelations to his early prophets, while the prophet Muhammad is believed to have been the ultimate and greatest of the prophets and messengers of God. And the Quran, the basic sacred scripture of Islam, is believed to be the literal text of God's revelations to Muhammad. From the point of view of modern westernized Muslims such as Fatima Zohra, many of the social regulations of the Quran are not essential to Islam, nor are they relevant to the modern world. Fatima Zohra rejects, for example, the Quranic rule that daughters should inherit half of what their brothers do (Quran IV: 11). From al-Hajj Muhammad's innately fundamentalist perspective, such rejection of the word of God is tantamount to apostasy.

The Islamic world view is outlined in the first or "opening" chapter (*al-Fatiha*) of the Quran. The prophet Muhammad is said to have referred to this chapter as "the mother of the book," and Muslims frequently contend that it "contains the whole of Islam compressed within it" (Khomeini 1981: 363). This short chapter of the Quran is the core of all of the five daily prayers as well as of

the congregational prayers said on Fridays and holy days. It is also
the first prayer learned by children.

AL-FATIHA

In the name of God [*Allah*] the merciful, the compassionate
praise be to God [*Allah*] Lord of the worlds
the merciful, the compassionate
master of the day of judgment
you do we worship and from you we seek assistance
guide us on the path of righteousness
the path of those whom you have favored
not of those who have incurred your wrath
nor of those who go astray.   [Quran I]

This fundamental prayer demonstrates that Islam, like Christianity, has inherited most of the world view of Judaism. All three of
the monotheistic religions share roughly the same conception of a
God who is both merciful and terrible in his wrath. They also share
the idea that this world is a test by means of which God determines
who shall go to heaven (*al-janna*) and who shall go to hell (*al-jahan-
nam*).

The concept of the ultimate day of judgment plays a particularly important role in the narrative of al-Hajj Muhammad. Whenever he speaks of someone having done an evil deed, he cites the
proverb "Everyone shall be hung by his leg" (*Kull wahid ghadi ikun
mallaq min rijlu*). This extremely common expression likens the fate
of the individual on the day of reckoning (*yawm ad-din*) to the fate of
sheep and goats hung by their hind legs after slaughter. The idea is
that people will be "hung" by their deeds, with the righteous being
allowed to enter paradise and the evil being condemned to hell.

The prophet Muhammad is also believed to participate in the
day of judgment by seeking to intercede on behalf of all good
Muslims. The idea of intercession (*ash-shafaa*) is belittled, although
not absolutely condemned, in the Quran (II : 48, 254–55). However,
the role of Muhammad as intercessor is accepted in many of the
hadith, or traditions, which constitute the second most important

source of Islamic law (Gibb and Kramers 1953: 511–12). And the idea of the prophet as intercessor has become an integral part of both orthodox and popular Islam (Munson 1980: 92). When Moroccan Muslims find themselves desperately waiting for assistance that they fear will be too late to avoid serious trouble of some kind, they often cite the proverb: "The prophet will not intercede on my behalf until after the affliction has overtaken me" (*ma iji an-nbi ishfa fiyya hatta ikun al-hamm fat fiyya*). Westermarck notes that when frightened by a thunderstorm, Moroccans sometimes exclaim, "Intercession, O messenger of God!" (*ash-shfaa ya rasul Allah*) (Westermarck 1968: I, 118). As these examples demonstrate, the role of the prophet as intercessor is not restricted to the day of judgment.

The Quran and fundamentalist ideologists tend to emphasize that Muhammad was the greatest of God's prophets without attributing to him any supernatural powers. In the Quran, God specifically commands Muhammad to tell his followers, "I am but a man like yourselves" (Quran XVII : 110). But other passages in the Quran are generally interpreted to mean that the prophet and his patrilineal descendants through his daughter Fatima and her husband Ali, the prophet's closest patrilineal kinsman, are all pure (*tahir*) and sinless. This is the meaning generally ascribed to the verse "and God only wishes to remove all abomination from you people of the house and to purify you completely" (*yutahhirakum tathiran*) (Quran XXXIII : 33). This idea led to the split between Shii and Sunni Islam, with the Shiis insisting that only the pure and sinless patrilineal descendants of Muhammad could serve as leaders of the Islamic world (Gibb and Kramers 1953: 534–36).

Associated with the concept of the purity of the prophet and his patrilineal descendants, known as *ash-shurfa* ("the honored ones") in colloquial Moroccan Arabic, is the concept of *al-baraka,* "the blessedness." During the course of the five daily prayers, Muslims beseech God to "bless (*barik*) Muhammad and the descendants of Muhammad." Elsewhere in the daily prayers, Muslims say: "Peace be upon you O prophet, and the mercy of God and his blessings (*barakatuhu*)" (Kamal 1978: 25–26). The belief that the descendants of the prophet are pure, sinless, and blessed has always been, and remains, extremely important in popular Islam. Most Jbala believe, for example, that the king of Morocco survived attempted coups in 1971 and 1972 because of the *baraka* he possesses by virtue of his descent from the prophet. And even though well-educated Muslims and fundamentalist ideologists emphasize that Muslims should be judged in terms of their actions rather than their ancestry, few of them would go so far as to say that descent from Muhammad is absolutely meaningless.

Generally speaking, the role of the prophet Muhammad is much less significant in the daily prayers than is that of God. After performing his or her ablutions, the worshiper begins the prayer with the phrase *Allahu akbar*, "God is greater" (i.e., greater than anything else), which is also said during most transitions from one position to another. Other phrases praising God include: "My Lord the almighty be praised," "Our Lord, praise be to thee," and "My Lord the most high be praised" (see Kamal 1978).

The five daily prayers can be said individually or congregationally in a mosque. But the Friday noon prayer should be performed congregationally, if possible. Al-Hajj Muhammad describes how congregational prayer is experienced from the believer's point of view:

> When I hear the call to prayer, I go to the mosque by the stream. And there I feel happy and clean. The whitewashed walls and the chanting of the Quran wash away the sadness and all the worries of this world. . . .
>
> The greatest part of the prayer is the touching of the floor with the forehead. The *imam* intones *Allahu akbar*, "God is greater." Then all the Muslims in the mosque respond *Allahu akbar*, and prostrate themselves with their foreheads and palms on the floor whispering *Subhana Rabbi al-ala*, "My Lord the most high be praised." The whole mosque is silent but for these whispered words of praise and supplication. It is then, when the Muslim touches his forehead to the ground in utter submission and humility before God, that he is closest to Him.

This is the best time for supplication, when the Muslim is lowest to the ground and closest to God the most high. This is the moment when the Muslim is purest and happiest and safest from the temptations of Satan. And it is then, with my forehead and my palms upon the floor and the praise of God upon my lips, that I forget that I am a poor peddler with no house and no son and with a wife who looks like a mule. [III. 10]

Clifford Geertz has suggested that the ideologization of Islam is due to the increasing inability of its classical symbols "to sustain a properly religious faith" (Geertz 1968: 102). Al-Hajj Muhammad's narrative demonstrates that this is not true insofar as most traditional Muslims are concerned. His faith has never been shaken and yet there is obviously an at least implicitly ideological dimension to his conception of Islam.

It should be emphasized that the five daily prayers are the basic ritual of Islam. They are said by illiterate peasants as well as by learned scholars, by Shiis as well as by Sunnis. They are said by people who visit the tombs of saints as well as by those who regard the saints as heretical. Their central role in everyday life demonstrates quite clearly that orthodox and popular Islam are variations on the same themes rather than two utterly distinct kinds of religion. And this same argument applies to the other "pillars" of Islam, three of which have yet to be discussed: almsgiving, fasting during the month of Ramadan, and the pilgrimage to Mecca.

The importance of almsgiving (az-zakat) reflects the emphasis placed upon charity in the Quran. Basically az-zakat involves giving one-tenth of a crop and 2.5 percent of the value of other possessions to the poor. (The details are discussed in Gibb and Kramers 1953: 654–56). The tithe on crops is called al-ashur in northwestern Morocco. Muslims are also supposed to give small amounts to the poor (especially poor relatives) at the end of Ramadan.

During the month of Ramadan, all adult Muslims in good health are supposed to fast from sunrise to sunset. While people are forgiven for not praying regularly when they are young, breaking the fast of Ramadan is viewed as a heinous sin by traditional

Muslims. This may be due to the fact that praying is usually an individual act whereas fasting is a familial and community one. At no other time of the year is the distinction between believer and infidel so conspicuously drawn as during Ramadan, when, theoretically, the only people eating and drinking in the daytime are infidels. From the perspective of the traditional Muslim, those Muslims who break the fast are symbolically severing themselves from the community of believers and joining the ranks of the infidels. The fact that most westernized Moroccans of the elite do not fast violates the most basic values of traditional Muslims—and it outrages them. Fatima Zohra discusses this issue while speaking of al-Hajj Muhammad's brother Mustafa, who is a waiter in a café:

> He says that during Ramadan, the month of fasting, the Fassis and other rich Moroccans in western clothes come to Abd ar-Rahman's ice cream parlor and order ice cream in French, pretending to be Christians. This makes Mustafa very mad and he tells them to leave before he calls the police. At any rate, this is what he says to the family. . . . Most older people still fast. And almost everyone pretends to fast. Most of the family would be shocked to know that my sisters and I do not fast any more. For them, not fasting during Ramadan is worse than lying, stealing or cheating their husbands and wives. Most Moroccan women cheat their husbands and most Moroccan men cheat their wives. But they would not think of breaking the fast. [II.7]

The fifth pillar of Islam is the pilgrimage to Mecca, which must be undertaken by all Muslims who are physically and financially able to do so. The *kaba,* or "cube," in Mecca is regarded as the first place of worship in the world built solely for the worship of God. Muslims believe it was built by the prophet Abraham and his son (al-Faruqi 1979: 32). During the course of the pilgrimage, the pilgrims in Arabia, as well as Muslims all over the world, commemorate Abraham's willingness to sacrifice his son at God's command by sacrificing a sheep or some other animal. This holy day is known as "the great feast" (*Id al-kbir*) in Morocco.

34

Anyone who makes the pilgrimage to Mecca is believed to have absorbed a great deal of *baraka*, or "blessedness," since Mecca is regarded as the holiest place in the world. When pilgrims return to Morocco, all their relatives of a traditional religious orientation kiss their right hand or their forehead so as to absorb some of their *baraka*. This is also done by close friends (Westermarck 1968: I, 136).

In "the honored sanctuary" (*al-haram ash-sharif*) of Mecca is a well that is believed to have been created by the angel Gabriel for Ismail and his mother Hajar, who were abandoned in the desert without water (Gibb and Kramers 1953: 178–79). The water of this well is said to possess considerable *baraka*. And traditional Muslims always try to bring back bottles of it to their countries. Because Fatima Zohra's father made the pilgrimage twelve times, her parents always had some of this water on hand. And any time a relative was sick, someone would come to their house and ask for a few drops of the water from Mecca, the *baraka* of which is believed to be more powerful than the spirits (*jnun*) who are believed to cause illness. Muslims like Fatima Zohra regard such ideas as a form of magic that has nothing to do with Islam. Muslims like al-Hajj Muhammad, on the other hand, continue to think this way.

Making the pilgrimage to Mecca is an extremely important status symbol in Moroccan society, outside of the westernized elite. To begin with, anyone bearing the title *al-hajj*, "the pilgrim" (*al-hajja* in the case of a woman), possesses a great deal of *baraka* and the purity that is associated with this concept. A *hadith* states that a Muslim who makes the pilgrimage "for God's sake, and does not talk loosely, nor act wickedly, shall return as pure from sin as the day on which he was born" (Westermarck 1968: I, 136). Moreover, the fact of having made the pilgrimage indicates that one is a pious "God-fearing" (*taqi*) Muslim.

The pilgrimage is also a status symbol in that it is an expensive undertaking that most Moroccans (and most Muslims) can never afford. Fatima Zohra's mother, al-Hajja Khadduj, spent over $1,500 on the pilgrimage in 1976. It would have taken most of the men of the family working in Morocco about two years to earn that much money, and they could not *save* that much in a lifetime. Al-Hajj Muhammad was the only other member of the family to have made the pilgrimage as of December 1978. (He went to Mecca with Fatima Zohra's mother.) Many of his relatives were astonished that he had saved enough for the trip because he had always appeared to be virtually destitute since his return from Belgium. And he has definitely been virtually destitute since his return from Mecca. Many of his relatives assert that he is in fact not a real *hajj* because he does not own his own house and barely manages to feed himself and his wife. This demonstrates to what extent the pilgrimage is associated with weath.

THE SAINTS

Having examined at least the most salient aspects of the five principal ritual obligations of Islam, which are as important in popular belief and practice as they are in orthodox doctrine, it is now necessary to examine a somewhat less orthodox phenomenon: the saints. There are two essentially synonymous words in Moroccan Arabic that may be translated as "saint." These are *siyyid* and *wali*. As used in northwestern Morocco, these terms refer to the spirits and shrines of pious Muslims whose tombs are believed to be imbued with their *baraka*. Anthropologists sometimes speak of the patrilineal descendants of such saints as saints also (Geertz 1968: 33, 45). But in northwestern Morocco, the patrilineal descendants of saints are referred to as *shurfa*, or patrilineal descendants of the prophet Muhammad, never as *sadat* (the plural of *siyyid*) or *awliya'* (the plural of *wali*).

The logic of the fusion of patrilineal descent from a saint with patrilineal descent from Muhammad derives from the fact that both the saints and the prophet are popularly believed to possess the power of intercession before God. And both the saints and Muhammad are believed to be pure and endowed with tremendous *baraka*, as are their patrilineal descendants (Munson 1980: 82–93). It is true that learned Moroccans in the cities of northwestern Morocco are often aware of the distinction between descendants of a saint and descendants of Muhammad. But for most people, this distinction does not exist.

However, it should be emphasized that only the patrilineal descendants of prominent saints whose tombs attract pilgrims and gifts are generally recognized as real *shurfa*. Virtually all Jbala belong to widely scattered patronymic clans (*uruq*) with vague traditions of common patrilineal descent from an eponymic saint. Most of the people of the house of Si Abd Allah, for example, belong to the B. clan (*irq* or *darat al-ummumiyya*). Al-Hajj Muhammad and Fatima Zohra's mother, al-Hajja Khadduj, claim that the patrilineal and eponymic ancestor of their clan was Sidi Ali B., a saint buried in Fez. And given the assumption that patrilineal descent from a saint is ipso facto patrilineal descent from the prophet, they claim to be *shurfa*. But no one takes this claim seriously, because the tomb of Sidi Ali B., if it exists, is unknown and attracts neither pilgrims nor gifts. (No one in the clan has ever seen it.) On the other hand, the patrilineal descendants of famous saints whose tombs are major pilgrimage centers—for example, Mulay Abd as-Slam bin Mshish, the patron saint of the Jbalan highlands—*are* regarded as *shurfa*. And the lineages and clans of the patrilineal descendants of such prominent saints are the only descent groups to have had any legal, political, or economic significance in the Jbalan highlands in recent centuries (Munson 1981).

The Islamic reformist movement associated with Moroccan nationalism from the 1930s until independence in 1956 criticized the popular veneration of saints as an anthropolatrous perversion of the monotheism of the Quran. This attitude is reflected in the narratives of both al-Hajj Muhammad and Fatima Zohra. Thus al-Hajj Muhammad declares:

> Sometimes ignorant Jbala who cannot read the Quran forget that the saints can only intercede on our behalf before God almighty. And it is as though they were worshipping the saints instead of God alone, like the Christians who worship

statues. This is forbidden (*haram*). This is not Islam.
[I.1]

But it should be noted that al-Hajj Muhammad himself often visits the shrines of saints when he feels sick or depressed (both conditions being attributed to the *jnun*).

Fatima Zohra describes the interior of a saint's shrine and the importance of saints in the lives of traditional Moroccan women:

> Saints' tombs are very beautiful. You kiss the pillars at the four corners of the sepulchre (*darbuz*) and you light a candle and place it next to the many candles flickering in a dark space in the wall above the tomb. And all around you old women whisper to the saint pleading with him to intercede on their behalf before God. And pleading with him to heal their pains and the pains of the people they love. Perhaps the *ulama'* (religious scholars) are right to say that this is *shirk*, that is, the attribution of God's attributes to his creatures. But I don't how many Moroccan women could bear their lives if they could not light candles for their saints. [VII.2]

As already noted, the saints are among the least orthodox institutions of popular Islam. But that does not mean that they can be understood without reference to the orthodox tradition. Although not mentioned in the Quran, the intercessory role of the saints, as well as that of the prophet, was incorporated into Islamic doctrine by many *hadith* during the early centuries of Islam (Gibb and Kramers 1953: 512). More importantly, the Muslims who visit saints also believe in God, Muhammad, and the day of judgment. They perform the orthodox rituals, at least in old age. And the process whereby descent from saints came to be confused with descent from the prophet cannot be understood without some awareness of the significance of Muhammad in both orthodox and popular Islam.

Another point to be emphasized is that those Muslims who seek the assistance of saints in times of distress do not think of themselves as "worshipping" them. The idea of "worship" in Islam is embodied in the concept of *ibada,* which also means "servitude." The last four "pillars" of Islam (prayer, almsgiving, fasting, and the pilgrimage to Mecca) are all referred to as *ibada,* which refers strictly to the relationship between man and God. (The masculine pronoun is always used in Islamic texts.)

BELIEVER VERSUS INFIDEL

The concept of *ibada* is of central significance in the Islamic world view and is directly related to the equally significant dichotomy of "believer" (*mu'min*) versus "infidel" (*kafir*). The term *ibada* is derived from the noun *abd,* which means "slave" in a secular context but has the additional meanings of "servant" and "worshiper" in the context of Islam. (*Abd* is the Arabic cognate of Hebrew *ebed,* which has the same range of meaning.) Thus the relationship between man and God is perceived as being analogous to that of the slave and his possessor (*rabbihi*). Like the slave, the true Muslim must submit unconditionally to his master (Munson 1980: 53–61). And just as the word *abd* means both "slave" and "worshiper," so too the word *rabb* means both "owner" and "Lord." The former meaning is found in secular contexts, the latter in religious ones. Thus, in al-Fatiha, the basic prayer of Islam discussed above, God is referred to as "Lord of the worlds," or *Rabb al-alamin* (Quran I). And when Moroccans visit the tombs of saints, they often begin their requests by saying, "O my Lord and this saint" (*ya Rabbi wa hadha as-siyyid*).

The idea of *ibada* also occurs in the Fatiha, in the phrase "you do we worship" (*iyyaka nabudu*), which actually implies the idea that "only you [God] do we serve and worship." Elsewhere in the daily prayers, the Muslim employs the plural of *abd—ibad*—in the phrase: "Peace be upon us and upon the righteous servants/worshipers of God" (*as-salamu alayna wa ala ibadi Allahi as-salihin*) (Kamal 1978: 26). For the overwhelming majority of Muslims, the phrase *ibad Allah* refers strictly to those who serve and worship Allah according to Islamic law. Only a small minority of modern Muslims would be willing to extend the meaning of this phrase to include infidels who serve and worship God according to their own rules. Fatima Zohra endorses this universalistic interpretation, but al-Hajj Muhammad would regard it as heretical.

The name *Abd Allah* is among the most common male names in the Islamic world because it symbolizes the paradigmatic relationship between man and God in Islam, a relationship of total "submission" analogous to that of the slave to his master. And insofar as the community of believers is referred to as "the house of Islam," the title of this book refers metaphorically to the community of all those who serve and worship Allah.

When we examine how the term *abd* is used in common Moroccan proverbs, we see that it is not only basic to the Islamic conception of the proper relationship between man and God, it is also basic to the popular Islamic conception of what it means to be human. In fact, in ordinary Moroccan usage, *abd* is the usual term for "human." Thus when traditional Moroccan Muslims want to say that they will never forgive someone for an offense, they often say, "I will not forgive him, not before God and not before man" (*ma nsmahlu shi la and Allah wa la and al-abd*). In this proverb, the phrase "before God" (*and Allah*) refers to the hereafter, whereas "before man" (*and al-abd*) refers to this world. Another proverb states: "Man (*al-abd*) begins and God (*Allah*) completes" (Westermarck 1930: 142). (The meaning of this proverb is basically that "God helps those who help themselves.") These examples demonstrate to what extent the traditional Muslim fuses the idea of being a Muslim with the idea of being human. It should also be noted, in this respect, that the Jbala always use the verb *mat*, "to die," when speaking of the death of a Muslim. But when speaking of the death of an infidel or an animal, they always use the verb *jaf*, literally "to choke to death." Modern westernized Muslims such as Fatima Zohra would never speak this way. But from the point of view of Muslims such as al-Hajj Muhammad, it is simply "common sense" to do so.

The tendency to view people of other religions and other cultures as less than fully human is found in all of the monotheistic

religions. And in Islam, as in Judaism and Christianity, this tendency is emphatically condemned by modern believers of a universalistic cultural orientation (see Rahman 1980: 162–70). But the fact
remains that many basic myths in all three of the monotheistic
religions portray all those outside the faith as intrinsically inferior to
those within it.

Much of the Quran, like much of the Torah-cum-Old Testa-
ment, depicts a state of "holy war" (*jihad*) between those who serve
the one true God and those who do not. The prophet Muhammad
and the fledgling Islamic community had to flee from Mecca to
Madina to escape the persecution of the infidels (polytheists) of
Mecca. The Quran relates in great detail the military conflict that
ensued until Mecca finally submitted to the Muslims in 630. This
conflict has served as a mythical paradigm in terms of which the
relationship between the believer (*al-mu'min*) and the infidel (*al-
kafir*) is perceived by the traditional Muslim.

All religions have a specific mythic structure. That is, they have
a set of narratives dealing with events in the primordial past which
involve divine powers of some kind. And the myths concerning
these events are believed to explain the nature of the world and of
the human condition. Moreover, such myths never cease to affect
the way the believer views the world and interprets history. The
devoutly religious Jew inevitably perceives the establishment of the
modern state of Israel in the context of the deliverance of the Jews
from their bondage in Egypt and the divine promise that all Jews
would ultimately be allowed to return from their exile to the land
granted them by God. Similarly, the traditional Muslim inevitably
perceives the struggle to free the Muslim world from European
domination (the state of Israel being considered part of this domination) in the context of the prophet Muhammad's *jihad* against the
infidels of Arabia. Modern Muslims such as Fatima Zohra regard the
idea of *jihad* as an anachronism that is completely irrelevant to the
modern struggle against foreign domination. But from the point of
view of Muslims such as al-Hajj Muhammad, such an attitude is,
once again, tantamount to apostasy.

However, while it is true that Muslims like al-Hajj Muhammad perceive the anticolonial struggles of the twentieth century as "holy wars," it is also true that the idea of anticolonial struggle has now become part of the meaning of the word *jihad*. Al-Hajj Muhammad, in describing his participation in the nationalist movement in the 1950s, declares, "I was a *mujahid* fighting the *jihad* (holy war) against the colonialism of the infidels." The word *jihad* has taken on a new semantic dimension that it did not have prior to the subjugation of the Islamic world by Europe in the nineteenth and twentieth centuries. And the same holds true for the words *Nisrani*, "Christian," and *Ihudi*, "Jew."

Both the Christian and the Jew are condemned in the Quran for having refused to accept Muhammad as the ultimate and greatest prophet of God (Quran II : 135–41). Various attitudes toward them are presented in different chapters. In the early chapters revealed to Muhammad in Mecca, there is an emphasis upon tolerance. A famous verse of the chapter of *al-Kafirun* ("the Infidels") states: "You have your religion and I have mine" (*lakum dinukum wa liya dini*) (Quran CIX : 6). This verse is often cited by modern westernized Muslims such as Fatima Zohra. However, the later chapters, revealed to the prophet in Madina when he was engaged in a prolonged *jihad* against the polytheists of Mecca, are less tolerant in spirit. Muslims are told that they must fight all infidels until they convert to Islam or pay the *jizya* tax (Quran IX : 29). (The *jizya* was a tax paid by Christians and Jews in the Islamic world until the twentieth century.) Both Christians and Jews are referred to as "people of the book" (*ahl al-kitab*) in the Quran because their sacred scriptures are regarded as having been revealed by God to early prophets such as Moses and Jesus. Thus, in the Quran, Christians and Jews are usually portrayed more favorably than are the polytheists. And whereas the polytheists were generally forced either to convert or die, "the people of the book" had the alternative of paying the *jizya* and becoming "the people of the covenant of protection" (*ahl al-dhimma*) (Gibb and Kramers 1953: 75). Christians and Jews (also Zoroastrians) thus had a specific legal position in Islamic society, a position that did not give them the same rights as Muslims but did accord them greater privileges than were granted to non-Christian minorities in medieval Christendom (Chouraqui 1973: 44–47).

However, certain qualities attributed specifically to polytheists (*al-mushrikun*) in the Quran came to be attributed to all infidels, including Christians and Jews. Thus the Quran states: "O you who believe, verily the polytheists are unclean" (*ya ayyuha al-ladhina amanu innama al-mushrikun najasun*) (Quran IX : 28). In the Shii sect of Islam that prevails in Iran, southern Iraq, and a few other scattered areas in the Islamic world, this verse is interpreted as referring to *all* infidels (Gibb and Kramers 1953: 432). And although this interpretation of this particular verse never became part of the dogma of Sunni Islam, the basic idea did. The dichotomy between Muslim and infidel implies a dichotomy between purity and impurity (*tahara* and *najas*).

The idea that the infidel is ritually unclean manifests itself repeatedly in al-Hajj Muhammad's narrative: "The Christians think we are dirty, but *they* are dirty. That is why we do not allow them in our mosques. Whenever I work for a Christian or a Jew, I feel dirty and I go to the *hammam* (public steam bath). But the cobblestone quarter is a clean neighborhood (*hawma nqiyya*). There are hardly any Christians or Jews in it now" (II.2). Edward Westermarck, who spent seven years in Morocco from 1898 to 1926, describes how *baraka*, or "blessedness," is polluted by contact with infidels:

> *Baraka* is considered to be extremely sensitive to external influences and to be easily spoiled by them.
> It is polluted by contact with infidels. One reason why the Sultan Mulai Abdl'aziz lost his *baraka* was the presence of Christians at court. The barbers of Andjra say that there is no *baraka* in the razors used by their colleagues in Tangier, because they are sharpened by Christians. A prayer said in a Christian's house or in the house or garden of a Jew is of no avail. If a Jew enters the house of a Moor, the angels will desert it for forty days. [Westermarck 1968: I, 229]

Modern westernized Muslims like Fatima Zohra regard such ideas as absolute nonsense. But the idea that the infidel is impure is often to be found in the writings of Muslim fundamentalist ideologists. In a sermon commenting on the significance of the attestation of faith, which he refers to as the *Kalima*, or "Word," the famous Pakistani fundamentalist Mawlana Mawdudi notes: "On uttering these words called *Kalima* a man undergoes a remarkable transformation. From a *Kafir* he turns into a Muslim. He was impure before and now he is pure. From being liable to Divine wrath, he becomes a beloved of God. He was destined for Hell before but now the gates of heaven are open for him" (Mawdudi 1976: 24).

The idea that all infidels are doomed to burn in the eternal fires of hell occurs repeatedly in the Quran (II : 24; XXXIX : 71) as well as in the narrative of al-Hajj Muhammad. But other passages of the Quran are far more universalistic in spirit:

> verily all those who believe
> Jews, Christians, and the Sabians
> all those who believe in God
> and the last day
> and who do good deeds
> they shall have their reward
> with their Lord
> and there shall be no fear upon them
> nor shall they grieve.   [Quran II : 62]

This verse is often cited by modernist Muslims to support the view that all those who believe in God and the day of judgment, infidels as well as Muslims, will be admitted to heaven on the basis of their deeds (Rahman 1980: 166). And Fatima Zohra extends this logic to assert that "good people will go to heaven no matter what they believe" (personal communication). Once again, al-Hajj Muhammad and most traditional Muslims would regard this universalism as being tantamount to apostasy.

In addition to the general idea that infidels are impure and doomed to burn in hell, there are more specific dimensions to the traditional conception of the Christian and the Jew in Moroccan popular culture. These dimensions demonstrate how the meaning of religious symbols is affected by economic, social, and political transformations. The Christian is perceived as being cruel and merciless. Thus, in speaking of a peasant in the village of the streams who burned his daughter's hand, al-Hajj Muhammad observes: "Only a Christian could do such a thing." Westermarck describes a Moroccan official who, upon hearing of a man who had slit his daughter's throat, exclaimed, "This was something so horrible that not even a Christian would have done it" (Westermarck 1968: I, 529). This image of Christian cruelty obviously bears the impress of twelve centuries of intermittent holy warfare, as does the European image of the Muslim (see Daniel 1960 and Said 1978). The Christian is also perceived as being "cheap and greedy," especially with respect to helping poor relatives.

The Jew, on the other hand, is regarded as being cunning and avaricious, especially with respect to his commercial transactions with the Muslim. Al-Hajj Muhammad declares: "There is nothing worse than the Jews (*ma kayin shi qbah min al-Ihud*). The Jew is only happy when he has cheated a Muslim." Westermarck recorded several similar proverbs in the first quarter of the twentieth century (Westermarck 1930: 130). This "Shylock" motif is the distinguishing feature of the popular conception of the Jew in the Islamic world. Although condemned by modern Muslims such as Fatima Zohra, it frequently recurs in the sermons, speeches, and writings of fundamentalist ideologists. Mawlana Mawdudi declared in a sermon given in India in the 1930s that "the people of Prophet Moses were narrow-minded, hankered after money, just as you see the condition of Jews even today" (Mawdudi 1976: 157). Sayyid Qutb, one of the most famous ideologists of the Egyptian Muslim Brotherhood, asserts in *Hadha ad-Din* (This Religion) that "usury is the basis of the economy of the Jews" (Qutb 1978: 60). And the Ayatollah Khomeini has declared that the Jews are "a cunning and resourceful people" who seek "to establish Jewish domination throughout the world" (Khomeini 1981: 127).

Lawrence Rosen has argued that in the Moroccan city of

Sefrou, "however much Jews are regarded as shrewd businessmen by the city's Moslems they are almost never characterized as dishonest or avaricious" (Rosen 1970b: 398). Rosen's observations certainly do not correspond to the image of the Jew that emerges from al-Hajj Muhammad's narrative. Al-Hajj Muhammad notes that "today a good Muslim woman is as hard to find as a generous Jew." Elsewhere, he refers to the miserly husband of his aunt Amina as a "Jew and a half" (*Ihudi wu nuss*). And this expression is the standard metaphor used to refer to a miser in northwestern Morocco.

However, it is true that the anti-Semitic motif of a conspiracy to extend Jewish domination throughout the world is not indigenous to the Islamic world, nor does it ever occur in al-Hajj Muhammad's narrative. This theme, which does often occur in the Muslim fundamentalist literature, has been borrowed from the anti-Semitic literature of Europe (Rosen 1970b: 394). It is also true that anti-Semitism in the Christian world has generally been far more virulent and fatal in its consequences than anti-Semitism in the Islamic world (Chouraqui 1973: 54; Goitein 1964: 87–88). In an interesting discussion of the Moroccan Muslim image of the Jew, Norman Stillman makes the important point that "most of the Moroccan stereotypes of Jews may be negative, but they are also peripheral" (Stillman 1977: 80). This point applies to al-Hajj Muhammad's narrative. Al-Hajj Muhammad's references to Jews, as well as the manner in which he once disrupted prayers in a synagogue of Tangier, demonstrate that he regards all Jews as utterly contemptible creatures. Like most traditional Muslims, he takes it for granted that they are avaricious, cunning, impure, and doomed to burn in hell. But he is far more vehemently hostile to the Christian than he is to the Jew. This is due to the much greater significance of the former in contemporary Moroccan society.

The evolution of anti-Semitism in both the Christian and Islamic worlds demonstrates how socioeconomic factors interact with religion and culture in history. The Jew is portrayed as an evil figure in the fundamental myths of both religions. In Christianity, the Jew is condemned not only for rejecting Christ but for "killing" him. In Islam, the Jew is condemned not only for rejecting Muhammad, but for deceitfully collaborating with his enemies (Quran XXXIII : 26; LIX : 2–4). Yet the descendants of the Romans who actually killed Christ are never called "Christ killers" and the descendants of the Meccans who actually fought Muhammad are not called "enemies of Islam." This is because the Romans eventually converted to Christianity and the Meccans to Islam. So the invidious role the Jew plays in the mythic structure of both religions is primarily due to his refusal to accept Christ as the son of God on the one hand, and Muhammad as the prophet of God on the other.

The exclusion of the Jew from the ranks of the believers resulted in his exclusion from the central economic, social, and political functions of the medieval Christian and Muslim societies that defined themselves in terms of common belief.

If the medieval church tolerated the Jews when she could have assimilated them by force or massacred them, it was because they filled a vital economic function. Accursed, they followed a cursed vocation; being unable to own land or serve in the army, they trafficked in money, which a Christian could not do without defiling himself. Thus the original curse was soon reinforced by an economic curse, and it is above all the latter that has persisted. [Sartre 1948: 68]

In the Islamic world, too, the Jew was *generally* excluded from occupations other than those that would defile a believer—notably, commerce associated with usury and artisanry associated with precious metals (Lapidus 1967: 82; Léon L'Africain 1956: 234; Stillman 1978: 120). Thus, onto the image of the Jew as impure infidel was grafted the image of the Jew as usurer. The originally strictly religious hostility was fused with, and exacerbated by, enmity of a socioeconomic character.

The process whereby religious enmity fuses with socioeconomic as well as nationalistic grievances is graphically illustrated by the semantic evolution of the terms *infidel* (*kafir*), *Christian* (*Nis-*

rani), and *Jew* (*Ihudi*) in the wake of the economic and political subjugation of Morocco by "the West" during the past century. After describing some of the jobs he has had working for Spaniards and Moroccan Jews in Tangier, al-Hajj Muhammad notes: "The Muslim lives on the money of the Christian and the Jew. In this world, they are always on the top and we are always on the bottom. But in the hereafter, God willing (*in sha' Allah*), we shall be on the top and they shall be on the bottom" (II.2). After condemning the westernized, that is, "Christian," culture of Fatima Zohra and her sisters, al-Hajj Muhammad declares:

> We should shut all the Christian schools in Morocco and teach our young people only the way of Islam. Until we return to the path of Islam, the Christians will continue to control our stores, our factories, our hotels, our mines and the minds of our young people.
>
> Some day, God willing, we shall arise and cleanse the house of Islam of all Christian filth. And when we do, all those Muslims who have become like parrots mimicking their Christian masters in this world will have to return to the path of Islam or be punished according to the word of God. [VII.8]

It is obvious that passages such as these involve more than mere enmity toward the infidel qua infidel. They involve resentment of "foreign" socioeconomic and political domination *as well as* strictly religious bigotry. The particularistic religious dichotomy of believer versus infidel has fused with socioeconomic and nationalistic dichotomies such as poor versus rich, colonized versus colonizer, and oppressed versus oppressor.

As we have seen, Morocco was governed by European powers from 1912 to 1956. And to this day Morocco remains a "client state" of France and the United States (Oualalou 1980). Referring to the continuing importance of foreigners in Moroccan society, the Moroccan historian Abd Allah Laroui observes that "the administration of *things* continues to be the province of foreigners; for Moroccans, there remains only the government of men" (Laroui 1976: 39). Fatima Zohra notes that "Europeans still control our biggest facto-

ries, our biggest hotels. They still occupy our biggest villas." Referring to the fact that the Europeans in Morocco are generally
wealthier than Moroccans whereas the Moroccans in Europe are
generally poorer than Europeans, al-Hajj Muhammad asks, "Why
does God allow the Christians to live like sultans in our land while
we are like slaves in their land?"

Resentment of the European economic and political domination of Morocco has exacerbated antipathy toward the Christian
insofar as the European (and the Euro-American) is perceived as a
Christian just as the Moroccan is perceived as a Muslim. For the
overwhelming majority of Moroccans, religious identity both tran-
scends and suffuses national identity. In everyday speech, traditional Moroccans (the great majority) do not speak of themselves as
"Moroccans" (*Mgharba*), but as "Muslims" (*Msilmin*). Similarly,
only an infinitesimal minority of Moroccan intellectuals ever refer to
Europeans by the literary term *Urubiyyun*. The standard word for
"European" is *Nisrani*, or Christian" (which becomes *Nsara* in the
plural). This is true even among modern westernized Moroccans
such as Fatima Zohra, who tends to use the terms "Muslim" and
"Moroccan" (*Maghrabi*) interchangeably in her narrative. Referring
to the economic and political dependence of Morocco upon Europeans and Americans, Fatima Zohra observes: "In one way or
another, all Moroccans spend their lives selling themselves to the
Christians." Such a statement does not imply religious bigotry when
said by a Moroccan like Fatima Zohra, although it would if it were
said by al-Hajj Muhammad. But even in the case of al-Hajj Muhammad, such a statement would involve resentment of foreign domination *as well as* particularistic animosity toward the Christian qua
Christian.

Abd Allah Laroui has stressed that the fact that Moroccans
generally refer to themselves as Muslims does not mean that they
lack a sense of national identity (Laroui 1980: 59). That is correct.
But it does imply that Islam is basic to that sense of national
identity, as is true throughout most of the Islamic world (Lewis
1981: 12, 17–18).

This relationship between religious and national identity is by no means a strictly Islamic phenomenon. Even in the most ostensibly secular societies in the world, there remains a specifically religious dimension to the national culture. This is illustrated by the role religious holy days play as national holidays. For example, every Christmas the President of the United States lights a "national" Christmas tree and non-Christian children in public schools are expected to sing (or pretend to sing) Christmas carols containing verses such as "O come all ye faithful, joyful and triumphant." Religious and national identity have been *legally* distinct in the West since the French and American revolutions in the late eighteenth century, yet *culturally* these two forms of collective identity have never been completely severed.

Given that religion continues to play an important role in the national cultures of the West, it is not surprising to find that this is even more true in the Islamic world. The idea that the individual's primary loyalty ought to be to "the nation" (*al-watan*), as opposed to the community of believers in Islam (*al-umma*), is a recent innovation borrowed from the West (Lewis 1981: 302). Fundamentalist ideologists condemn this innovation as being contrary to the laws of God (al-Banna 1965: 102–112; Khomeini 1981: 302). And it has not altered the way in which most Muslims continue to define themselves.

It should also be emphasized that the role of religion in the evolution of a national culture is typically heightened in the case of countries dominated by other countries with different "national" religions. Thus, just as the role of Roman Catholicism in Irish nationalism has been magnified by the fact that England is Protestant, so too the role of Islam in Arab nationalism has been enhanced by the fact that Europe is Christian (Geertz 1968: 65). And as in northern Ireland, traditional religious animosities have been aggravated by nationalistic as well as socioeconomic factors.

The fact that European domination of the Islamic world was, and is, widely perceived in terms of the domination of "the house of Islam" by the infidel has tended to accentuate the alienation of the

Christian and Jewish minorities of the Islamic world from their Muslim "compatriots." Moreover, these minorities, like "pariah" minorities throughout the third world, generally welcomed European colonialism as a means of escaping their subordinate position in precolonial Muslim society (Chouraqui 1973: 260). In Morocco, European rule greatly improved the legal and socioeconomic position of Moroccan Jews, most of whom naturally found it difficult to sympathize with the nationalist struggle of a nation to which they had never really belonged (Stillman 1978: 121). Thus, the Moroccan Muslim increasingly perceived the Moroccan Jew as being on the side of colonialism. Speaking of the general strike in Tangier on March 30, 1952, al-Hajj Muhammad states: "The Independence party and the other political parties organized a general strike to demand independence. All Muslim stores were closed that day. But all the big modern stores remained open because they were owned by Christians and Jews." And Fatima Zohra, who condemns al-Hajj Muhammad's anti-Semitism, states: "When Tangier was an International Zone, all of *la ville nouvelle* was a European city which Muslims only entered to serve the Europeans and the Jews who lived there." The Moroccan Jew was in fact caught in the middle of the struggle between the colonized and the colonizer, with both sides ultimately rejecting him as "foreign" (Memmi 1972: 17, 37). This position was analogous to that of the Indian minorities in black Africa and the West Indies.

The Moroccan Jew became even more closely identified with European imperialism after the establishment of the state of Israel in 1948. The Arab perceives Israel in the context of the subjugation and displacement of the Palestinians. Moshe Dayan, who more than any other man symbolizes the significance of Israel in terms of Jewish history, has observed: "It is not true that the Arabs hate the Jews for personal, religious, or racial reasons. They consider us—and justly, from their point of view—as Westerners, foreigners, invaders who have seized an Arab country to turn it into a Jewish state" (cited in Chomsky 1974: 53). As we have already seen, there are in fact many Arabs who *do* hate Jews for religious reasons.

However, the primary cause of Arab hostility toward Israel is that Arabs perceive it as an artifact of European imperialism created on the premise that Europeans have the natural "God-given" right to colonize the lands of the "natives" of the third world (Said 1980).

But while anti-Semitism is definitely not the principal cause of Arab hostility to Israel, it nonetheless suffuses this hostility in the case of traditional Muslims like al-Hajj Muhammad. Such people interpret colonial domination in terms of traditional religious symbols. And traditional particularistic stereotypes affect the way they perceive all forms of colonial domination, just as this domination adds new meanings to these stereotypes. Thus many traditional Muslims link the conflict between the Israelis and the Palestinians to the conflict betwen Muhammad and the Jewish tribes of Madina described in the Quran and assert that the Jew has always sought to harm Islam (Khomeini 1981: 27, 89, 127).

As has been already noted, this tendency to interpret modern events in terms of ancient religious myth is not an exclusively Islamic phenomenon. From the believer's point of view, myth explains the present as well as the past. Just as many zealous fundamentalist Muslims justify the slaughter of Jews by citing the extermination of the men of the Jewish tribe of Bani Qurayza by order of the prophet Muhammad (Quran XXXIII : 26–27), so too many zealous Orthodox Jews justify the slaughter of Palestinians by citing the extermination of all of the Amalekites, including women and children, by order of the prophet Samuel (I Samuel 15; Chomsky 1974: 109). And devout, God-fearing Christians have also always been able to cite a verse or two of scripture to justify the slaughter of "the enemies of Christ."

It should be emphasized, once again, that not all Muslims perceive Jews as does al-Hajj Muhammad. And most well-educated and relatively secular Muslims do distinguish between condemnation of what they perceive as the European colonization of Palestine and hatred of the Jew qua Jew. In fact, in Morocco at any rate, relatively secular Muslims tend to be more outraged by the statelessness and dispersion of the Palestinians than are Muslims of a more traditional religious orientation. Fatima Zohra, for example, feels far more strongly about the Palestinian issue than does al-Hajj Muhammad. And yet she generally gets along better with relatively secular Israelis and American Jews than she does with devoutly religious Muslims.

Prejudice is always easy to see when one is its victim. It is considerably less obvious when it is in one's own mind. In the words of a Moroccan proverb, "The camel does not see his hump, only that of his father's sister" (*Aj-jmil ma kayshuf shi kurrtu, ghayr d ammtu*). Many westerners outraged by the bigotry of Muslims such as al-Hajj Muhammad do not perceive the ethnocentrism in their own conception of the Muslim, and of the Arab in particular. Aside from the manifest bigotry of Christian fundamentalists, who are just as certain as al-Hajj Muhammad that all infidels are evil, the image of the Muslim and the Arab that prevails in Western culture is a highly prejudiced one. The only Arabs one usually sees in American movies are corrupt sheiks or vicious terrorists. And Islam is thought of as a primitive religion utterly unlike the "humane" religions of "the civilized world," when in fact all three of the monotheistic religions share the same basic assumptions concerning the meaning of human existence.

It should be noted that when al-Hajj Muhammad speaks of Christians as being "dirty," he usually does so after observing that "the Christians think we are dirty, but. . . . " He generally uses the words *dirty* (*musakh*) and *clean* (*nqi*) in the sense of "impure" (*najis*) and "pure" (*tahir*). This dichotomy is at least implicitly associated with the distinction between European and non-European in Western culture generally.

A Moroccan once described to me what happened when he went to a movie theater (the Mauritania) in the European "new city" of Tangier before independence. He had bathed at a public bath and had put on his cleanest and purest white jillaba, which he usually wore only for congregational prayers, in order to have the privilege of seeing a movie in a Christian (i.e., European) movie theater. But he was apparently the only Muslim in the theater. As he waited in line for a ticket, the Christians (Europeans) stared at him and whispered to each other about this insolent Muslim who had dared to enter their theater. And they carefully avoided physical contact with him, as though they did not want to be soiled or defiled. Aware that the Christians thought all Muslims were dirty, the Muslim had done his best to cleanse and purify himself in order to enter their domain. But their conception of cleanliness-cum-purity differed from his. From their point of view, he was dirty and impure simply by virtue of being a Muslim wearing Muslim clothes. Perhaps if he had been wearing "civilized" European clothes, the "native" might have been able to "pass" for a swarthy Spaniard. But his white jillaba symbolized the fact that he was an Arab rather than a European, a Muslim rather than a Christian, a "native" rather than a colonist. And he was therefore by definition "dirty."

The Moroccan (a friend of al-Hajj Muhammad's brother Ahmad) wanted to run out of the theater when he felt the eyes of the Christians staring at him, but he stayed in line and saw the movie in order to defy these foreigners who controlled his country. However, he did not attempt to enter another movie theater in the new city until after independence, when the de facto segregation of this part of Tangier was eliminated. In recounting this story, the Moroccan emphasized that he would never forget the expressions of revulsion on the faces of the Christians near him in the theater for as long as he lived. Such experiences have obviously infused new meaning into traditional Muslim antipathy toward the infidel.

CONCLUSION

Both al-Hajj Muhammad and Fatima Zohra are Muslims. It is true that many Muslims would argue that Fatima Zohra is in fact not a Muslim at all because she does not conform to the rules of Islam. She neither prays nor fasts. She wears a bikini at the beach. She drinks wine with her food. And she refuses to accept the idea that women should only inherit half as much as their brothers despite the fact that this rule is prescribed by the Quran. But she still thinks of herself as a Muslim. And she continues to believe in the basic concepts of Islam, notably God, the prophet Muhammad, and the day of judgment. She interprets these concepts more universalistically than al-Hajj Muhammad, but she nonetheless remains a believer.

However, being a Muslim is not simply a question of religious belief. It is also a question of cultural and national identity. A number of French intellectuals assumed Moroccan citizenship after independence without converting to Islam. Legally, these people are citizens of Morocco with the same rights as any other Moroccan. But culturally they remain foreigners. Regardless of their atheism or agnosticism, they remain *Nsara*, or "Christians." All Europeans are referred to as *Nsara* regardless of their religious belief or legal citizenship—unless they specifically identify themselves as Jews. The idea of being a Christian is inseparable from the idea of being a European (or Euro-American) in Moroccan culture, just as the idea of being a Moroccan is inseparable from the idea of being a Muslim.

And given that the Muslim/Christian dichotomy implies the Moroccan/European dichotomy, it has absorbed new meaning as a result of the European domination of Morocco since the late nineteenth century. Al-Hajj Muhammad notes that "the Christians are rich and powerful and we Muslims are poor and weak. So we think they are better than we are." No Muslim in his or her right mind would have suggested that an infidel could be in any way superior to a Muslim prior to the subjugation of the Islamic world by Europe. Nor would Moroccans of the early nineteenth century have felt obliged to harp on the spiritual superiority of the Muslim vis-à-vis the infidel, as does al-Hajj Muhammad. This would have been taken for granted. But after over a century of European ("Christian") domination, the idea of spiritual superiority has become a refuge from the sense of inferiority felt by the Muslim in the economic, technological, and political aspects of modern life. Fatima Zohra notes that "everything from the West is considered better than what is from Morocco—except when it comes to religion, of course." By interpreting the world in an Islamic framework, the secular superiority of the infidel can be inverted. This is an important source of the appeal of Islamic fundamentalist ideology to educated young Muslims, who tend to be far more tormented by a sense of inferiority than are Muslims like al-Hajj Muhammad.

Another source of the appeal of Islamic fundamentalist ideology to educated young Muslims is that Islam represents their "authentic" national culture, whereas westernization represents the assimilation of the culture of the foreign powers that have dominated their country for over a century. Many Muslims bitterly resent the assumption that "modernization" and "westernization" are synonymous. They argue that they want technological, economic, and political modernization without having to replace their own authentic culture by the culture of the industrialized West. For such people, "the revival of Islam" is primarily a means of resisting what they regard as a form of "cultural imperialism."

But Muslims like al-Hajj Muhammad are not in search of authenticity. When al-Hajj Muhammad condemns Moroccan women who wear bikinis at the beach, he does so because he regards such behavior as contrary to the laws of Islam, not because he views the bikini as a form of western cultural domination. (However, these attitudes are often intertwined.)

The traditional Muslim generally rejects cultural modernization, which does typically involve assimilation of the culture of the West, insofar as it is perceived as being contrary to the laws of God. And the outrage provoked by perceived violations of divine law can assume considerable political significance, as is demonstrated by the importance of the issues of abortion and public school prayers in contemporary American politics.

But the appeal, or potential appeal, of Islamic fundamentalist ideology to Muslims like al-Hajj Muhammad does not derive solely from the outrage provoked by perceived violations of the laws of God. Such Muslims are also outraged by social inequity and foreign domination, as al-Hajj Muhammad's narrative makes abundantly clear. And the fundamentalist ideologist articulates all of these grievances in terms of the basic sacred symbols that shape the way the traditional Muslim perceives the world. The fundamentalist ideologist speaks the language of the traditional Muslim, albeit with a different accent.

However, while al-Hajj Muhammad's conception of Islam is relatively traditional, and Fatima Zohra's relatively modern, both bear the impress of the recent history of Morocco—the distinctive feature of which has been domination by "the West." Just as Islam has played an important role in determining how Moroccan Muslims have interpreted and participated in this history, so too has this history played an important role in determining how Moroccan Muslims interpret and participate in Islam.

I

Si Abd Allah

(1870–1932)

Peasant of the Village of the Streams

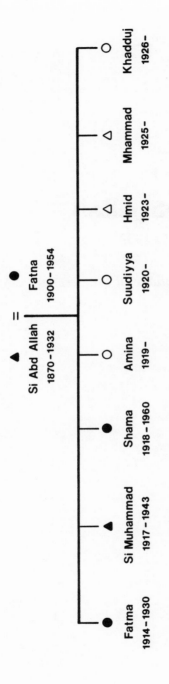

KEY

△ Male
○ Female
▲ Deceased
= Marriage Bond

Genealogical Diagram I: Si Abd Allah and His Eight Children

1. Al-Hajj Muhammad the peddler
on his grandfather, Si Abd Allah

S I ABD ALLAH (Slave of God) son of Si Amar son of al-Arbi B. was born in the village of the streams not long after the Spanish desecrated the mosque of Sidi Abd Allah al-Baqqali in Tetuan and turned it into a church (1860–61). God damn the infidels. This was the time of violence (*as-siba*) in the hills of the Jbala. Muslim killed Muslim for the slightest reason: a cow, a goat, a piece of land or a woman. A man who found his wife or his daughter lying with a man would kill them both. If we still did this today, there would be no Muslims left in Morocco.

In those days, the *qayyids* did not care if the Jbala killed each other so long as they paid their taxes. Two men would argue as the *fqih* would wake the village by the call to the dawn prayer. And by the sunset prayer, all the men in the village would be shooting at each other. But the Jbala never killed the way the Rifis used to kill. The Rifi would kill his own brother over an onion.

Much has changed since the time when Si Abd Allah was born in the village of the streams. But much is still the same. We Muslims are still so busy eating each other that we do not see the Christians eating us all. We no longer kill our neighbors in our village. Now we kill our brothers in the Sahara. And they kill us. And the Christians laugh while we do their work for them. But they shall not laugh on the day of reckoning, when God shall condemn them to the eternal fires of hell.

> fear the fire
> the fuel of which
> is man and stone
> the fire lit
> for the infidels
> who cover
> the signs of God   [II : 24]

The hills of the Jbala (mountain people) are full of the bounty of God. We sow wheat, barley, and broad beans in the valleys after the start of the winter rains in October. We harvest them in early summer, after the death of the land (*mut d al-ard*) in May. During the winter rains, the soil of the valleys is black and moist. But after May, the land is parched and cracked. In the winter, the rain falls in torrents, turning every mule path into a rushing stream. But in the summer, even the biggest streams slow to a trickle.

In the winter we sit around the *mijmar* (an earthenware brazier) fanning the charcoal embers and drinking hot mint tea. And we listen to the rain pounding on the roof and pray that it will not wash away the wheat. When a man has to take his mule down to the Tuesday market of Jbil Hbib or to Dar Shawi, he prays the mule won't slip on the muddy paths going down to the valley. If a mule breaks a leg, it dies. And a man cannot live in the hills without a mule. Nowadays you cannot buy a mule for less than 200,000 francs ($444). Most Jbala never see that much money in their entire lives.

Before independence (1956), poor Jbala with little or no arable valley land would grow barley and even wheat on village communal land in the scrub forest of the hills. The soil in the hills is sandy and less fertile than the black soils of the valleys. But poor Jbala would burn the scrub brush off a field and the ashes would give strength to the soil. After two years, a man would leave that field and go burn another one. And after fifteen or twenty years, after the scrub forest had grown back, he would return to the old field again. In this way, even poor Jbala could feed their families. But after independence, the government said this was illegal. And they said the Jbala could only graze their goats in certain areas near their village. And they said that the Jbala could no longer make charcoal. They do not want us to kill the forest but they do not care if we, the sons of Adam, die of hunger.

We fight to free the house of Islam from the Christian colonialists, and our Muslim brothers in their air-conditioned offices in Rabat make it impossible to live in the hills. Now, nobody cuts and burns fields in the hills anymore because the forest rangers patrol the woods. But many Jbala still make charcoal because you can make a mound of charcoal in a week to ten days. And if you are lucky, they won't catch you. If they do, you pay a fine or you go to jail. Each time you are caught, the fine and the jail sentence get bigger. And sooner or later, the poor Jibli gives up and brings his family down to Tangier where he will try to work as a day laborer with a shovel and a pick (*bi il-palu wa al-piku*). This is what happened to my uncle Hmid.

> verily
> God is with those
> who patiently endure   [II : 153]

Life is hard in the hills. But still the hills are full of the bounty of the Lord. We grow wheat, barley, and broad beans in the valley fields, and tomatoes, potatoes, green peppers, and mint in village gardens in the hills. We have figs, plums, apples, and pears from our village orchards. We have buttermilk, butter, and cheese from our goats and our cows. We have the meat of our goats, the eggs of our chickens, and fish from the sea.

> if you were
> to count
> God's bounty
> you could not
> for God is
> forgiving and
> merciful   [XVI : 18]

In the days of Si Abd Allah, my grandfather, Muslims were content with the bounty that God granted them. Today, the Muslim wants to live as the Christian lives. We buy Christian food. My aunt Khadduj and her daughters are not satisfied with bread and stew (*gwaz*) anymore. Now they buy *bocadillos* (hero sandwiches) like Christians and Muslims with no family. Everyone wants to buy Christian clothes, Christian shoes, Christian cigarettes. In the days of Si Abd Allah, the Jbala used to make their own soap from olive oil, lime, and the ashes of green lentisk wood. Now they buy the Spanish *sabun d Sibta* in the weekly markets.

The Christians are rich and powerful and we Muslims are poor and weak. So we think they are better than we are. But the Christians have their paradise in this world only. We Muslims have our paradise in the hereafter. And it will last forever.

The village of the streams lies high in the hills of the *qbila* of Bni Msawwar. Perhaps the original Bni Msawwar were the sons of a man named Msawwar. God knows best. But today there are people from all over Morocco in Bni Msawwar. The two original clans of the village of the streams were the B. clan and the Y. clan. The B. clan is descended from Sidi Ali B., a saint buried in Fez. But no one has ever seen his grave. The Sons of Y. claim to be descended from a saint named Sidi Y. But there are many saints named Sidi Y. No one knows which of them is the ancestor of the Sons of Y. The Sons of Y. used to be carpenters as well as farmers. They made plows, yokes, winnowing forks, and spoons. Luhsin son of Qasim still makes spoons sometimes. The others do not carve wood anymore. But they still have beehives and make honey, especially Si Muhammad Qasim, my aunt Amina's husband.

When Si Abd Allah was still young and strong, other men came to live in the village. Sidi al-Ayyashi and Sidi al-Mahdi of the Baqqali clan came from the village of the weavers in the nearby *qbila* of Jbil Hbib. They were originally from the village of Fijj Hanun in the *qbila* of Bni Yidir. And Muhammad F. came from the village of the reeds in Bni Msawwar. He had killed a man and had left his village to escape the vengeance of the dead man's brothers. The F.s are poor and they have no value. But Si Abd al-Ali F., the village *fqih* (teacher of the Quran), is a good Muslim.

The Baqqalis are *shurfa* descended from the saint Sidi Allal al-Hajj al-Baqqali, who is buried in the *qbila* of Ghzawa. The patron saint of Tangier is also a Baqqali: Sidi Bu Araqiyya. And there are Baqqalis in every *qbila* of the Jbalan hills. In the time of *as-siba* the Baqqalis, like all *shurfa*, would make peace between feuding families.

We of the B. clan are also *shurfa*, but we do not want to show off (*ma khassna shi ndahhru rasna*). So people do not know that we are *shurfa*.

Shurfa are pure (*tahirin*). It is said that if a *sharif* drinks wine, it becomes honey in his mouth so that he does not sin.

Maybe the Baqqalis of the village of the streams are not true *shurfa* because they have always been a pack of thieves and whores. Every summer Sidi Muhammad son of K. and his brothers bring sacks of wheat up to the village on their mules. But they own no land in the valley. Muslims are supposed to give alms to *shurfa*. And some say these sacks of wheat are alms collected in many villages. Others say they steal this wheat. God knows best.

But those Baqqalis are no good. Sidi Mustafa son of K. pretends to be a good Muslim. But one day his daughter was screaming. So he lit a match and burned her hand. And she was a little baby girl. Only a Christian could do such a thing.

La Ftuma al-Baqqaliyya has been a whore and dancing girl all her life, as was her mother La Shama. One day my aunt Khadduj asked her, "La Ftuma, how many men have you gone with?" La Ftuma laughed and said, "Hundreds." My aunt asked, "Do you not fear God?" And La Ftuma pointed to the hole between her thighs and said, "God is good. And He gave us this thing to enjoy it, not just to have it eaten by worms after we die." Ah La Ftuma! She is a big woman with breasts so big she can sling them over her shoulders and her buttocks are like watermelons. She has given many men pleasure. Even now, although she is old and wrinkled, she still dances at weddings. And she still goes with men, sometimes for money and sometimes because the fire still burns in that hole between her legs.

And La Ftuma is a thief, like all the Baqqalis in the village of the streams. One day, she and her husband were having dinner at my brother Mustafa's house in the cobblestone quarter. And they stole some gold bracelets that belonged to Mustafa's wife Rahma. Since then, we do not let her into our homes.

But at least La Ftuma is not a hypocrite (*munafiq*) like Sidi Muhammad and Sidi Mustafa, the sons of Sidi K. al-Baqqali. She does not pretend to be anything but a whore. They are liars and thieves but they try to pretend that they are good Muslims. Everyone will be hung by his leg on the day of reckoning.

Si Abd Allah, my mother's father, built and lived in the house we now call "Grandmother's house" (*dar d al-aziza*), because my grandmother lived in it when we were children. It is near the stream of Maymun, where Si Abd Allah had a grain mill. The grindstone was turned by the water of the stream. It turned fast in the winter and slowly in the summer. Everyone in the village brought their wheat and barley to this mill to be ground into flour. Now only the rocks of its foundation are still there and everyone uses Si Muhammad Qasim's mill farther up the stream.

In those days Si Abd Allah was the richest man in the village. Now Si Muhammad Qasim is, but he is a thief and he will pay for his actions on the day of reckoning. Si Abd Allah owned about four hectares of land in the valley. Some near the stream of ar-Rmilat, and some near where the town of Dar Shawi is now. He also owned the gardens and orchards near Grandmother's house. He would bring plums, pears, figs, and apples down to the Tuesday market of Jbil Hbib in the late summer and fall. And he made some money this way. He also owned four cows, two mules, about thirty goats, and about the same number of chickens. And now his children are poor because of my uncle Hmid and Si Muhammad Qasim. Everyone will be hung by his leg (*Kull wahid ghadi ikun mallaq min rijlu*).

Si Abd Allah was no longer young when he married my

grandmother Fatna daughter of Si Ahmad B. of the village of the reeds in Bni Msawwar. This was about the time the Spanish colonized northern Morocco (1912).

Bir-Raysul was governor of the hills of the Jbala (mountain people) in those days. Bir-Raysul was a *sharif* descended from Mulay Abd as-Slam son of Mshish, the possessor of the land (*mul al-blad*) of the Jbala. The Jbala say that seven pilgrimages to the tomb of Mulay Abd as-Slam on Jbil Alam (Mount Alam) are equal to one pilgrimage to Mecca the holy. But this is not true.

> verily
> we worship
> only God
> and with Him
> we associate
> no other
> and we take not
> from amongst
> ourselves
> lords
> other than God   [III : 64]

Sometimes ignorant Jbala who cannot read the Quran forget that the saints can only intercede on our behalf before God almighty. And it is as though they were worshipping the saints instead of God alone, like the Christians who worship statues. This is forbidden (*haram*). This is not Islam.

The Christians think we are primitive savages and they think our religion is primitive. But *they* are the primitive savages worshipping statues in their churches and saying that Jesus was the Son of God.

> in the name of God
> the merciful
> the compassionate
> say He is the one God
> the eternal God

He has never begotten
nor was He begotten
and there has
never been
anyone
like Him   [CXII]

Jesus was a prophet, not the son of God. The Christians control this world. They send men to the moon. They build great buildings, great bridges, great ships, and great bombs. But when it comes to understanding the word of God, they are ignorant savages. Thus does God seal the hearts of those who do not know (XXX : 59). They shall burn in hell while we bask in the softness of heaven.

Anyway, Bir-Raysul was a *sharif*. One of his ancestors is one of the greatest saints in Tetuan. The Jbala say that Bir-Raysul had such great *baraka* (blessedness) that bullets could not kill him. He used to boast that he had brought peace to the hills and that he had made it safe for a woman or a Jew to walk all the way from Tetuan to Tangier (through the hills of the Jbala) without being touched. But Bir-Raysul was a traitor who sold the house of Islam to the Christians. Everyone will be hung by his leg.

We could not have defeated the Spanish even if Bir-Raysul had not been a traitor. Abd al-Krim and the Rifis could not stop them in the Rif. What is written is written. Nothing afflicts us but what God has written for us.

Why did God allow the Christians to rule over the house of Islam? Why did God allow the Jews to take Palestine and holy Jerusalem? Why does God allow the Christians to live like sultans in our land while we are like slaves in their land? This is God's punishment. And this is God's test. Muslims have left the path (*kharju min at-triq*) of Islam. Young people do not pray. The rich do not pray. Muslim girls bare their bodies like Christian women. And they walk hand in hand with their lovers on the *bulivar* (le Boulevard Pasteur, the main street of Tangier). The rich Muslim does not fast during Ramadan. And he drinks wine and whiskey. And he asks why it is that the house of Islam is like a toy in the hands of the Christian. The Christian domination is the wrath of God.

And the Christian domination is God's test of our submission (*islam*) to His will.

> be sure
> that We
> shall test
> you
> by fear
> by hunger
> by loss of goods
> by loss of lives
> by loss of the
> fruits of your
> labor
> and bring
> glad tidings
> to those
> who patiently endure
> those who say
> when affliction
> afflicts them
> to God we belong
> and to Him we shall return   [II : 155–56]

To God we belong and to Him we shall return. Praise be to God who created the heavens and the earth and the darkness and the light.

2. *Al-Hajj Muhammad the peddler on his aunt Fatma,* *daughter of Si Abd Allah (1914–1930)*

S I ABD ALLAH'S FIRST CHILD, my mother's sister Fatma, was married by my father Abd as-Slam B., may God have mercy upon him, not long after she began bleeding as a woman. My father was a poor shoemaker from the village of the rocky places in Bni Msawwar. He was also of the B. clan and many men of the B.

clan were once shoemakers. My aunt Fatma died giving birth to their first child, who died at the same time. May God have mercy upon them. To God we belong and to Him we shall return (*Inna li Il-lahi wa inna ilayhi rajiun*). Later, my father married Fatma's younger sister, my mother Shama, may God have mercy upon her.

3. Al-Hajj Muhammad the peddler on his uncle Si Muhammad, son of Si Abd Allah (1917–1943)

THE SECOND CHILD of Si Abd Allah B. was my mother's brother Si Muhammad, may God have mercy upon him. Si Muhammad was a *talib*. Like all *tulba*, he made a little money chanting the holy book on the seventh day after birth, at circumcisions, at weddings, and at funerals. He was a good Muslim who prayed every prayer at its time (dawn, noon, mid-afternoon, sunset, and evening). He helped Si Abd Allah with the valley crops and the village gardens and orchards.

My uncle Si Muhammad married Khadduj A., the daughter of a peasant and charcoalmaker from the village of the big rock in the *qbila* of Bni Yidir (just east of Bni Msawwar). They had one daughter, my cousin Rahma, who is married to my brother Mustafa.

Si Muhammad died during the great war of the Christians (World War II). May God have mercy upon him. Khadduj A. caused him to die because she is cursed (*maskhuta*). Anyone who has been cursed by his parents will be hated by everyone. He will always be poor in this world. And he will burn in the eternal fires of hell in the hereafter. And this is also true of a woman who has been cursed by her husband. The curse of the husband is as strong as the curse of the parents. When a woman has been cursed by her parents or her husband, no one can help her. Not even the saints.

Khadduj A. used to disobey and torment Si Muhammad the

way her daughter Rahma now disobeys and torments my brother Mustafa. The women say that Rahma too is cursed.

After Si Muhammad died, Khadduj A. returned to her village of the big rock, where she married the *fqih* Muhammad A., of her own clan. But after two years he divorced her. He said that she was possessed by a *jinniyya* (an evil spirit).

Later, the *fqih* married another one of his cousins of the A. clan in the village of the big rock, where he taught the Quran and led the prayers in the village mosque. He had a daughter with this woman. And this daughter is my present wife Rahma, daughter of the *fqih* Muhammad A. She looks like a mule. And sometimes she shouts at me and complains when I have no money and the grocer will not give us any more credit because we owe him so much money already. But she is really a good woman. Now that I am growing old and fat, I could not find a better one who would be willing to marry a poor peddler who owns nothing but a rickety old baby carriage full of plastic dishes and cups, blankets and brushes. Even her flesh is hard and muscled like that of a mule that has spent its life carrying heavy loads. It is not soft, fresh, and smooth like the flesh of a young girl. But what is written is written. And she is a good woman.

The *fqih*, may God have mercy upon him, used to live with us in Tangier. And sometimes he would stay with his son, who is a barber in the Bni Makada quarter. He was always whining like a sick kitten: "Oh, I am so cold! Oh, my stomach hurts! Oh, my children do not care if I live or die! Oh, why must we eat *baysar* (mashed broad beans, lentils, or peas with olive oil, cumin, and paprika)?" He would have liked to eat meat every day! I would tell him, "Say praise be to God that you have bread to eat and water to drink." Sometimes I would tell Rahma to send him up to the roof so I wouldn't have to listen to him complain. But he was a good Muslim who prayed every prayer at its time (*kan kaysalli kull as-sla fi waqta*). He died not long ago. May God have mercy upon him.

As for Rahma, the daughter of my uncle Si Muhammad and Khadduj A., she was first married to a cousin of hers on her mother's side. He was a poor Jibli. He made charcoal. He divorced her after two years because she bore him no children. Three months later, my brother Mustafa married her. And she has caused him nothing but sorrow ever since the day they were married. It is said that she is cursed like her mother.

Khadduj A. still lives with them in the cobblestone quarter (of Tangier). She is very old and wrinkled. She no longer knows what she says and the children of Mustafa laugh at her. The women of the family are afraid to show her their children because she has the evil eye.

4. Fatima Zohra on women who are said to be cursed

WHEN A WOMAN HAS HAD A HARD LIFE, it is said that she has been cursed by her parents or her husband because of some evil that she has done. When a man has had a hard life, it is said that he is unlucky.

II

Shama, Daughter of Si Abd Allah

(1918–1960)

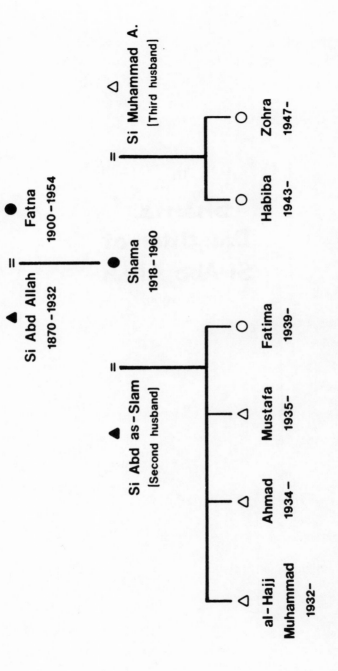

Genealogical Diagram II: Shama and Her Six Children
[Shama had no children by her first husband.]

1. Al-Hajj Muhammad on his mother, Shama, and her three husbands

THE THIRD CHILD OF Si Abd Allah was my mother Shama, may God have mercy upon her. When she was still a young girl, Si Abd Allah gave her in marriage to a wealthy government official, a *khalifa* in Casablanca. The marriage was arranged by Si Abd Allah's brother, who was a *fqih* in that city. The *khalifa* was a very old man. And my mother was very young. He died two years after they were married. May God have mercy upon him. They had no children.

After the *khalifa* died, my mother was very rich. When she returned to Tangier from Casablanca on the train, one whole car of the train was full of her gold, her clothes, and her furniture. Si Abd Allah and my uncle Si Muhammad met her at the station with mules. They had to borrow extra mules to carry all her treasure up to the village of the streams. Our Lord preserved them and they were not robbed on the way up to the village. Praise be to God. Then my mother Shama lived with her parents once again in the village of the streams. Many men wanted to marry her because they knew that she was rich even though she was still very young. Among the men who wanted to marry her was the *qayyid* al-Ayyashi Zillal, may he burn in hell with Bir-Raysul and all the other Muslims who have sold the house of Islam to the Christians.

When Zillal first came to Bni Msawwar from the Jbalan *qbila* of Bni Zarwal (around 1890), he owned nothing. No land, no house, no cows, no goats. Nothing. But then he became a cattle thief with Bir-Raysul. They would steal a man's cattle and then force him to pay them money to get his cattle back. In this way, both Bir-Raysul and Zillal became very rich. But the more money they had, the more they wanted. Oh sons of Adam, everything satisfies you except money. The more you have the more you want (*qadd ma andak qadd ma khassak*). Nothing fills the eye of the sons of Adam except dirt (after death).

Zillal paid millions of pesetas to the sultan Mulay Abd al-Aziz (1894–1908) to become *qayyid* of Bni Msawwar. He earned much more than this from his share of the taxes he collected from the people of Bni Msawwar. When a Msawri could not pay the taxes Zillal demanded, Zillal would take his land and send him to Bir-Raysul's terrible jail in Arzila. Everyone will be hung by his leg.

Like Bir-Raysul, Zillal helped the Spanish control the Jbala. And the Spanish made him *qayyid* of Jbil Hbib and Amar Fahs in addition to Bni Msawwar. And they built him an administration building near their garrison in Dar Shawi. Before the Spanish came, there was nothing in Dar Shawi but a small market on Wednesdays. The Spanish built their garrison there and many shops sprang up on both sides of the road.

Zillal was like a sultan until he was very old. His son al-Hajj Muhammad Zillal replaced him a few years before independence (1956). Then after independence, the government removed al-Hajj Muhammad from office because he had always been a Spanish puppet, like his father. But they did not take his land. Al-Hajj Muhammad Zillal is still the richest man in Bni Msawwar today. He owns over fifty hectares of land while most Jbala own less than one hectare. And he still owns the biggest house in Dar Shawi.

Anyway, al-Ayyashi Zillal heard about my mother's gold and so he told Si Abd Allah that he wanted to marry her. But he already had several wives and concubines. And like most Jbalan women, my mother did not want to be one of several wives. So she refused to marry Zillal.

There was another reason she refused to marry Zillal. Some years before the Spanish came (1912), my mother's maternal uncle had killed a kinsman of Zillal's because he had been speaking freely with a woman of the B. family during the holy month of Ramadan. Zillal was very angry. My mother's uncle fled to Tangier. Then Zillal burned his house down and threatened to imprison one of his brothers unless he returned to Bni Msawwar. So my mother's uncle (*hbibi*) returned to the hills and Zillal sent him to Bir-Raysul's prison by the ocean in Arzila. He stayed in this prison for many years. Maybe six, maybe ten. He had scars on his wrists and ankles for the rest of his life from the chains. And he walked with a stoop because of the chains. This is justice in Morocco.

> and verily the hereafter
> will be better for you
> than the present   [XCIII : 4]

So my mother Shama hated Zillal because of what he had done to her mother's brother. And she hated him for the same reasons everyone hated him. He was a cruel, greedy *qayyid* who grew rich on the backs of the poor Jbala he governed. He would force people to sell their land for almost nothing. He helped his brother's son, Si Ahmad Zillal, buy most of the land in the village of the streams by force.

Zillal made the pilgrimage to Mecca many times. But the Spanish paid for his pilgrimages. The Prophet, may God bless him and grant him peace, intercedes on behalf of all *hujjaj* (those who have made the pilgrimage to Mecca). But Zillal's pilgrimages will be of no avail because he was worse than a Christian.

Zillal was very angry when Si Abd Allah told him that Shama refused to marry him. Si Abd Allah said that since she had already been married, she had the right to refuse a man she did not want to marry. Zillal put Si Abd Allah in jail in Dar Shawi because he would not force Shama to marry him. Then, after a month, Zillal let my

77

uncle Si Muhammad take Si Abd Allah's place in jail. And Si Abd Allah returned to the village of the streams. Shama still refused to marry Zillal and Si Abd Allah still refused to force her to do so. But Si Abd Allah told her to marry someone else so that Zillal would leave them alone. So my mother Shama married my father Abd as-Slam B., who had been married to my aunt Fatma before she died, may God have mercy upon her. And my mother and father moved to Tangier to escape from Zillal. Zillal was like a sultan in Bni Msawwar because the Spanish *Interventor Comercal* let him do whatever he wanted so long as he maintained order and collected taxes. But Tangier was an International Zone in those days, and Zillal had no power there.

When Zillal learned that my mother Shama had married my father and that they had escaped to Tangier, he realized that he had lost. And he released my uncle Si Muhammad from jail. Si Abd Allah died shortly after this. I never knew him. May God have mercy upon him. This was after the Spanish had defeated the last of the *mujahidin* (fighters of the holy war) in the hills of the Rif and the Jbala (1926), and before the war between Franco and *los rojos* in Spain (1936–39).

My mother Shama was still rich when she and my father moved to the cobblestone quarter of Tangier. She bought three houses on the Road of the Mountain (*at-triq d aj-jbil*). But my father, Abd as-Slam B., may God have mercy upon him, liked to spend money. And he did not like to work. He was a shoemaker, but he did not make many shoes. At least once a week, he would have parties with musicians (*awwadin*) and dancing girls. In this way, he spent my mother's money. And as the years passed, she had to sell her houses and her gold.

My mother and father had four children that did not die in infancy. I, al-Hajj Muhammad, am the oldest. I was born in about 1932. Then comes my brother Ahmad, who was born in about 1934. Then comes my brother Mustafa, who was born about a year after Ahmad. And then comes my sister Fatima. She was born near the end of the war between Franco and *los rojos* (1939).

My brothers and I were born in the cobblestone quarter. We were not born in the hills (*aj-jbil*). So we are not really Jbala (mountain people). But just before my sister Fatima was born, my father and mother moved back to the village of the streams, and Fatima was born there. By then, my mother had sold all her houses in Tangier. But she still owned a house in the village of the streams, and we lived in it. It is shameful (*hshuma*) for a man to live in his wife's house. But my father lived in my mother's house.

One day my father went to a spring to drink some water. And a *jinniyya* (female spirit) pulled his arm until it ached. And it ached for the next few days until he died, may God have mercy upon him. This was when I was a little boy and just before my sister Fatima was born (1939). My aunt Khadduj says that God punished my father for causing my mother so much sorrow. God knows best. But it is not right for a Muslim to speak badly of his father.

After my father died, may God have mercy upon him, my mother married her third husband, Si Muhammad A., a peasant from the village of the big rock in the *qbila* of Bni Yidir. Si Muhammad A., who is still alive today, is a kinsman of Khadduj A., the widow of my mother's brother Si Muhammad, may God have mercy upon him. And he is also a kinsman of my present wife Rahma, the one who looks like a mule. May God forgive me for saying so. Si Muhammad A. used to make a lot of money as a bandit in the time of violence before the Christians came. But by the time he married my mother, he was poor and came to live in my mother's house in the village of the streams. This is shameful.

God granted my mother and Si Muhammad A. two daughters that lived. The first one was my sister Habiba, who was born between 1943 and 1945. And the second was my sister Zohra, who was born between 1945 and 1948.

Si Muhammad A. was very poor and very lazy. And life was hard in the village of the streams. My mother Shama decided to sell her house in the village and bring us back down to Tangier. In those days, Tangier was even more full of Christians and Jews than today. And where there are Christians and Jews, there is money for the Muslim.

My mother's brothers Hmid and Mhammad helped Si Muhammad A. build us a *barraka* (tin shack) in the cobblestone quarter.
My mother had sold her houses in the cobblestone quarter many
years before. And when you do not have the money to buy or build a
real house, you build a *barraka* and live in it until God grants you
money for a house of bricks and mortar. It was a nice *barraka* of
sheets of corrugated tin. Really poor people make their *barrakas*
out of flattened oil cans.

Then my mother divorced Si Muhammad A. He was no good.
He wanted to sit at home and in cafés while my mother and my
brothers and I worked. This is not right. Si Muhammad A. went
back to his village of the big rock, where he now has a young wife
who probably goes with young men whenever he is not home. Si
Muhammad A. comes down to Tangier every summer when my
sister Habiba comes home from Belgium for her August vacation.
He lives on the money she gives him. And no matter how much she
gives him, he always wants more. Nothing fills the eye of the sons
of Adam except dirt.

Like many poor Muslim women with no husband, my mother
began to make and sell bread. She would have it baked at the public
oven (*farran*) of the Rifi on the Road of the Mountain. Then she
would put on her *jillaba* and her veil, and she would walk to the
place of the fountain (*as-Saqayya*) in the old city. This is where poor
women sell bread.

It is shameful for a Muslim woman to sell anything in the
street. A woman should stay at home, hidden from the eyes of men.
But what is written is written. The money my brothers and I earned
when we were young boys was not enough. So my mother sold
bread. This is a very sad thing for any woman. But it was especially
sad for my mother because she had once been the richest woman in
Bni Msawwar and the cobblestone quarter.

After selling bread for many years, my mother finally saved
enough money to buy a real house in the cobblestone quarter,
decades after selling the houses she used to own on the Road of the
Mountain. This is the house my brother Mustafa now lives in. My

mother died in this house in the year of independence (1956). May
God have mercy upon her.

> and verily
> the hereafter
> will be better
> for you
> than the present
> and your Lord
> will give
> unto you
> and you
> shall be
> content   [XCIII : 4–5]

2. Al-Hajj Muhammad on himself (1932–)

I WAS BORN IN THE COBBLESTONE QUARTER in about 1932. God
knows best. I began studying the holy Quran in a *msid* (Quranic
school) when I was a little boy. Then, when I was about seven,
we went to live in the village of the streams, where we lived for
seven years. So although I was born in the city, I grew up in the
hills. I studied the holy Quran in the mosque of the village of the
streams. But when we moved back to Tangier, I had to go to work as
an apprentice in a Spanish candy factory. So I had to stop studying
the holy book and I never became a real *talib*. But I know most of
the holy Quran by heart. And I have read many *hadith* and many
books about religion. Whenever anyone in the family (*al-a'ila*) has a
question about religion, he asks me.

Whenever I visit the village of the streams (at least two or three
times a year), the village *fqih* Si Abd al-Ali lets me chant the call to
prayer standing on the boulder in front of the village mosque (*jama*).
Si Abd al-Ali's call to prayer (*ta'din*) is good. He has a good, strong

voice. But just ask anyone in the village and he will tell you that no one chants the call to prayer like al-Hajj Muhammad. Grown men cry when I chant the call to prayer. The call to prayer is the most beautiful sound in this world.

Allahu akbar	God is greater
Allahu akbar	God is greater
Ashhadu al-la ilaha illa Allah	I bear witness that there is no god but God
Ashhadu al-la ilaha illa Allah	I bear witness that there is no god but God
Ashhadu anna Muhammadan rasulu Allah	I bear witness that Muhammad is the messenger of God
Ashhadu anna Muhammadan rasulu Allah	I bear witness that Muhammad is the messenger of God
Hayya ala as-sala	Come alive to prayer
Hayya ala as-sala	Come alive to prayer
Hayya ala al-falah	Come alive to success
Hayya ala al-falah	Come alive to success
Allah akbar	God is greater
Allahu akbar	God is greater
La ilaha illa Allah	There is no god but God
La ilaha illa Allah	There is no god but God

Sometimes I feel sad because I have no son and no house of my own. Then I hear the call to prayer and it washes my heart. And I perform my ablutions and pray. I was never happy working in France and Belgium because I missed hearing the call to prayer at dawn, noon, midafternoon, sunset, and evening time. Praise be to God who created the heavens and earth and the darkness and the light (VI : 1).

Anyway, we moved back to the cobblestone quarter in the year of hunger after the great war of the Christians. I was thirteen or fourteen then. My mother sold bread in the old city. And I worked as an apprentice (*mitallim*) in a Spanish candy factory (*mamal al-halawiyyat*). Then I worked in a Spanish ice cream factory (*mamal al-ladu*). And then I worked for a Jew unloading bags of cement from trucks. The Muslim lives on the money of the Christian and the Jew. In this world, they are always on the top and we are always on the bottom. But in the hereafter, God willing (*in sha' Allah*), we shall be on the top and they shall be on the bottom.

In those days, we Muslims began to smell the scent of independence. Our great sultan, Muhammad V, may God have mercy upon him, led the Moroccan people in the struggle for independence. In 1947, he made a great speech in Tangier. In it, he told the French that we are Muslims and Arabs, not animals. The French were very angry because they wanted us to thank them for colonizing us. He kept refusing to be a traitor to his people and to Islam. And the French exiled him to Madame Gascar (Madagascar) for two years (August 1953 to November 1955). But the Moroccan people demanded his return. And he did return and he led us to independence (1956). He was a great sultan, may God have mercy upon him. He would dress in an old *jillaba* and walk the streets to see how the poor lived. And he would help them.

One day when I was still young and the Spanish still controlled the north (until 1956), I took the bus to Dar Shawi, where my uncle Mhammad waited for me with his mule to ride up to the village of the streams. It was a hot summer day and the dust of Dar Shawi was in my mouth. So I asked a Spanish shopkeeper for a glass of water. He said no and looked at me as if I were a dirty animal that had no right to drink from the glass of a Spaniard. I punched that Christian in the face and his white shirt was red from the blood of his nose. The Spanish soldiers put me in Zillal's jail for three days.

The Christians think we are dirty, but *they* are dirty. That is why we do not allow them in our mosques. Whenever I work for a Christian or a Jew, I feel dirty and I go to the *hammam* (public steam bath). But the cobblestone quarter is a clean neighborhood (*hawma nqiyya*). There are hardly any Christians or Jews in it now.

Not long after I punched that Spaniard in Dar Shawi, I was

83

walking near the mosque of the Jews in Tangier. And I felt a big fart aching to come out. So I entered the mosque of the Jews and farted three times in the faces of the old Jews praying. Oh you should have seen them screaming and running like chickens whose throats have been cut. I had to spend three days in jail and pay a fine of 18 riyals for this. One day in jail and six riyals for each fart.

There is nothing worse than the Jews (*ma kayin shi qbah min al-ihud*). The Jew is only happy when he has cheated a Muslim.

Not long after this, I went to jail again because of the infidels. The Italian manager of the Spanish ice cream factory where I worked said that Muslims are stupid and dirty. I told him *he* was stupid and dirty and I wrecked his face. And I wrecked the ice cream factory. This time a Christian judge sent me to the *qasba* jail for six months. My mother and my brothers would bring me bread and stew (*gwaz*) every day. I was a *mujahid* fighting the *jihad* against the colonialism of the infidels. But they did not understand. They kept telling me to stop getting into trouble.

I don't know why I have always gotten into trouble while my brother Ahmad never has. I am his older brother. But he is rich and I am poor. But people like me because I bring laughter and happiness wherever I go. Ahmad is always thinking about how to make money. How to save money. He laughs like a Christian—from his mouth not from his heart. May God forgive me for saying so.

Then there was the thirtieth of March (*tlatin mars*) 1952, a day that everyone in Tangier remembers or has heard about from his parents. The Christians in their villas pray to their statues that we will not arise again as we did on that day and drive them from the house of Islam. But we will, God willing.

The thirtieth of March 1952 was the fortieth anniversary of the signing of the Treaty of Fez. This treaty turned most of Morocco into a French "Protectorate," while northern Morocco became a Spanish "Protectorate" and Tangier became an International Zone. The Independence party and the other political parties organized a general strike to demand independence. All Muslim stores were closed that day. But all the big modern stores remained open because they were owned by Christians and Jews.

There were many Muslims in the *Suq al-barra* (the Outer Market). One Muslim tried to cut down the French flag, and the Christian police arrested him. The Muslims became very angry and the Christians began shooting at us. Then we all started running. Some ran down the Street of the Jewelers (*as-Siyyaghin*) toward the *Suq ad-dakhil* (the Inner Market). Some ran down the calle de Italia. And some ran up toward the *bulivar* and the new city.

Many of us stayed in the *Suq al-barra* and threw stones at the Christian police. We also threw stones at all Christians and at their stores and their cars, which we also burned.

The police could not stop us because there were so many of us. God knows how many Muslims the Christian policemen killed that day. They lined up on the rooftops above the marketplace and mowed us down with machineguns. But all the Muslims who died went straight to heaven because they died fighting the *jihad* against the infidels.

I grabbed the pistol of a policeman near me and I was going to kill him. But four other Christian policemen grabbed me and beat me. It took five of them to push me down on the ground. I felt as though I were on fire. I was shouting, "There is no god but God" (*la ilaha illa Allah*). And God filled me with the strength of five men. But the five of them finally shoved me to the ground and beat me with their wooden clubs. My blood was smeared all over their clothes. But finally they beat me until I was unconscious. And I woke up in jail with hundreds of other Muslims who had fought the Christians.

Later, a French judge sentenced me to six months in jail. When he said this, I spit at him and told him in French, "Vous n'êtes pas grand Président, vous êtes grand tapette" (i.e., a homosexual). I tried to break loose from my guards and kill him. But the Christian policemen, and some Muslim traitors who had sold their place in the hereafter for a few pesetas, grabbed me and dragged me out of the courtroom. I smashed the glass doors of the courtroom with my feet as they dragged me out. They made me stay three extra months in jail because of these things. So I spent nine months in jail.

Not long after the thirtieth of March, the bodies of eighteen Muslims were washed ashore on the beach of Tangier with their hands tied behind their backs. This was the work of the Christians.

On the day after the thirtieth of March, there was a great funeral for seven martyrs who had died for Islam and the independence of their country during the battle. Thousands of Muslims joined the funeral march from the mosque of Msalla, down the calle de Inglaterra to the charcoal market and the Suq al-barra, and from there to the cemetery of Sidi Bu Araqiyya, where the seven martyrs were buried. May God have mercy upon them. I was in jail at this time. But some Muslim guards and relatives told us about it. The coffins of the martyrs were covered by Moroccan flags. The Christian police guarded the procession to prevent another battle. The Christians did not understand that we would keep fighting until we were free.

In those days, we thought that once we obtained independence everything would be wonderful. We thought we Muslims would live the way the Christians live, with villas, cars, and servants. But now we are no better off than we were under the Christians. Now the Fassis rule as the Christians used to. *They* have villas, cars, and servants. But those of us who toil for a mouthful of bread have gained nothing since independence.

And the Fassis and the other rich Moroccans have forgotten their religion. They have become like Christians. Sometimes they speak French among themselves. They send their children to French schools. They marry French women. And even their Muslim wives and daughters bare their bodies like Christian whores. They wear bikinis at the beach and short skirts and low-cut blouses in the streets. They do not fast during the month of Ramadan. They drink wine and whiskey in the Café de Paris. They are those who buy the life of this world at the price of the hereafter (II : 86).

And even today the Christians still control Morocco. The biggest villas on Jbil al-Kbir (the Big Mountain) still belong to Christians. The factories are still controlled by Christians. The best parts of the beach of Tangier are still reserved for Christians. The law says everyone on the beach must wear a bathing suit. But this is just a trick to keep good Muslims away from the beach, because good Muslims do not allow their women to bare their bodies like Christian whores.

My cousins Fatima Zohra, Rhimu, and Nufissa wear bikinis at the beach. And their mother, my aunt Khadduj, never wears a veil. And she is a Hajja who has been to the holy places of Islam. May God guide them.

After I stopped working in the Spanish ice cream factory, I started selling popsicles (*polos*) from a bicycle pushcart. Then I worked with a shovel and a pick (*bi il-palu wa al-piku*). And for many years I sold old clothes, kerosene lamps, dishes, radios, and other things in the *Jutiyya* (flea market). Some days, I would make four or five thousand francs ($9 to $11 in 1977). And many days, I would make less than 500 francs ($1.11). Sustenance is from God (*ar-rizq min and Allah*). Some days you eat *baysar*, and some days you eat meat. Everything is in the hands of God (*kull shi fi yidd Allah*).

For many years before and after independence, I also made magic charms (*hjuba*) for people. I learned magic (*as-shur*) from an old *fqih* when I was young. I don't do it any more because it is forbidden by Islam. But in those days, people would pay me between one and three thousand francs ($2 to $7 in 1977) for a charm. I would sell one or two each week. Most of the time, I wrote *mahabbat*, which cause a woman to want a man: "Oh God let the heart of ———— daughter of ———— surge, soften and break with love for ———— son of ————." I could make a woman walk from Rabat to Tangier to be with a man.

I also made charms to ward off the *jnun*. There used to be an *afrita* (a powerful spirit) who haunted my aunt Khadduj when she lived by the stream of the Jews in the cobblestone quarter. I sold her a charm for 1,500 francs ($3.33) and that *afrita* never came back. But magic is evil and I do not make such charms any more.

In the years before and after independence, I worked for the Istiqlal (Independence) party and for the Moroccan Union of Labor. They didn't pay me, but they promised me a passport so I could go to work in Europe. All Moroccans dream of getting a passport and working in Europe. But it is hard to get one, very hard, unless you are rich.

In 1960, I handed out papers and told people to vote for the Istiqlal candidates in the local elections. I had my stall in the Jutiyya flea market then. I worked hard for the party. But the years passed and still I had no passport. So I started working for the new party, the National Union of the Popular Forces (*al-Ittihad al-Watani li il-Quwat ash-Shabiyya*). In those days, I lived in the quarter of the vegetable gardens, which I organized for the 1963 elections. Ninety-six percent of the people of this quarter voted for the National Union of the Popular Forces.

Then I had a lot of trouble. The Istiqlal people were mad because I was working for the National Union party and they tried to kill me. And the king was mad because so many people voted for the National Union of the Popular Forces in the 1963 elections. So he claimed that the leaders of the National Union had been plotting to kill him, and he had them arrested. I was afraid and escaped to the village of the streams. But after a month my brother Ahmad sent word to me that the police were not looking for me and that the Istiqlal people did not want to kill me any more. So I came back to Tangier. I still had my stall in the Jutiyya where I sold the garbage of the Christians (*az-zbil d an-Nsara*). After all this trouble, I decided to have nothing to do with politics anymore. It is too dangerous.

But I finally obtained my passport in 1964, after trying for many years. Some friends of mine at the *Amala* (City Hall) helped me get it. Morocco is not like the Christian countries. In Belgium, if you want a passport or any other document from the government, you go to the office and you fill out a form and you get what you want. Here, you must *know* many people, and you must *bribe* many people in order to get the slightest paper.

In 1964, I went to France where I drove a train in a coalmine. They paid me 6,500 francs ($14.44) a day. But I did not like it and I came back to Tangier after a few months. Then I took my wife Fatma with me to Brussels in Belgium, where my brother Ahmad was working in a car factory. Ahmad is not like me. He has worked at that car factory ever since 1964. But I cannot stay at one job for many years. I always want to change. But I worked for many years in Belgium. I worked with a pneumatic drill for five years. Then I worked as a stonecutter. I was making good money in those days. But I came back to Tangier in 1973. I was tired of cold winters. And I was tired of being in the land of the Christians.

When I returned to Tangier, I tried to get back my stall in the Jutiyya, but I couldn't. So I started selling the garbage of the Christians in the other markets of Tangier and in some of the rural weekly markets: the Sunday market of al-Gharbiyya, the Monday market of Sidi al-Yamani, and many others. Now I sell mostly in the little market of the cobblestone quarter.

Sometimes I smuggle merchandise from Sibta (Ceuta, a free-port Spanish presidio about seventy kilometers east of Tangier). And sometimes I buy merchandise in Tetuan, where everything is cheaper than in Tangier.

Sometimes I work as a painter for Christians and Jews in the city. And sometimes I build tables and stools and sell them in the little market of the cobblestone quarter. Every day has its sustenance (*kull an-nhar bi rizqu*).

When I was still young, before the events of the thirtieth of March (1952), I was married to my first wife, Aysha daughter of M. A. She was a Jibliyya from the *qbila* of Wad Ras, next to Bni Msawwar. She had already been married and divorced. She worked with me in the Spanish ice cream factory in the Bni Yidir quarter in the old city of Tangier. My mother paid 25,000 francs ($55.56) in *sdaq* (brideprice) for her to her father, who still lived in the hills.

I had gone with many women before I married my first wife, with money and without money (*bi l-flus wa bi la flus*). I used to waste money on the whores in the brothels of the Bni Yidir quarter. In those days, I was young, handsome, and strong. And many women wanted me. The Moroccan woman wants a big *zibb* (penis) or money from a man. Sometimes I have money. Sometimes I don't. But I have always had a big *zibb*.

My first wife Aysha loved a man from Bni Millal who worked with a shovel and a pick in Tangier. She would go with him while I was selling *polos* from my bicycle pushcart. So I divorced her a year and eight months after we were married, and she married the man from Bni Millal.

I remained single for about four months. And I was sick and my mother took me to visit Sidi al-Arbi, the saint of Arzila. Then I was better.

Not long after the French exiled our great sultan, Muhammad V (August 1953), may God have mercy upon him, I married my second wife Awisha daughter of Muhammad D., a Jibliyya born in the village of the weavers in the *qbila* of Jbil Hbib (just west of Bni Msawwar). Her family lived next to us in the cobblestone quarter. She was still young and her breasts were still small and firm. Her skin was dark and she was very beautiful. She said that she was pregnant with my brother Ahmad's child. But Ahmad said that he had never gone with her. And most people believed him because he has always seemed so reasonable.

When people think of Ahmad, they think of money. They do not think of him lying with a woman. Even when he was a boy, he would save every peseta he earned working for the Spaniard. He never bought candy. And he never went with the whores in the brothels of the Bni Yidir quarter. But he likes weaving (sex) as much as any other man. No man thinks only of money.

But he insisted that he had never touched Awisha. God knows best. I married her to protect the honor of our family and because I loved her. Oh, she was beautiful! I used magic to make her love me. My mother paid 25,000 francs in *sdaq* for her. Some people in the family were ashamed because she was already big with the child when we were married. But I was happy.

The baby was born a month after the wedding. She gave it to some neighbors in the cobblestone quarter. I don't know what they did with it. We remained married for four years. But I sent her back to her parents three times before I finally divorced her a year after independence (1957). She was a whore. She was like a bitch always in heat. Even when I locked her up in the house while I was busy selling in the Jutiyya, she still found ways of going with men. If a woman wants a man, she will give it to him even through the keyhole of the door (*al-mra ida habbat ar-rajil, tatihlu min at-tuqba d al-bab*).

One night, long after we had been divorced, she and her father came to have dinner at my brother's house. We stayed up late laughing and talking. Then everyone went to sleep in the same room. And after I was sure everyone was asleep, I went over to her and we did some weaving. Oh, the sweetness (*Ya al-halawa*)!

Now she has a husband and children in Casablanca. I am sure that she is cheating him just as she used to cheat me. That is the nature of a woman. A woman has ninety-nine devils tempting her while a man has only one.

A few weeks after I divorced my second wife Awisha, I married my third one, Fatma daughter of Muhammad Z. from the *qbila* of Bni Yidir. She had been divorced by her first husband, a Susi grocer. She had a son by this Susi. After he divorced her, she worked as a servant for a Christian family in a villa on the Big Mountain, where all the rich Christians of Tangier live. All the Muslim women in the cobblestone quarter dream of working as servants for the Christians on the Big Mountain.

Although Fatma worked as a maid in the villa of the Christians, her family lived in a *barraka* in the Bni Makada quarter. I paid 20,000 francs in *sdaq* for her. I was still selling the garbage of the Christians in the Jutiyya market at this time. Then, in 1965, I took her to Brussels with me. She worked as a cleaning woman and I was working in construction with the pneumatic drill. But she was cheating me like the others. So I divorced her. Later she married another man who took her to Belgium where she still works as a cleaning woman. They have three children.

Then I married my fourth wife, Ftuma daughter of Si Ali M., from the Urubiyya lowlands near Qsar al-kbir. She was born and grew up in Tangier. She worked in the Hotel Rif, where Christians stay. Her first husband had divorced her. And I divorced her after three months.

Then, in 1966, I married my fifth wife, Fatma daughter of Idris S., a barber from Mulay Idris who lived in the Msallah quarter. No man could love a woman more than I loved this one. But she cheated me like the others. I paid 25,000 francs in *sdaq* for her. Her first husband had divorced her.

Fatma was a beautiful woman with big milky breasts and big buttocks, even though she was only seventeen years old when I married her. I took her with me to Belgium in 1966. I was working ten hours a day with the pneumatic drill and she worked as a cleaning woman.

On March 13, 1967, God granted us a beautiful baby girl. I named her Fatima Zohra, after my cousin Fatima Zohra. She is a big girl now, may God bless her. She lives with her mother in Belgium, but I see her in August, when her mother comes home for her vacation.

But Fatma was cheating me like the others. And she tried to colonize me like the others. So I divorced her in 1971. Then she married an Algerian she used to go with when I was not home. I thought he was my friend and I let him live with us when he couldn't find any other place to live. And he would lie with my wife while I was at work. What is written is written.

After I divorced Fatma, I married my sixth wife, Juma daughter of Muhammad the Maknassi (man from Meknes), a day laborer in Tangier. I paid 15,000 francs in *sdaq*. She had been married and divorced. And like most women, she was a whore. I divorced her after a month.

Then I remarried my fifth wife Fatma. Everyone in the family said I was crazy. Maybe she had used magic to make me love her. But I did love her. The Algerian had divorced her. This time we stayed together for two years. I only paid 1,000 francs ($2.22) in *sdaq* because we had already been married. I was working as a stonecutter in a cemetery in Brussels and she was still working as a cleaning woman.

One day, I came home early and found her in my bed with another man. I beat them both and then I cried like a baby. I brought her back to Tangier and divorced her in 1973. Then she went back to Brussels and took my daughter with her. Sometimes she sends her relatives to ask me to take her back. But I gave her two chances and she cheated me both times. So even though I still dream about her almost every night, I cannot take her back. I see my daughter Fatima Zohra every August, but I do not see Fatma. Once I did see her on the street in Tangier and I turned around and walked away. She thinks she can use me. But she is wrong.

After I divorced Fatma for the second time, I came back to Tangier. Belgium was sad. So I started selling in the markets of Tangier and the nearby weekly markets in the country. And I married my seventh wife, little Rahma (*Rahma as-stituwa*) daughter of Abd as-Slam A., from the village of the big rock in the *qbila* of Bni Yidir. She is a cousin of my brother Mustafa's wife Rahma and of my half-sister Habiba. I paid 10,000 francs in *sdaq*. She had been married to a cousin of hers from the big rock who is a cook in a little restaurant in Tangier. They had two children. He divorced her and she left the children with him. What kind of a mother would do that? I met her when she was working in Abd ar-Rahman's ice cream parlor, where my brother Mustafa works. Mustafa and Abd ar-Rahman told me I was crazy because everyone knew that she was a whore. But what a delicious whore she was! She had big soft breasts and smooth firm thighs that would squeeze me as I entered her. There are some women who make you want them every time they move. She was like that. Weaving with her was sweet. Oh, the sweetness! But she would go with anyone. I divorced her after two months.

Now she works as a whore in a bar near the *bulivar*. Sometimes I walk by there at night to see her in her tight *jillaba* with slits half way up her smooth, firm thighs. She drinks whiskey and laughs the laugh of a whore. God knows how many men she goes with every night. Every time I see the big war ships of the Christians in the harbor, I think of how many Christians will enter little Rahma before the next morning. She will squeeze the infidels with her smooth, firm thighs as they taste of her sweetness. And she will earn more from one night of weaving than I earn in a month of peddling.

In 1975 she had a son. The father could be any one of a thousand men: Muslims, Christians, maybe even Jews. She is without shame. She sent the boy to live with her father in the big rock. What kind of life will that poor little bastard have? I still see her sometimes in August when my sister Habiba comes back from Belgium. Habiba is her cousin and brings her back to the house to eat with us. We do not speak to each other. She hates me because I used to beat her when she went with other men. One day she was riding in the car of my cousin Fatima Zohra's husband with Habiba and Fatima Zohra. And as they were driving along the *bulivar,* she pointed out to them the bar where she works as if she were a teacher pointing out the school where she teaches. She is without shame.

After I divorced little Rahma, I married my eighth wife, my present wife Rahma, daughter of the *fqih* Muhammad A. from the village of the big rock. She was first married to her cousin, al-Hsin son of Hmid A., her father's sister's son, who was a poor charcoal-maker in the big rock. He died after a year. May God have mercy upon him. Then she lived many years in the big rock taking care of her father the *fqih*. I married her in 1974. I paid 17,000 francs ($37.78) in *sdaq* for her.

My wife Rahma looks like a mule. May God forgive me for saying so. When a man is ascending (*tala*) he can have beautiful, delicious women. But when he grows older and he is descending (*hawwad*), he is lucky to find a woman at all, especially if he is poor. And I am descending (*wa ana hawwad*). And I am poor. I have a big belly, my sideburns are turning gray, and I own nothing in the world except the rickety old baby carriage I carry my merchandise in when I go sell in the market. I live in my brother Ahmad's house. I am growing old and I do not own my own house. And I have no son. When I die, people will say "he lived and acquired nothing and he died and left nothing" (*ash ma ksab mat ma khalla*).

But, God willing, they will also say that al-Hajj Muhammad was a good Muslim who prayed every prayer at its time, who fasted during Ramadan, and who made the pilgrimage to Mecca the holy.

3. *Fatima Zohra on her cousin al-Hajj Muhammad*

I LOVE AL-HAJJ MUHAMMAD as though he were my brother. He is like a little boy. Sometimes he would come to our house by the stream of the Jews in Tangier and he would draw with my little children. The three of them would sit at the table together for hours drawing.

Al-Hajj Muhammad is sterile and he has always been sad because of this. People see him laughing, singing, and joking and they think he is very happy. And in some ways he is happy. But sometimes he feels sad and he lies in bed and refuses to see anyone. Whenever he divorces his wives, or they divorce him, he becomes strange. He talks fast and he does not know what he is saying. My aunt Shama used to take him to visit Sidi al-Arbi, a famous saint in Arzila who is said to cure those who are possessed by the *jnun*. Once his brothers took him to the Polyclinique in Hasnuna.

Everyone in the family avoids upsetting him because when he is upset he becomes strange. That is why we don't say anything when he talks about "his daughter" Fatima Zohra. Everyone knows this girl is the daughter of his Algerian friend who used to go with his wife Fatma when he was at work. I think he knows it too in his heart. But people often pretend not to know what they really know. Like children.

Al-Hajj Muhammad loves children. He kept divorcing his wives hoping that they were sterile, not him. But often they divorced him. They used him.

People say that there are two kinds of girls: good girls and bad girls. All of al-Hajj Muhammad's wives were bad girls. A good girl is one who obeys her parents and does not go with men until she is married. Such a girl usually marries a cousin or a boy from her neighborhood. It is said that the cousins on the father's side and the cousins on the mother's side are first (*ulad al-amm wa ulad al-khalat huma al-ulin*) when it comes to obtaining a girl for a wife. But no one in the family would let al-Hajj Muhammad marry his daughter because everyone knows he is unstable. That is also why none of the neighbors would let him marry their daughters, except for Awisha when she was pregnant. He had to marry women from other places who had been divorced or who were pregnant like Awisha. Maybe if he had had a good wife, he would have become more stable.

Al-Hajj Muhammad is a wonderful man. Although he is very religious, he is also a clown. The family gets together about once a week in Tangier. Usually, we gather at Mustafa's house in the cobblestone quarter. When al-Hajj Muhammad arrives, he greets everyone in the customary way: "Peace be upon you" (*as-salamu alaykum*). "How are you? All right? And your father? Your mother? Your brothers? Your sisters? Your children?" And so on. Every time Moroccans see each other, they spend a long time asking each other such questions. But al-Hajj Muhammad follows such questions, in the same tone of voice, with questions such as: "Did you shit today?" (*khriti shi al-yawma?*) "How was it? Soft? Hard?" No one speaks this way except al-Hajj Muhammad. And the contrast between these questions and his conventional tone of voice causes everyone to laugh. My uncle Hmid says it is wrong to speak this way, especially since al-Hajj Muhammad is a Hajj who has been to Mecca. But most people love to listen to al-Hajj Muhammad.

Al-Hajj Muhammad often jokes about the naiveté (*an-niyya*)

of Jbala when they come to the city. One of his favorite stories is about a Jibli who came to Tangier to see a doctor. He claims this is a true story.

This Jibli was sick and his brothers in his village had told him to go see the doctor whose office is on the fourth floor of the building my mother lives in, in downtown Tangier near the *bulivar*. He found the building and entered the lobby looking lost. A young man saw him and asked him what he wanted. "I want to see the doctor," said the Jibli. "Oh, then you must have an x-ray first," said the young man. And the young man told the Jibli that the elevator was the x-ray machine. And he told him to take off all his clothes and enter the elevator. So the Jibli took off all his clothes, including his little money pouch (*zabula*), and entered the elevator as naked as the day he was born. Then the young man told him to push the button next to the number "4." The Jibli did so. And the elevator started to ascend. The Jibli was terrified and screamed, for he had never been on an elevator before. Meanwhile, the young man grabbed the Jibli's clothes and money pouch and disappeared.

When the elevator reached the fourth floor, it stopped and the Jibli stopped screaming. He thought the x-rays were finished. And he waited for the doctor. Hours passed and he just stood there waiting in the elevator with no clothes on. Finally, a door opened and a nurse saw the naked Jibli and started to scream. She had never seen a naked Jibli in an elevator before.

Another one of al-Hajj Muhammad's favorite jokes concerns a Jibli who went to the movies for the first time. He had seen the queue of people waiting for tickets and he had assumed that the government was giving out free food. So he waited in line. When he finally reached the ticket window, the girl asked: "Balcony or orchestra?" (*Balcon aw butaka?*) Having never heard these words before, the Jibli assumed that they were some kind of Christian food. So he told the girl, "Give them both to me in half a loaf of bread" (*atihumli bi juj fi nuss d al-khubz*).

Al-Hajj Muhammad can go on for hours telling such jokes

while we all laugh until our eyes water. Everyone knows these jokes. But no one tells them as well as he does.

Al-Hajj Muhammad is also a wonderful singer and a poet. Speaking of his wife Fatma, he once noted, "Love is a malady for which there is no cure other than the beloved one for whom the heart yearns" (*Al-hubb da' ma lahu dawa' sawa' al-habib alladhi talabahu al-fu'ad*). This sounds like a line from a love song by Abd al-Wahhab or Umm Kultum (famous Egyptian singers). He often sings Egyptian love songs. I remember one day when we were in the village of the streams for a wedding, al-Hajj Muhammad, my husband, and my cousins Abd as-Slam and Hmidu were coming to the village from Hmidu's garden. And they were all singing Abd al-Halim Hafidh's song "I want you and hope that if I forget you, I forget myself as well as you" (*Ahwak wa atamanna law ansak ansa ruhi wa iyyak*).

Al-Hajj Muhammad always sings when he is happy. Often, we would take him with us when we drove to Tetuan. He and I would sing and my husband would listen. Even my husband would sing with us when he knew the words. And whenever we saw a Jibliyya (mountain woman) walking by the side of the road, al-Hajj Muhammad would tell my husband to slow down a little, and he would stick his head out of the car and shout, "O daughter of my father's brother, how are you today?" Then he would laugh and the Jibliyya would laugh.

If we passed an old Jibliyya carrying a heavy load, he would ask us to stop and give her a ride, even if we were already crowded. And several times when we took him with us to the Tuesday market of Jbil Hbib, he would ask us to stop for an old Rifi who had lived in the village of the rocky places for over sixty years. He was a wonderful old man. He chanted a long *qasida* (traditional poem) for us on the way to the market. Al-Hajj Muhammad has a good heart. Everywhere he goes, he brings happiness to people.

On the way to Tetuan, we would stop at the spring of al-Hisn. There was a stream there and a little tea shop with wonderful mint tea. We would order glasses of mint tea and eat bread and goat's cheese and look at the mountains. Al-Hajj Muhammad would always be very happy here. The children would play by the stream and al-Hajj Muhammad, my husband, and I would look at the hills and the valleys. It was wonderful.

Sometimes, we would take al-Hajj Muhammad and his wife Rahma with us to the beach. I would wear a bikini and my husband wore a bathing suit. Sometimes al-Hajj Muhammad would wear a bathing suit too. But Rahma, never. The Jbala think it is shameful for a woman to show her body. Al-Hajj Muhammad looks funny in a bathing suit because his big belly hangs out. He would build castles in the sand with our children. And he would go in the surf. But he doesn't know how to swim. We would roast balls of chopped meat (*kifta*) over a fire and eat them with bread and hot mint tea. He would make fun of me sometimes because I like to make tea with just mint leaves and no tea. He called this "the tea of the weeds" (*atay d al-ushub*). Those days were wonderful.

Even Rahma was very sweet on those days at the beach. Usually, she and al-Hajj Muhammad shout at each other a lot. She has a good heart. But often they have no money and she complains. Some days, we would go to their house and she would give us cold tea because they had no money to buy charcoal or gas for the *Butagaz,* so she couldn't heat it. And sometimes she would offer us stale bread. It is not her fault. Al-Hajj Muhammad does not give her much money.

Some days, he makes a lot of money selling old dishes and clothes in the little market of the cobblestone quarter. But he spends it. He doesn't know how to save money. As he says, when he has coins in his pocket, they shout, "We want to get out! We want to get out!" (*Khassna nkharju! Khassna nkjarhju!*) But when his brother Ahmad has coins in *his* pocket, they say, "We want to hide! We want to hide!" (*Khassna nitkhabu! Khassna nitkhabu!*). That is why al-Hajj Muhammad is poor and Ahmad is rich.

Al-Hajj Muhammad is like a brother to me. But when it comes to money, he cannot be trusted. In October of 1977, my mother sent 50,000 francs ($111.11) to him to give to my sisters. About a month later, she came back from Belgium and I went with her to al-Hajj Muhammad's house. My sisters had never received a single franc. "What did you do with the fifty thousand francs?" my mother asked. "I never got fifty thousand francs," he said. Then my mother showed him a letter from his brother Ahmad telling him to give my mother back her fifty thousand francs. He is afraid of Ahmad because he lives in Ahmad's house. So he admitted that he had the money. But he said he needed it. He said he was using it to buy sheep that he was going to sell at a profit because it was almost the time of the Feast of Sacrifice (*Id al-kbir*) when every family sacrifices a sheep or a goat. He offered to give my mother 10,000 francs now and 40,000 later, after he had sold all the sheep. I said no. And I made him give my mother fifty thousand francs. He was angry, as though we were taking *his* money when in fact he had tried to take my mother's money. Everyone in the family thinks my mother has a lot of money so they think it is all right to cheat her. They have always tried to use her. When al-Hajj Muhammad went on the pilgrimage to Mecca with my mother, she was always very careful to hide her money. And she always told him she had less than she really had, because he always tried to use her money instead of his. I don't know how he saved enough money for the pilgrimage. My mother spent over $1,500 on the pilgrimage. He didn't spend that much. But he must have spent over a thousand dollars. How did he get that much money? He never saves. Or at least he never seems to save. And his brother Ahmad is very tight with his money. So I don't think Ahmad lent him the money. I think he was secretly saving over the years. Some people say that he did not have the right to make the pilgrimage because he does not own his own house. They say this about my mother too, because she doesn't own a house either. But this is just envy. Other people in the family are envious because they do not have the money to make the pilgrimage.

Al-Hajj Muhammad is very proud that he is a Hajj. He has always resented the fact that everyone respects his younger brother Ahmad because he owns many houses and a Volkswagen bus.

Everyone loves al-Hajj Muhammad but they do not respect him because he is poor. As much as you possess so much you are worth (*Qadd ma andak qadd ma tiswa*). So making the pilgrimage was very important for him because it meant people would respect him more than before.

When al-Hajj Muhammad and my mother came back from the east (i.e., Mecca) they did not have the customary feast of the *dakhla*. So Rahma, al-Hajj Muhammad's wife, said they were not true *hujjaj* (pilgrims). And she called my mother and al-Hajj Muhammad "monkeys"! This made my mother very angry. Rahma said these things because she was angry that al-Hajj Muhammad had left her very little money when he had left for the east. She had had to borrow and beg from her brother who is a barber in Bni Makada. And I would help her sometimes. She has a bad mouth but she was right to be angry. Al-Hajj Muhammad wanted the honor of being a Hajj, but he didn't stop to think how his wife would eat while he was gone. I feel sorry for any woman married to an irresponsible man like al-Hajj Muhammad. But in his heart he is good, very good.

4. Al-Hajj Muhammad on his brother Ahmad (1934–), factory worker in Belgium and landlord in Tangier

MY BROTHER AHMAD is about two years younger than I am. He was born about 1934. When he was a little boy, he studied the holy Quran with me for over a year in the mosque of the village of the streams. But he did not study as long as I did. And he only knows the short *suras* of the Quran used in prayer. But he is a good Muslim. He prays every prayer at prayer time. He doesn't drink. And he doesn't smoke hashish or even cigarettes.

When we came back down to Tangier after the great war of the

Christians, he went to work as an apprentice in a Spanish store. And when he was about eighteen, he began driving a minibus for a Spanish wholesale dealer. He would deliver packaged and canned food to grocery stores from the Spanish warehouse.

We could make a lot of money working together in the rural weekly markets because he has a Volkswagen minibus. We could fill it with merchandise. But I don't think he wants to. He doesn't trust anyone, not even his brothers.

I married my second wife Awisha because she said she was pregnant with Ahmad's child. Ahmad was very young then. And he denied the child was his. And he refused to marry her. When people see Ahmad with his bow tie and his gold-rimmed glasses, they think he is a Muslim who thinks only of God and of money. But he likes weaving like all men. Everyone was surprised when he brought the Christian woman from Belgium. But not me.

In about 1955, Ahmad married our father's sister's daughter from the village of the rocky places. She had three miscarriages. So Ahmad divorced her in about 1959. She then married another cousin from the *qbila* of Bni Arus. She died the following year while giving birth to a dead baby. May God have mercy upon them. The women in the family say she died because she loved Ahmad and did not want to live without him.

Less than a week after he divorced his first wife, Ahmad married his second wife Fatma, with whom he has remained ever since—about twenty years. Just as he has remained in the car factory ever since he went to Belgium in 1964, he has remained with Fatma ever since they were married in about 1960 or 1961. God knows best.

Fatma's mother worked with Ahmad in the Spanish warehouse. She is a Ghmariyya (from the Ghmaran highlands east of the Jbalan highlands). She saw that Ahmad worked hard and would one day be rich. So she told him that her daughter Fatma was very beautiful. Fatma was sixteen years old then. Ahmad wanted children and his first wife had not borne any children that lived. So he divorced his first wife to marry Fatma. Fatma's family lived in a *barraka* (tin shack) in the shanty town of Bu Khashkash. She is no good. She always insults the B. family.

One day, when they were in Tangier for Ahmad's August vacation, Fatma couldn't find some silk panties she had bought in Brussels. And she started calling all of us a "family of thieves" (*a'ila d surraq* and *tasila d surraq*). She always talks as if we were a family without value. But what is she? Nothing. She is just a poor Ghmariyya whose family left the mountains of Ghmara to come and live in a dirty little *barraka*, where her mother still lives when she comes back from Belgium. She is proud (*katihyal*) now because Ahmad is rich. But she is nothing. It is only thanks to Ahmad that she has those gold teeth and those gold bracelets on her arm.

I don't know why Ahmad didn't divorce Fatma many years ago. I could kill her every time she opens that rotten mouth of hers. She is even tighter and greedier than Ahmad. Whenever you put a piece of their bread into your mouth, she winces as though you had driven a nail into her heart.

My aunt Khadduj stayed in the attic of their building in Brussels in 1977. Every time that Fatma went out, she would tell the children not to give my aunt Khadduj any food while she was gone. She is worse than a Christian.

Fatma's mother is worse than she is. She works as a cleaning woman in Brussels. She lives in the same building as Ahmad. Everyone in this building is Moroccan. My sister Habiba has an apartment in this building too. Ahmad hates his mother-in-law (*nsibtu*). She is always at their apartment and she and Fatma talk the way women talk for hours. But Ahmad does not speak to her and she does not speak to him. It is like a war. I cannot relax in their house because I always feel the hatred. The hatred between Ahmad and Fatma. And the hatred between Ahmad and his mother-in-law. And I always feel strange with Ahmad.

Fatma's mother has nothing to worry about. She has saved millions of francs during the many years she has been mopping floors and washing windows in Brussels. When she comes back to Tangier every August, she goes back to her old *barraka* in Bu

Khashkash. She could buy her own house and live like a Christian if she wanted to. But she is tight like Ahmad. She doesn't spend a franc unless she has to. So when she will be too old to work, she will be able to live on the millions (one million francs = $2,222) she has saved. She keeps her money in the bank like Ahmad.

Ahmad and Fatma have five children. Muhammad, the first-born and the only son, was born in Tangier in 1963. Then came the four daughters, who were all born in Brussels, in hospitals like the Christians. Samira was born in 1965. Najat was born in 1966. Fatima was born in 1967. And Nadia was born in 1968. All of them study in Belgian schools. Muhammad is a good boy. He is studying to be an accountant. He is a very good boy. May God bless him (*tabarraka Allah alayh*). But he laughs like Ahmad, and like the Christians: from his mouth not from his heart. May God forgive me for saying so. Like his father, his blood is heavy and tasteless (*basil*). I never heard him tell a joke. And like his father, he wears glasses and he is always using French words when he speaks Arabic. But he is a good boy. May God bless him. The girls are good too. They all read and write French. And they even speak to each other in French some-times—like the Fassis. Ahmad worries that they will forget Islam in Belgium. And one year he came back here to live. But he could not make a living. So he went back to the car factory in Brussels. The Muslim must leave Morocco to feed his family.

Even when he was very young, Ahmad saved every franc he earned. He helped my mother pay for the house my brother Mustafa now lives in. He paid half the money for the house. And after my mother died, may God have mercy upon her, he bought my sister Zohra's share. But Mustafa, Habiba, and I still own our shares. In 1976, Ahmad said he wanted to sell the house and the land it is on for five million francs ($11,111). But the house is not his alone. It is all of ours. We were very angry. I do not wish to speak badly of my brother Ahmad. But sometimes he thinks money is more important than his brothers and sisters. This is the house where my brother Mustafa and his children always lived. This is the house where the family gathers almost every week because it is easy to get to from all of our homes. He has no right to sell it just because his share is greater than anyone else's. Sometimes his heart is as hard as that of a Christian.

Ahmad says he wants to buy or build a house for each of his five children. And he already owns four houses. Mustafa used to collect the rent from three houses for him. But sometimes Mustafa would use a little of the money for himself and his family. So Ahmad told his tenants to pay their rent directly to his bank. And the bank people put the money in his account. Ahmad does everything through his bank, like a Christian or a Jew. He does not trust his brothers.

The house I live in belongs to Ahmad. But I built it for him. He would send me the money and I hired some workmen and I did most of the work myself. Ahmad is mad because I built the house on the wrong lot. His lot is right next to this one and looks just the same. So we are trying to exchange lots with the man who owns the lot next door. It was a simple mistake. The two lots look the same. But Ahmad is still very angry. He has never thanked me for all the work I did to build this house. He just complains because I built it on the wrong lot. And he says that he and his family will live here when he returns from Belgium after he retires and they give him a pension. I will have to leave then, he says. What kind of a Muslim would put his own brother in the street?

In the summer of 1976, Ahmad bought a piece of land near the cobblestone quarter for three million francs ($6,667). Most of the men in the family have never earned more than 30,000 francs ($66.67) a month. In their eyes, Ahmad is as rich as the king. When he returns from Belgium every August, everyone comes to visit him. The *muqaddim* comes. The *qadi* Muhammad B. comes. Si Muhammad Qasim and my uncle Muhammad come down from the village of the streams. And their mouths are all full of honey.

If the rich man farts, for them it is as though a canary had sung. If the poor man farts, they insult him and add to that a beating (*At-tajir ida hzaq, andum fhal al-kalanyu ida ntaq. Al-maskin ida hzaq izibblu fih wa iziduh ad-daqq*).

105

And everyone in the family comes to the house when Ahmad returns from Belgium in August. Not out of love for Ahmad, but out of greed (*at-tma*). He always brings gifts for everyone in the family. And for the *muqaddim* (petty official who represents an urban quarter or a village). And he usually brings a gift for the village of the streams. Once he gave the village a big kettle as *hbus* (inalienable property of mosques and other Islamic institutions). Any time anyone in the village has a feast on the seventh day after birth (*saba*), or a circumcision (*tahara*), or a wedding (*urs*), or a funeral (*gnaza*), he can use the kettle to cook the food for his guests. Another time, Ahmad brought an aluminum ladder for the village *hbus*. People use it when they want to fix their roofs or cut high branches from a tree.

And Ahmad lends people money. He lent Si Muhammad son of at-Tayyib 100,000 francs ($222.22) to buy a mule. And I don't think Si Muhammad ever paid him back. And Ahmad lent my mother's sister's son Hmidu 50,000 francs ($111.11) to start his vegetable garden. Later Abd ar-Rahman lent Hmidu more money and became his partner in this garden. Hmidu sells his tomatoes, potatoes, onions, green peppers, and watermelons at the Monday market of Bni Harshan and the Tuesday market of Jbil Hbib. And he is making a lot of money now from that garden. But he never paid Ahmad back a single franc. So Ahmad does not lend people money any more.

People think Ahmad gives me a lot of money because I am his brother. But he hardly ever gives me money.

Sometimes I think Ahmad can smell money from far away just as the jackal smells the flesh of the goat. No matter what he does, he ends up richer than when he started. He always figures out exactly what a thing will cost and how he can profit from it. Every August, when he spends his vacation in Tangier, he buys much of the food he and his wife and children will eat for the next year in Belgium. He goes out to the Tuesday market of Jbil Hbib and other weekly markets and he buys at least a hundred kilos of wheat, thirty kilos of broad beans (*al ful*), and fifteen kilos of green peppers. His Volkswagen bus is mostly full of food when he goes back to Belgium at the end of August. He could afford to give his children meat every day. Yet they eat like the children of a poor charcoalmaker in the hills. Most of the time they eat *baysar*. And he does not even give them the *baysar* of peas *(julban)*, just the *baysar* of broad beans *(ful)*. *Miseria!* He is like a Susi. He eats stale bread and drinks weak tea in order to save money. What kind of life is that? He is always telling the children to put out the lights to keep the electricity bill low. What good is being rich when you live like that?

We do not even know if we are going to live until tomorrow. Everything is in the hands of God *(kull shi fi yidd Allah)*. So what is the point of saving and saving and living like a Susi? Me, I do not eat *baysar* when I have money in my pocket. I eat meat. But most of the time I have no money in my pocket. So the only time I eat a lot of meat is at feasts on the seventh day after birth, at circumcisions, at weddings, and at funerals. Everything is in the hands of God.

5. *Fatima Zohra on her cousin Ahmad*

MY COUSIN *(wild khalti)* Ahmad is not at all like al-Hajj Muhammad, except that they are both extremely religious. They both pray every prayer at its time. And they have both been to Mecca. Ahmad made the pilgrimage in 1979. But I have not seen him since 1977 and I am not used to calling him al-Hajj Ahmad. But he is now a Hajj like al-Hajj Muhammad.

In his heart, Ahmad is good. But he does not have the sweetness of al-Hajj Muhammad. He cannot laugh and make people happy the way al-Hajj Muhammad does. But he is good. Every year when he returns from Belgium, he brings a gift for everyone in the family. Usually, he brings clothes he buys at the flea markets of Brussels. My sisters laugh at him and say he just brings garbage *(az-zbil)*. But for most of the people in the family, the old shirts,

107

pants, dresses, and shoes he brings are very useful. Most of them spend their lives wearing threadbare clothes they buy at weekly markets. So they do not see Ahmad's gifts as garbage. But my sisters have lived in the States. So they see things differently.

Because Ahmad has worked hard all his life and saved his money, everyone in the family tries to stick to him (*yilsaq fih*). They try to use him and squeeze as much money as they can from him. Naturally, he is not stupid. And he does not let people trick him out of his money. So people say he is stingy (*mijwa*). And it is true that he is very tight with his money. But he has provided his children with a secure future.

One thing I admire about Ahmad is that he is a very good father to his children. He is like a European or American father. He washes them. He makes sure they do their homework. And he buys them nice clothes. And he always thinks about their future. He says he wants to buy or build a house for each of them. I think the only reason he hasn't divorced Fatma a long time ago is because of the children. She has a terrible mouth and she always insults him and our family. And she is lazy. Ahmad wakes up at five every morning in Belgium. And my mother says that he sweeps and cleans the house before he goes to the car factory because Fatma never cleans. Most Moroccan men would never do housework like this. And then when he comes home late at night, she starts complaining. And he endures her because of the children.

Ahmad is a rather vapid (*basil*) man. May God forgive me for saying so. He does not laugh like al-Hajj Muhammad. If it were not for his money, he would probably have no friends. And he is rather ridiculous. He always wears a bow tie and a clean white shirt, even when he visits the village of the streams for a wedding in late August. With his gold-rimmed glasses, his bow tie and his big ears, he does look quite funny. My sisters find it very difficult not to laugh when they see him. He tries to look like a big businessman. And this is the way most of the family sees him. He is not stupid. Not at all stupid. He was once just a poor Jibli who used to watch his mother's goats when he was a little boy in the village of the streams. Now he owns four or five houses and land and he will soon be eligible for a pension from the car factory where he works. Then he will come back to Tangier and start a little business (*shi haraka*), probably a store. Or maybe he will buy a taxi and a taxi license. And he will make even more money, God willing (*in sha' Allah*), in addition to the rents from his houses and the money from his pension.

"Be active and you will receive bounty" (*taharraku wa turzaqu*). Ahmad often quotes this proverb when his brothers ask him for money. He does give them money sometimes. But he says, "I have worked hard all my life. I work eight hours a day at the factory and I often work extra hours. And I save the money I earn for my children. I cannot support my brothers. I can help them from time to time. But I cannot support them!" Unlike al-Hajj Muhammad, Ahmad is not very interested in Islamic socialism, because he understands socialism to mean that people who work hard (such as himself) have to support people who do not work hard (such as al-Hajj Muhammad).

But like al-Hajj Muhammad, Ahmad is always talking about how Muslims have left the path (*kharju min at-triq*) of Islam. He tells my mother that she should wear a veil and that my sisters and I should also wear *jillabas* and the veil. That is a joke. I cannot imagine my sisters wearing a *jillaba,* let alone a veil. And he condemns the Fassis and other rich Moroccans for baring their bodies at the beach. And he criticizes my sisters and me because of this too. Yet, one year, it was about 1973 I think, he brought a fat, ugly Belgian woman back with him from Belgium. She rode in the VW bus with his wife and children. I would like to have seen Fatma's face. He would go to the beach with the fat Belgian woman and leave his wife at home. He would wear a bathing suit and the fat Belgian woman wore a little bikini. My mother says that she looked like a white elephant and Ahmad looked like a hairy mouse next to her. I wish I could have seen them. I can't imagine Ahmad without his bow tie and his gold-rimmed glasses.

He was thinking about divorcing Fatma and marrying the Belgian elephant. But he decided not to. Probably because of the children. He took the Belgian woman back to Brussels and no one in the family has ever seen her since. That is the only strange thing he has ever done. The old women say he was possessed by a *jinn* then.

All Moroccan men dream of having Christian women. They think they can show that they are equal to Christian men in this way. And when you look at the rich Fassis who have studied in Europe or in the States, they almost all have Christian wives. But the Christian women who marry poor Moroccan workers are usually fat and ugly ones who cannot find a decent man in their own country. So they latch on to a handsome Moroccan. But the European wives of the rich Moroccans with villas are often beautiful. And most Moroccan women hate them. That is natural. Christian women take the finest men in Morocco. Most of the important officials in the government and most of the professors at Muhammad V University have Christian wives. And everyone considers this natural. But when a Muslim woman marries a Christian man, everyone condemns her.

My sister Rhimu used to have a boy friend from a famous old family of the Moroccan elite. He is now a professor at the Muhammad V University in Rabat. He wanted to marry Rhimu, but she said no. Before she said no, my husband and I visited him and his family. And he showed us an album of pictures of all the European girls he had known in Europe. I couldn't believe it. He was bragging about them like a little boy bragging about how many candies he had stolen. I was disgusted. Not because he had had so many European girl friends, but because he bragged that way in front of me, the sister of the girl he wanted to marry. I don't like the way Moroccan men think about women.

This boy friend of my sister's was like all the professors and students at Muhammad V University. He was always talking about "the revolution" (*at-tawra*) and how everything would be wonderful in Morocco once we got rid of the king. It is very dangerous to say such things, but he would say them anyway. Like all such Moroccans, he is full of big words about "the oppressed masses" (*al-jamahir al-kadiha*). These are just words, empty words in their

110

mouths. The closest such people have ever come to "the oppressed masses" is through the servants who cook their food, wash their clothes, and mop the floors of their villas. And when it comes to women, such people think much the way the Jbala do. This great revolutionary who wanted to marry my sister wanted her to live with his family so that his mother and sister could treat her as their servant!

We used to have a neighbor in Tangier. He was a schoolteacher with a *licence* from Muhammad V. He would often talk with my husband. And he would talk about how religion was "the opium of the masses." He refused to fast during Ramadan. And he would angrily condemn Morocco's dependence (*tabiiyya*) upon Europe. But he never let his wife wear western clothes outside of their apartment. And he hardly ever let her leave their apartment at all. I would see him on the *bulivar* with other women or sitting in a café with his friends. Once I took his wife with me to the movies. And before the movie started, all she did was stare at all the men coming into the theater, like a bitch in heat. I couldn't believe my eyes. But then I realized that not only do Moroccan men think of their women as bitches in heat that would go with the first male that approaches them, but most Moroccan women accept this conception of themselves. This is what they have been taught ever since they were little girls.

Women in Morocco live empty lives as the prisoners of men. Their only purpose in life is to provide their husbands with food, a clean home, sexual pleasure, and children—preferably sons. It is true that now things are changing a little bit. There is a woman judge in Tangier. And I know a woman professor. But they are two out of thousands.

When I complain about the position of women in Morocco, everyone in the family (except my sisters) looks at me as if I had been possessed by a *jinniyya*. And they say that I have forgotten my religion. They say I have become a Christian. But I hope things will gradually change. Now there are thousands of Moroccan girls who have grown up in Europe. And there are more and more women schoolteachers. So, God willing, things will change in time. But it is very hard to change the way men think about women.

Like al-Hajj Muhammad, Ahmad sometimes talks about how the Christians still control Morocco and about how Muslims should expel them and return to the true path of Islam. Like al-Hajj Muhammad, he speaks angrily and proudly about how we must free Morocco from Christian domination. But like almost all Moroccans, when he speaks *with* Christians, he is like a little puppy rubbing its neck on its master's pants. Whenever Moroccans speak with Christians, they become fawning sycophants. It makes me sick. But it is not their fault.

Europe has controlled Morocco for over a century. From 1912 to 1956, we were ruled by Europeans on the grounds that we were too primitive to rule ourselves. Still today, Europe and the United States control almost every facet of Moroccan society. The rich send their children to French schools and speak French among themselves. Government documents, the major newspapers, and much of what we see on television is still in French. Europeans still control our biggest factories, our biggest hotels. They still occupy our biggest villas.

So the Muslim hates the Christian. But he also admires and envies him. Rich Moroccans, especially the Fasiyyin, are imitation Frenchmen. They wear French clothes. They marry French women. They drink French wine. When they write books, they write them in French. And yet, they are haunted by the knowledge that they can never really be French. But at the same time, they can never again really be Moroccan.

All Moroccans feel inferior to the Christians. The cars we drive, the clothes we wear, the rifles our soldiers shoot, the television sets we watch, and the radios we listen to were all made by Christians. But this feeling of inferiority is much greater for the intellectuals than it is for working people who still believe in their religion. The poor peasant or laborer who retains his faith in Islam can say: "As for the Christians, they have their paradise in this world. As for us Muslims, we have our paradise in the hereafter" (*An-nsara andum aj-janna diyalum fi ad-dunya. Amma hna al-msilmin, andna aj-janna diyalna fi al-akhira*). But the intellectual cannot accept this logic. So he has nothing to soften his sense of inferiority.

When you have been controlled by foreigners all your life, you know only two ways of acting toward them: either you fawn upon them or you fight them. Most Moroccans spend their lives fawning upon them because, as my mother says, "It is by means of them that we live" (*hnaya ayshin bihim*).

6. Al-Hajj Muhammad on his brother Mustafa
(1935–), waiter in an ice cream parlor in Tangier

MY BROTHER MUSTAFA was born in about 1935. He studied the Quran in the mosque of the village of the streams for a year or two before we returned to the cobblestone quarter in about 1946. He worked as an apprentice to a Spanish confectioner (*halawi*). And he worked in a Spanish ice cream parlor near the beach. He still makes pastry in a little shop off the Road of the Mountain in the winter. And in the summer, he still works as a waiter and counterman in the ice cream parlor—which now belongs to his friend Abd ar-Rahman.

In the winter rainy season, Mustafa and Abd ar-Rahman spend a lot of time together in Abd ar-Rahman's café in the quarter of the lemon tree. The Christians don't come to Tangier when it rains, so business is slow in the ice cream parlor. And Mustafa and Abd ar-Rahman sit in the café. Sometimes ag-Grini the taxi-driver joins them. Sometimes I join them. And my cousin Hmidu joins them when he comes down to the city from the village of the streams. They sit and play cards or dominoes. They drink mint tea, café au lait, or Coca Cola, and they watch soccer on the television in the café. Whenever people want to find Mustafa during the winter rains from October through March, they look for him in this café.

If he is not there, they look in his little shop off the Road of the Mountain. If he is not there, he is probably home. But he is hardly ever home because his wife Rahma is always insulting him and complaining that he doesn't give her enough money. I don't know why he didn't divorce that woman many years ago.

Sometimes, Abd ar-Rahman, Mustafa, and ag-Grini go fishing on the Straits of Gibraltar between Tangier and Sibta (Ceuta). I go with them sometimes. We go in Abd ar-Rahman's car. It is wonderful there. The big waves crash on the rocks. Across the water you see Spain. And no one bothers us. We cook the fish over a fire with a stew of tomatoes, potatoes, and green peppers. We drink hot mint tea and we smoke hashish. It is nice.

Abd ar-Rahman is a Rifi, although he was born in the town of al-Ara'ish (Larache). He is smart like Ahmad. He has a nose for money. He started working as an apprentice in the ice cream parlor after Mustafa. And he is younger than Mustafa. But he saved his money over the years and bought the ice cream parlor from the Spaniard after independence. People say the Rifis are cutthroats. "The Rifi killed his brother over an onion" (*ar-Rifi qtil khah ala basla*). But Abd ar-Rahman is a good Muslim. It is true that he does not pray and he does drink whiskey. But every time he visits the village of the streams, he spends a hundred thousand francs ($222.22) for a night of the *tulba*. He buys sheep for a feast (*zirda*) and he gives money to all the *tulba* to chant the Quran. Every time Mustafa visits the village, the men ask him when Abd ar-Rahman will visit again. Jbala love to eat meat bought by money from another man's pocket.

Abd ar-Rahman always stays in the house of my aunt Amina's husband, Si Muhammad Qasim, when he visits the village of the streams. This is the biggest house in the village. It has two floors and a tile roof and carpets in the guest room on the second floor. Whenever rich, important people visit the village, this is where they stay.

Abd ar-Rahman is also a good friend of Si Muhammad Qasim's son, my cousin (*wild khalti*) Hmidu. He put up the money for

Hmidu's garden (*al-gharsa d Hmidu*). Hmidu cleared this garden on village communal land on a hill above the village. It was just scrub (*al-harish*) before. It is about six-tenths of a hectare in size. I have never seen such a big garden in the hills. My brother Ahmad lent Hmidu 50,000 francs ($111.11) to start this garden. And Hmidu never paid him back—so far as I know. But Abd ar-Rahman has lent him over 450,000 francs ($1,000) to pay his workers and buy seed. Once Hmidu pays him back out of the money he is making selling his vegetables, they will share the profits from the garden fifty-fifty. It was a good deal for both of them. Hmidu could never have raised that much money without Abd ar-Rahman. And Abd ar-Rahman will be making money for years without doing any work. But he was really just doing Hmidu a favor. He doesn't need the money from that garden.

Abd ar-Rahman is still young. He is about thirty-five or thirty-six, I think. He is married to a Rifiyya and they have a baby. And he has a Jibliyya mistress who works as a cashier in the ice cream parlor in the summer. He pays the rent on her apartment near the *bulivar*. And he gives her money to live on in the winter when she is not working. She is not so pretty. A man like that could have just about any woman in Tangier. He is young, handsome, and rich. May God bless him.

> and He
> has raised
> some of you
> over others
> so as to
> test you
> in what
> He has
> given you   [VI : 165]

May God guide him back to prayer. All the wealth of this world will be like nothing on the day of reckoning when we will all be called to account for all that we have done and all that we have not done.

My brother Mustafa is older than Abd ar-Rahman by a few years. But they have always been very close friends. Mustafa's wife Rahma complains that Mustafa spends too much time with Abd ar-Rahman and not enough time at home. If I had a wife like her, I would *never* go home. She says that he doesn't give her enough money. She is without shame (*ma kathishim shi*). In the summer, from May through September, he works from 10:30 every morning until 2:00 or 3:00 the next morning. During this time, he makes about 45,000 francs ($100) a month, of which he gives 30,000 francs a month to Rahma. Say "Praise be to God"! There are many months when I do not earn that much, let alone give that much to my wife Rahma. And she doesn't complain. Well, at least she doesn't complain as much as Mustafa's Rahma does. In the winter, of course, Mustafa doesn't make much money. It is rare that he makes 30,000 francs ($66.67) a month from his pastry in the winter. But he gives as much as he can to Rahma. And her arms are heavy with gold. I think she uses some of the money he gives her for food to buy gold.

Mustafa was first married in about 1958 to a Ghmariyya named Fatima Zohra. He divorced her eight months later. And in about 1960, he married Rahma, the daughter of my mother's brother Si Muhammad. May God have mercy upon him. Rahma had been married to a cousin of hers on her mother's side in her mother's village of the big rock. But this cousin divorced her after two years because she did not bear him any children.

Mustafa and Rahma have four children that did not die in infancy: (1) Latifa, a daughter born in about 1961; (2) Muhammad Said, a son born in about 1963; (3) Fatima Zohra, a daughter born in about 1970; and (4) Hannan, a daughter born in about 1973. Rahma's mother Khadduj A. lives with them. She is a shriveled old lady now. But she has the head of a little baby.

A man must control his wife firmly or she will control him. My brother Mustafa has never controlled his wife Rahma. And because of this, he is sad. She is possessed by a *jinniyya*, that woman. And it is said that she is cursed (*maskhuta*) by her first husband. One day, she wanted to go up to the village of the streams for the wedding of my uncle Mhammad's son Abd as-Slam. Mustafa said no because Si Muhammad Qasim sent word to everyone in the family not to attend the wedding. And Si Muhammad Qasim said he would not allow anyone to stay at his house for the wedding. He wanted to shame my uncle Mhammad. Anyway, Mustafa said no. And Rahma was furious. She grabbed a carving knife and tried to stab Mustafa. Praise be to God she missed him. Then she went to stay with a kinsman of hers on her mother's side in Bni Makada. She took her senile old mother with her.

Everyone in the family told Mustafa to divorce that mad woman (*dak al-masura*). He should have divorced her long ago just for the way she insults him in front of guests. When people of the family used to come to Tangier from the village for a few days, they always used to stay at Mustafa's house because it is big and easy to get to from all the other houses of the family. But now they stay with my aunt Khadduj near the *bulivar* or with me in the quarter of the lemon tree, because they are ashamed to see a Muslim be insulted by his wife. It is disgusting. She is worse than a Christian woman.

For a woman to try to kill her husband with a knife, that is forbidden (*hram*). She should be put in the crazy house in Bni Makada. She should be in chains. One day the *jinn* will possess her and she could try to kill one of her children. God forbid (*Allah yihfad*).

She often insults her children in front of me and other kin. She says Muhammad Said is stupid and lazy. What kind of mother would speak this way about her son? And Muhammad Said is a good boy. May God bless him. He and his sister Latifa are always arguing with their mother. It is true that a Muslim must always obey and respect his parents. But who would obey and respect a woman who tries to kill her husband because he won't let her go to a wedding?

Some people say that Mustafa has no self-respect (*qlil an-nifs*) because he did not divorce Rahma after she tried to stab him. Hmidu says he is ashamed to look Mustafa in the eye now. He is too ashamed to stay in Mustafa's house any more. I told Mustafa he should divorce her but he said the children needed their mother and he didn't want to be without his children. It is true that he loves those children. God bless them. But they know their mother is no good. They would be happier without her. I think Rahma used magic (*as-shur*) to control Mustafa. Maybe she fed him donkey ears. Anyway, he did not divorce her. And a week after she tried to kill him, she came back from Bni Makada. And since then, no one talks about that day in front of Mustafa or Rahma. It is shameful.

Mustafa used to collect the rent from my brother Ahmad's tenants. But when Mustafa used a little of the money to feed his children, Ahmad had his tenants pay their rent directly to the bank. Mustafa was very angry. And Ahmad was wrong to do this. A Muslim must help his brother. We are not like the Christians. We help each other. Ahmad should say "Praise be to God" (*al-hamdu li Illah*) that he is able to help his brothers. Brotherhood is neither sold nor bought (*Al-khawa ma katinba ma katin-shra*). The Muslim who gives to his brother has much *ajar* (spiritual reward the accumulation of which leads to admittance to heaven). Instead of giving kettles and aluminum ladders to the village mosque, Ahmad should give to his brothers. Charity to kinsmen first (*As-sadaqa fi al-muqarribin awla*).

But he wants everyone in the village of the streams to say what a good Muslim he is. Maybe someday he will try to use those people. Maybe he will try to be elected to the parliament or something. Then he will remind everyone of the kettle and the aluminum ladder. And everyone will vote for him because he is a good Muslim. But his brothers cannot sleep at night for fear that he will put them out in the street. Mustafa knows that Ahmad wants to sell the house he lives in, even though Mustafa, Habiba, and I still own our shares. And I am afraid that Ahmad will put me out into the street when he retires from the car factory and returns to Tangier to live. He even says he is going to. He is not ashamed to say that he is going to put his own brother out in the street! He says I have been living in the house rent-free for years and he will not let me stay when he comes back. He thinks like a Christian man. He insults me because I built the house on the wrong lot. But it was not my fault, I thought this was his lot.

Every time he comes back in August for his vacation, he and his bitch of a wife and their children, may God bless them, take over the house. And Rahma and I are like mice in a corner! Everyone in the family comes to see him and to receive a gift from him. But he doesn't give me any money to feed them. He has millions in the bank. But he expects his poor peddler brother to provide a feast of meat for the entire family, not to mention the *muqaddim* and all the others who dream of squeezing a little money out of him. It would be easier to squeeze water from a rock! I have to beg him for money to feed them. And he is my younger brother. I have to listen to him insult me and call me an idiot before he gives me a franc. Every August the family is happy and excited because Ahmad and Habiba are coming from Belgium. But I cannot sleep at night thinking of how Ahmad will insult me before he will give me any money with which to feed them. He knows I have nothing. Nothing! But he pretends not to know so he can watch me squirm.

It is wrong to speak badly of your brother. May God forgive me. May God forgive me.

Mustafa has a white (i.e., good) heart. May God guide him. He stopped praying when he was a boy. His son Muhammad Said says that he has started to pray again. But I have not seen him pray since he was a boy. But now he is growing older. And when a man grows older he begins to fear God for he knows that death is getting closer and closer.

> everything dies
> except His face
> to Him
> is the Judgment
> and to Him
> you shall return   [XXVIII : 88]

When a man is young, death (*al-mawt*) is just a word. The young man dreams only of the sweetness between the thighs of a woman. His flesh is hard and muscled. But the old man whose flesh sags from his bones dreams of death. Of the worms that will eat his

119

flesh. Of the dirt that will fill his eyes and his mouth. Of the fire that will burn the evil. And the old man fears God and prays. All men pray once they start to feel the strength of their bodies dying.

Mustafa is not really old. He was only born in about 1935. If he were a rich Christian with Muslim servants to work for him, he might still look young. But when you spend your life working from dawn to dusk for a mouthful of bread (*shi luqma d al-khubz*), you die fast. Especially because there are many nights when you go to sleep and your stomach aches from hunger. Everything is in the hands of God.

When Mustafa takes out his plastic teeth, his sunken cheeks and toothless mouth make him look very old. And he has a big belly like me. He would look a lot younger if he didn't have that bitch of a wife. May God reward patient endurance. I think Mustafa will start praying and stop drinking whiskey soon. May God guide him (*Allah yihdih*).

7. *Fatima Zohra on her cousin Mustafa*

MY COUSIN MUSTAFA IS A GOOD MAN. May God bless him. Al-Hajj Muhammad sometimes insults him because he does not pray and because he drinks whiskey with Abd ar-Rahman. But al-Hajj Muhammad didn't pray when he was young. And he used to drink whiskey too. He would be extremely disturbed if I said this in front of him, so I would not do so. Because when he is upset, he starts talking fast and he doesn't know what he is saying.

Mustafa has had a hard life. He and his wife Rahma argue a lot, mostly about money. She says she cannot feed the children on what he gives her. Most women in the family say she is cursed (*maskhuta*) by her first husband. This is a terrible thing to say. It is cruel because when a woman hears that people believe that she is cursed, then she will believe it too. And because she believes it, she will expect bad things to happen. And she will cause them to happen. And then the women will say, "Ha, you see? Didn't we say that she was cursed?" Rahma was wrong to try to stab Mustafa when he wouldn't give her money to go to the wedding. She didn't know what she was doing. But she has always been good to me. We have never argued in all the years I have known her. And I have known her all my life. When my sister Zubida was forced to leave her husband for over a month, she stayed with Rahma and Mustafa. And Rahma was very nice to her. It is true that she complains because Mustafa does not give her enough money. But when a man does not give his wife enough money to feed their children, why should she not complain?

Mustafa is good, but he still thinks the way men thought a hundred years ago. Most Moroccan men do. He took his daughter Latifa out of school in 1976, and he enrolled her in a government vocational center to learn to sew, knit, and embroider. In 1977, she received a fifty kilo sack of flour a month. That's $10.56-worth. (A kilo of flour was 95 francs, or $.21, in 1977). But she had to pay a dollar a month in tuition, so her net income was about $9.50 a month in 1977. But Mustafa would say that some day she would make over 20,000 francs ($44.44) a month. And she was learning a craft. In school she was just wasting her time, he would say. And he was wasting money on her books, paper, and pencils.

Latifa was an excellent student at the school of the stream (*al-mdrasa d al-wad*), which I also attended when I was a little girl. This is the elementary school where most children in the cobblestone quarter go. Latifa was also a good student at Zinab secondary school, which she attended for three years. After one more year of school, she could have taken and passed the exam for the *brevet* (*ash-shahada d at-tanawi*). With this diploma, she could have worked as a secretary or a clerk or she could have gone to the *Ecole Régionale d'Instituteurs* for a year and become an elementary schoolteacher. She could have had a secure white-collar job for the rest of her working life, with a pension after that. She could be making anywhere from 50,000 francs ($111.11) a month as a secretary to 120,000 francs ($266.67) a month as a schoolteacher with five or six years' experience. My mother and I tried to explain all of this to Mustafa. We tried to explain to him that it was in his interest to let her stay in school.

But he kept saying that he could not afford the books and pencils. So I said I would pay for them. But he said he wanted Latifa to start bringing home some money now. Not in the future. And then he started to tell us how a woman should be at home with her kin, not in public places. "Secretaries, schoolteachers, and clerks who wear western clothes bare their bodies to strange men every day and men and women cannot work together every day without thinking of more than work," said Mustafa. "Such women are corrupt (*mafsudin*)," he said. "They are little better than whores. It is not natural for men and women to work together, especially when the women are almost naked." We told him that the world had changed and that now it is perfectly all right for a woman to wear western clothes and work in an office or as a teacher. No man would dare molest her. But he said that he would never let Latifa work at such a job.

In some ways, Mustafa is right. I hate to say it, but it is true. Most Moroccan men still think that a woman who works in western clothes is as loose as the Christian movie stars they see on Friday and Saturday nights. And often, when a Moroccan man hires a woman to work for him, he thinks he has the right to sleep with her. It is not always this way. It is not usually this way for rich women with powerful fathers, husbands, or brothers. And if a woman is ugly, she too is fairly safe. But a pretty woman from a poor family has a hard life in Morocco if she works for a man, even if she wears a *jillaba* and a veil.

Latifa was very angry when Mustafa forced her to leave school. She wants to wear western clothes and drive a car like me. And maybe she will some day. Some women make a lot of money as seamstresses. A girl I went to school with now has her own shop and four girls who work as her apprentices. She bought a big house in

Marshan, where she lives with her parents. And she drives her own Fiat. She is divorced and sad because she has no husband. But she is rich and she has no one to answer to. And her father was just a poor Jibli with charcoal dust in his ears.

When I was last in Morocco, Mustafa was talking about taking his son Muhammad Said out of school too and putting him to work as an apprentice to an electrician. Muhammad Said, who was about fourteen then, is a very nice boy with curly light brown hair and light skin. He looks like a French boy. He was never as good a student as Latifa and he had to repeat the last year of elementary school (*al-mutawassit at-tani*). Many students are failed at the end of this year because there is not enough room for them in secondary school. But in 1977, Muhammad Said was in the first year of secondary school.

Rahma would insult Muhammad Said in front of me and say that he was lazy and stupid. A mother should not speak this way about her children at any time, but especially not in front of other people. I felt sorry for Muhammad Said when his mother said these things. I think she and Mustafa just wanted him to start working and bring home some money. It is hard to make people like Mustafa and Rahma understand that it is in their best interest to keep their children in school so that some day they will earn good salaries and be able to help their parents when they are old. By now they have probably put Muhammad Said to work as an apprentice (*mitallim*).

Mustafa says school is only for the rich. He says the poor need the money their children can earn as apprentices. And he says that only the children of the rich are passed year after year. The poor man sends his boy to school year after year and pays for his books and paper. But then he doesn't have enough money to bribe his boy's teacher to pass him into secondary school. And all those years of school are wasted and the boy starts to work as an apprentice at the age of fifteen when he could have started when he was eight or nine so that by the age of fifteen he could be bringing home ten thousand francs ($22.22) a month or more.

Again I am very sad to say that Mustafa is right—to *some*

degree. It is true that rich fathers bribe their sons' teachers (although they would not waste their money to bribe their daughters' teachers) to pass them. And people say that rich parents even bribe teachers to pass their sons on the *baccalauréat* exam! But it is also true that if a poor boy or even a girl is a very good student, he or she will pass even without a bribe. Latifa, for example, was always one of the best students in her class. Mustafa would never have had to bribe anyone for her to become a schoolteacher. But it is hard to get a new idea into an old head.

Mustafa's third daughter, Fatima Zohra, is also very smart like Latifa. She was in the first grade in 1977, at the school of the stream. Mustafa will probably take her out of school at an early age too, and she too will probably become a seamstress like Latifa. And they will both probably marry husbands who will never let them leave their homes except to visit relatives and to go to the steam bath (*al-hammam*). (They will sew in their own homes.)

Although Mustafa does not pray like al-Hajj Muhammad and Ahmad, he thinks the same way they do. And like all men, he will start to pray as his hair starts to whiten. Like al-Hajj Muhammad and Ahmad, he condemns the Fassis because they have become like Christians. He says that during Ramadan, the month of fasting, the Fassis and other rich Moroccans in western clothes come to Abd ar-Rahman's ice cream parlor and order ice cream in French, pretending to be Christians. This makes Mustafa very mad and he tells them to leave before he calls the police. At any rate, this is what he says to the family. But I am sure that he sells ice cream to many rich Moroccans during Ramadan because they are rich and powerful. Many rich young people buy Coca Colas and *bocadillos* (hero sandwiches) in grocery stores in downtown Tangier during Ramadan. And the police do not arrest them. They ask for the food in French and the Susi grocer answers them in French, pretending to believe that they are Christians. But they are the children of powerful government officials or wealthy businessmen. No policeman is going to arrest them! He would lose his job if he did so. But if a Muslim in a dirty, threadbare *jillaba* is caught eating between dawn and sunset during Ramadan, he is immediately arrested and jailed. I have *seen* poor men being dragged off to jail for not fasting. Usually, they are young men. Most older people still fast. And almost everyone pretends to fast. Most of the family would be shocked to know that my sisters and I do not fast any more. For them, not fasting during Ramadan is worse than lying, stealing, or cheating their husbands or wives. Most Moroccan women cheat their husbands and most Moroccan men cheat their wives. But they would not think of breaking the fast.

8. *Al-Hajj Muhammad on his sister Fatima* *(1939–), wife of a flower vendor in Gibraltar*

MY SISTER FATIMA was born in about 1939 near the end of the war between Franco and *los rojos*. My father died a few months before she was born, may God have mercy upon him. She was born in the village of the streams not long after we moved back there from Tangier. After we came back down to Tangier in about 1946, she would help my mother knead the dough for the bread my mother sold in the old city. May God have mercy upon my beloved mother.

When she was about seventeen years old, Fatima married Mshish H. He is about nine years older than she is. He looks old now because he has spent his life drinking whiskey and smoking *kif* (marijuana) and hashish. His father came to Tangier from the village of the mint leaves in Bni Msawwar. And he died when Mshish was still a little boy, may God have mercy upon him. Mshish's mother sold flowers in the New Market (*Plasa aj-Jdida*) near the *bulivar*. Mshish and his brothers and his sister helped her. She made a lot of money from the flowers because most of the Christians in the new city of Tangier used to do their marketing here. And the Muslim grows rich selling to the Christian. Only the Christians bought their flowers. As Mshish says, we Muslims do not spend our money on flowers the way the Christians do. We are lucky to have enough to eat. Mshish's mother would buy the flowers from a Christian in Casablanca and Mshish bought a car and he would bring the flowers himself, after wasting thousands of francs on the whores of Casablanca.

My mother refused to let Fatima marry Mshish. Everyone knew how he spent money on whores, whiskey, and hashish. And he never prayed. Even today, he still does not pray. He has probably not been inside a mosque since he was a boy. But Fatima insisted upon marrying him. So my aunt Khadduj's husband, al-Hajj M.B., and *al-Qadi* (judge) Muhammad B. arranged the wedding.

Fatima went to live with Mshish and his mother in the quarter of the little mosque. Mshish's mother built a house there, a nice whitewashed two-story house with a terrace on top and a little garden. From this terrace you can see the big villas of the Christians. And you can see the cobblestone quarter far below on the slopes of the valley. Just across the road is the villa of an Englishman. He has a big wall around his garden with broken glass on top to prevent poor Muslims from stealing. After Mshish's mother died, may God have mercy upon her, Mshish and Fatima and their children remained in the house.

Mshish was never a good husband. He was always wasting his money on the whores of the Bni Yidir quarter. And he was always drunk or full of hashish. What kind of a Muslim would let his children see him drunk?

After they had been married for about ten or twelve years, we found out that Mshish had a second wife who lived in another part of Tangier. One day, my aunt Khadduj saw him carrying a bag of food for this second wife and the child he had with her. And my aunt told Fatima and showed her the house where the second wife lived. Fatima was very angry and told Mshish to divorce the second wife or she would divorce him. He divorced the second one. This second wife was from the *qbila* of Ahl Srif. After she had been divorced by her first husband, she sold *qasbur* (coriander) and *maadnus* (parsley) in the Suq al-barra. That is where she met Mshish. He started giving her money so she wouldn't have to sell in the market any more. But after Fatima made him divorce her, she probably started selling coriander and parsley again.

People used to respect Mshish because he owned his own car as well as the house his mother left him. He made a lot of money from his flowers. And if you have money in your pocket, everyone is your friend, but if you have none, no one is your friend. The words of the possessor of property are pure silver while the words of the poor man are covered with shit (*Mul al-mta klamu safi an-nuqra wa al-maskin matli bi l-khra*).

And Mshish was very strong when he was young. He lifted iron bars with iron plates on both ends every morning. So his arms were like iron. And women always wanted him. He attracts women the way my brother Ahmad attracts money.

But one day in about 1974 or 1975, Mshish was drunk and he was driving down the winding road from the Big Mountain. And his car hit a man. The man went to the hospital but he didn't die. Muhammad K. the policeman told Mshish to pay him a lot of money or he would go to jail. Mshish didn't pay and he spent six months in jail. And the police took away his license. He was stupid not to pay Muhammad K. But maybe he didn't have the money. After he got out of jail, he was ashamed to let people see him walking downtown from the quarter of the little mosque. He would walk at night and on little side streets so on one would see him. The great Mshish had to walk his own two feet.

But Mshish's brother lent him some money and they started selling flowers together in Gibraltar. They take turns running their flower stand there. One of them stays in Tangier for ten days or so while the other one sells flowers in Gibraltar. But sometimes Mshish tells Fatima that he is in Gibraltar and then someone sees him in the Bni Yidir quarter, where he wastes his money on whores and whiskey while his wife and children have nothing to eat.

But somehow he managed to save 80,000 francs ($178) to buy a motorcycle. He was very proud of his motorcycle and he rode it everywhere so that everybody could see that he did not have to walk or ride the bus anymore.

He doesn't give my sister Fatima enough money to feed their children. They have eight children that lived, plus six who have returned to God. May God have mercy upon them. The living children are: (1) Rashid, a son born about 1960; (2) Naima, a daughter born in about 1964; (3) Huriyya, a daughter born in about 1966; (4) Fathiyya, a daughter born in about 1968; (5) Fu'ad, a son born in 1969; (6) Muhammad, a son born in 1972; (7) Murad, a son born in 1975; and (8) a baby born in 1977.

Rashid is a good boy. He lifts the iron bars with iron plates on both ends the way Mshish used to. And he knows karate. He is strong and handsome. Even though he is still young, there are probably many women who would go with him without money. But he is not like Mshish. He doesn't drink whiskey and he doesn't smoke hashish. And he gives most of the money he makes to his mother. He went to school for five years. Then Mshish put him to work helping him sell flowers. In 1976, my sister Habiba took him with her to Belgium. He studied French at a school that Habiba paid for. But he couldn't find work. In the old days when I was in Belgium, it was easy to find work, even without papers (*bi la kwaghat*). But now it is very hard. So after about a year, Rashid came back to Tangier and started helping Mshish sell flowers in Gibraltar. Then he was supposed to be drafted into the army. But Mshish bribed the *muqaddim* of the quarter of the little mosque so he didn't have to go. In this world, a little money takes care of all problems. Like most Moroccans in Gibraltar, Rashid stays in a big dormitory in Gibraltar. He pays 1,850 francs ($4.11) a week. He sleeps in a big room with forty-nine other Muslims. He is a good boy, not like his father. Unfortunately, he does not pray. May God guide him (*Allah yihdih*).

9. *Fatima Zohra on her cousin Fatima*

MY COUSIN (*bint khalti*) Fatima used to be beautiful. Now of course, after fourteen children, six of whom died (including a set of triplets), her body is flabby. But she is still beautiful. She is very sweet. And I could sit and laugh with her for hours. She loves to joke and laugh. And when you hear her laugh, it is hard not to laugh yourself. Sometimes I wonder how she can laugh living the life she has led with Mshish. He is no good. But she still adores him after twenty years of seeing him come home drunk and stinking of the perfume of the whores of the Bni Yidir quarter.

One day, I was visiting Fatima with my mother and Mshish staggered through the door and up the stairs without even greeting us or his wife or his children. He stank of whiskey. And his seven little children were sitting there watching their drunken father crawl up the stairs on his hands and knees. What kind of memory is that to put in the head of a little child? If Fatima's brothers were really men, they would beat Mshish until he swore to never drink whiskey again. But she wouldn't let her brothers touch him. They would have to fight her to get to him. And anyway he could beat them altogether, even drunk. Mshish is very strong and he often fights when he is drunk. I cannot imagine Ahmad or Mustafa fighting, although al-Hajj Muhammad used to. Anyway, Fatima adores that drunken bum. And, in his strange way, Mshish adores her too. But that is not a good way to love. If he really loved her like a decent man, he would not have married the coriander and parsley woman in secret and he wouldn't go with the whores of the Bni Yidir quarter. And he would give her money to feed the children.

I want to cry when I see the children of Fatima. They are always dirty. They always have runny noses. They are usually without shoes and their clothes are torn and threadbare. Mshish never gives her enough money to feed them. She gets some money from Ahmad and from Habiba, who sends her checks from Belgium. Mustafa and al-Hajj Muhammad cannot help her because they are as poor as she is. Like all poor Moroccans, they buy food on credit. Those children are lucky if they eat meat once a year! Thank God Rashid is a good boy. Now that he is working in Gibraltar, he gives her most of the money he makes. He is a very good boy. When my husband and I spent a day in Gibraltar, Rashid insisted on paying at the restaurant where we had lunch. Everybody else in the family was always trying to squeeze money from my husband. But Rashid is proud. I hope he finds a good wife and lives a happy life.

Rashid used to be crazy about my sister Nufissa and she was crazy about him. He would take her to ar-Rmilat on his father's motorcycle. People in the family said this was shameful. But that is nonsense. When people are young, they should enjoy life. And if Nufissa enjoyed riding on Rashid's motorcycle, that is fine. He drives carefully. He is not crazy like many of the young men who have motorcycles. But after a while, Rashid and Nufissa drifted apart. They no longer live in the same worlds. Nufissa studied and graduated from the American School in Tangier and she lived for several years in the States. She is, in many ways, more American than Moroccan. She writes poetry. She has probably not worn a *jillaba* more than two or three times in her life. Next year, she will be going to a university in the States, God willing (*in sha' Allah*). Rashid did not finish elementary school. He will marry a woman who will never leave their house without wearing a *jillaba* and a veil. Nufissa usually wears blue jeans and T shirts. Or else she wears western skirts and blouses. I cannot imagine her wearing a veil. She could never be the wife of a Moroccan flower vendor.

When I was in Morocco in 1977, Fatima was talking about putting her oldest daughters Naima and Huriyya to work as apprentices in a lingerie factory (*mamal nilun*). They cannot go to the government vocational center for seamstresses because they have never been in school. They are sixteen and fourteen years old now and they do not even know how to write their own names! But the third daughter, Fathiyya, and the son Fu'ad are both in school. Fu'ad is a cute little boy with blond hair and rosy cheeks, like a little Dutch boy. And his little brothers Muhammad and

Murad have black hair. They are also very cute, may God bless them.

Fatima once asked me about using some form of birth control. After fourteen children, six of whom died, it is not surprising that she should be interested. Especially with that bum of a husband. But when I tried to take her to a clinic, she was afraid and refused to go. Women are ashamed to let some strange doctor see their bodies. And they are afraid that birth control is a sin and that they will be punished by God. The government should push the *ulama'* (religious scholars) to tell people that birth control is not sinful. They should tell men this at Friday prayer. But the government is doing very little to change people's ideas about such things. So women like Fatima keep making babies year after year.

10. Al-Hajj Muhammad on his half-sister Habiba (1943–), cleaning woman in Belgium

AFTER MY FATHER DIED, may God have mercy upon him, my mother married Si Muhammad A. from the village of the big rock. And their first child was my sister Habiba, who was born in 1943 or 1944. She was born in the village of the streams. She was always in trouble. When her breasts started to swell when she was about thirteen or fourteen, she started going with men. It is not right to speak badly of my sister, but she is without shame.

In about 1960, when she was about sixteen, she met a motor-cyclist-stuntman named Ahmad W. who used to perform at the *imarat* (carnivals in celebration of saints) around Tangier. She ran away with him to Casablanca, where they were married. He taught her how to ride a motorcycle. And she would ride the motorcycle at the *imarat* wearing tight, sexy clothes like women acrobats in a circus. She is without shame. She also did tricks with a snake.

Ahmad W. used to beat her because she would go with other men. So she divorced him.

Then Habiba married a laborer named Abd al-Qadir S. He was originally from the village of the cold spring in Bni Msawwar. They went to Belgium in 1967. He worked in a factory and she worked as a cleaning woman. Most of the Moroccan women in Belgium mop floors and wash windows. After about five years, Habiba divorced Abd al-Qadir. Since 1972, she has been living with Luhsin, a factory worker from Meknes. He comes back from Belgium with her every August. They live in the same building as Ahmad in Belgium. They live together and they are not married. And she is not ashamed. No one in the family insults her for living with Luhsin because she is rich. And Luhsin is too, compared to most people in the family anyway. The rich man is loved even if he is bad; the poor man is hated even if he is good (*Mul al-flus ihibbuh wa law ikun qbih; al-maskin, ibaghduh wa law ikun mlih*).

Habiba is rich like Ahmad. She probably owns over four and half million francs ($10,000) worth of land in Tangier. She owns a big plot of land near the little market of the cobblestone quarter. And she owns the land and the house where my sister Zohra lives, right next to Mshish's house in the quarter of the little mosque. Zohra and Habiba are both the daughters of Si Muhammad A. Habiba sends Zohra money from Belgium.

Habiba often spends a lot of money for nights of the *tulba* in the village of the streams and in her father's village of the big rock. She pays for the sheep, the tomatoes, the potatoes, the olive oil, the tea, and the sugar cones. And she pays the *tulba* for chanting the Quran. Whenever someone who has a lot of money visits the village, he or she is supposed to have a night of the *tulba* especially if he or she has not been to the village in a long time.

Habiba is not only rich, she has a permanent visa and working papers, so she can stay in Belgium as long as she wants. And she has the right to bring her husband to Belgium. So many men in the family and in the village of the streams want to marry her in order to go to Belgium. Everyone thinks that if he goes to Belgium, he will come back rich like Ahmad and Habiba. My cousin Abd al-Aziz did marry Habiba for about a week in order to get a passport.

But I have one cousin on my father's side who wanted to marry Habiba for love, not for money. He is still young and he is already a *qadi* (judge). He studied law at the Muhammad V University in Rabat. He is very smart. He has a library with many books in Arabic, French, and Spanish. His father is just an ignorant Jibli, but he is rich, with about fifteen hectares of land in Bni Arus. But what does a rich, well-educated (*qari*) young *qadi* want with a chubby old whore like Habiba who cannot read or write anything more than her name? God forgive me for speaking badly of my sister. She has a white heart and she is good to her sister Zohra and to her no-good father in the village of the big rock. But who can respect a woman like that? She probably cannot even remember all the men she has gone with. What would a *qadi* want with such a woman? Moreover, she is older than he is. And fatter. She used to have a beautiful body when she was young, but now she is getting heavy. And the *qadi* is skinny and small. Wear clothes that fit you and mix with those who are like you (*Lbis qaddak wa khlat mitlak*). The *qadi*, who is educated, could not understand these things. But Habiba, who is uneducated, did. And she refused to marry him. And she is still living with Luhsin the factory worker even though they are not married. Everyone will be hung by his leg (*Kull wahid ghadi ikun mallaq min rijlu*).

11. *Fatima Zohra on her cousin Habiba*

MY COUSIN HABIBA is a sweet, wonderful woman. In some ways, she is al-Hajj Muhammad in the form of a woman. Like him, she is sterile. And this makes her sad. Maybe the reason she has gone with so many men is that she could never have children. But she would go with men even when she was still a young girl and her mother was still alive.

In those days, they lived in the house where Mustafa now lives in the cobblestone quarter, near the village fountain (*sabila aj-Jmaa*). (The cobblestone quarter used to be a village before it became part of Tangier.) Habiba's breasts developed early and men would stare at her. Al-Hajj Muhammad says men like a woman with a lot of meat on her bones. And men always liked Habiba. And she always liked men. Everyday she would put on rouge and lipstick and a tight *jillaba* and she would leave the house before the call to the sunset prayer. Her mother would scream at her and beg her not to go, but she went anyway. And she would meet men and stay out until late at night. I don't know where she went with the men, maybe in their cars.

My aunt Shama was very sad because Habiba did these things. One day, she cut Habiba's hair while she was asleep so that she would be ashamed to leave the house. Oh Habiba was mad! She was screaming like a madwoman. She tried to tape her hair back on her head, but that didn't work. Then she tried to burn herself. She was on fire. So she ran to the village fountain and pushed aside the girls who were waiting in line with their buckets and bottles. And she doused the fire under the fountain. She was very strong then and she used to beat other girls when she was mad. People said she was possessed by a *jinniyya*. And nobody wanted his son to marry such a woman, which is why none of her husbands were cousins or neighbors.

The men in the family say that Habiba is "hot" (*skhuna*) and needs to have sex all the time. And of course all women need to be with men, just as all men need to be with women. But sometimes I think Habiba did some of the things she did to revolt against her mother and the family. I think she enjoys shocking people. And she certainly did when she was riding the motorcycle in the *imarat* wearing black stockings and a sexy little outfit covered with gold spangles. Most people in the family insult my mother for not wearing a veil, so you can imagine what they thought of Habiba. And now she is living with Luhsin without being married to him! People whisper about it behind her back. But no one insults her to her face because they all want her money!

Like al-Hajj Muhammad, Habiba is always joking and laughing.

I think she is the funniest woman in northern Morocco. One day when she had just come back from Belgium for her August vacation, all the women in the family were crowding around her at al-Hajj Muhammad's house and she kept having to say *la bas* ("no harm," i.e., "all right"). How's your mother? *La bas?* How's your father? *La bas?* And one has to do this for everyone in a person's family. And when you have to do this for all the relatives of about twenty women, it gets to be a nuisance. But this is the custom. After about an hour of saying *la bas?*, Habiba shouted, "Hey, what is this? I didn't come back all the way from Belgium just to spend my vacation saying *la bas?*" But she said it in a funny, sweet way, the way she says almost everything. So the women were not mad. Like al-Hajj Muhammad, Habiba says things no one else would say. But everyone loves her sweetness and laughter.

Habiba brings back clothes for everyone in the family when she returns to Tangier for her August vacation, just as Ahmad does. This is the custom. When my mother lived with us in the States, she was always collecting old clothes. My sisters and I would tell her to throw out all that garbage. But she had to bring gifts for everyone in the family or people would say that she had become cheap and greedy like a Christian. And when she went to Mecca, she brought everyone gifts, which made them all very happy because anything from Mecca is said to be full of *baraka,* or blessedness.

Habiba lets her sister Zohra live rent-free in a house she owns in the quarter of the little mosque, right next to Fatima's house. She sends Zohra money to live on because her husband ach-Chino is a bum. And she helps Fatima too. But sometimes she is tight with her money. When my mother asked to ride with her in Luhsin's car to go to Belgium in 1977, she made my mother pay thirty-five thousand francs ($77.78). And my mother helped my aunt Shama raise Habiba and her brothers and sisters when they were little children in the village of the streams. And when my mother was in Belgium, she tried to borrow some money from Habiba and Habiba said no. "Her daughters are married to husbands with cars, so why should I lend her money?," Habiba said to Ahmad while my mother overheard them from outside the door to Ahmad's apartment. My mother was very angry.

But Habiba is really good. And everyone in the family tries to use her because she has money. I remember one day we went to the *imara* of Sidi Qasim near Tangier. Habiba was there with my cousins Muhammad, Abd al-Aziz, and Rashid. She paid for their food, their tea, and their bus tickets home. When they got on the bus, they all pointed toward Habiba when the conductor asked them to pay. It was disgusting. Rashid would never do that now because he is making money selling flowers. But Abd al-Aziz and Muhammad are not ashamed to let a woman pay for them.

I hope Habiba has enjoyed the many men she has been with. And I am glad she jokes and laughs. Because she is really sad. Luhsin is no good. He is very tight with his money. And he does not really love her. He is just using her. He sleeps with her and she cooks for him, and he didn't spend a franc for a wedding or for *as-sdaq* (brideprice). He is younger than she is. And as she gets older and fatter, he will start looking for a young beautiful wife. And she will be alone with no husband and no children when she is old. I hope I am wrong. I hope Luhsin really does love her. Or else I hope she finds a man who really does. Because it is sad to grow old alone, no matter how rich you are.

12. *Al-Hajj Muhammad on his half-sister Zohra* (1947–), *wife of a laborer in Tangier*

MY YOUNGEST SISTER ZOHRA was born between 1945 and 1948. She says she was born in 1948. God knows best. She has always been in trouble like Habiba. But she is poor and Habiba is rich. She is skinny and Habiba is fat. She is always whining and Habiba is always laughing. And she is missing two front teeth so she looks older than she is. Her husband knocked out her teeth. She says she is only two years older than my cousin Fatima Zohra. But she looks like an old woman while Fatima Zohra looks like a beautiful young woman. God has punished her for going with so many men and causing her mother so much sorrow.

She always went with men, as did Habiba. My mother tried to stop her. But it was useless. My mother would often cry because of Zohra and Habiba. Shortly before my mother died, may God have mercy upon her, Zohra married Mihjub, a day laborer from Casablanca. Like all her other men, he was a good-for-nothing bum (*silgut*). They had two children that lived: Muhsin, a boy born in about 1963, and Zinab, a girl born in 1964. They were always arguing and he would beat her and the children. Sometimes a man has to beat a woman, but not all the time. He died after four years, in 1966. Zohra says that he was poisoned to death by another woman. But nobody believes what she says.

After Mihjub died, Zohra went with many men, all of them bums (*slagat*). In 1971, she became pregnant with the child of one of these men. God knows which one and only God knows. But Zohra says the father was a laborer named Hasan. He was from Casablanca like her first husband. But he refused to marry her. So she told another one of her bums that *he* was the father. This was ach-Chino (the Chinaman). They call him Chino because of his slanted eyes. He is a day laborer from the Ghmaran hills. He believed Zohra and married her. She looked like she had a big watermelon in her stomach when they were married. Some of the old men in the family said that before the Christians colonized Morocco, such a woman would have been stoned to death. But today a good Muslim woman is as hard to find as a generous Jew.

Zohra's baby was born three months after she married Chino. It was a girl and they named her Miryam. God bless her (*tabarraka Allah alayha*). She is a sweet little girl. How could such a bitter mother have such a sweet little girl? God bless that sweet little girl and grant her a good life in this world.

Chino found out that Miryam was not his daughter. He probably knew all along. I think he just married Zohra because he knew that Habiba always sends her money and lets her live in her house in the quarter of the little mosque without paying rent. Some days he works, some days he doesn't. But he spends most of his money on whores, whiskey, and hashish. Zohra says he takes strange pills too. His brain has rotted from all the whiskey and the drugs. He beats Zohra and Miryam all the time—whenever his head is full of whiskey and hashish.

Zohra always comes to my house and complains about Chino. And she asks me to lend her some money. If you lend Zohra money you never see it again. And she gets more money from Habiba than I do peddling. So why should I give her money? Habiba gives *her* money, not me. So she should help me instead of asking me to help her. She is always begging everyone in the family for money; me, Mustafa, Fatima Zohra, my aunt Khadduj. But never my sister Fatima.

Zohra and Fatima live right next door to each other and they are sisters even though they have different fathers. But they hate each other. Sometimes they fight and the neighbors have to pull them away from each other. As for Chino, he wouldn't dare fight Mshish. Mshish would kill him. Chino is small. But he always carries a knife, so he is dangerous. He is big and strong when it comes to beating his wife and her little children. But he needs a knife to fight a man.

Zohra brought her troubles upon herself. She has been going with bums ever since she was a young girl. She could have left Chino a long time ago, but she keeps going back to him. Maybe she likes being beaten. Or maybe she is afraid that no other man would have her. I do not want to speak badly of my sister. But she is impossible. Sometimes when she knocks on the door, Rahma and I pretend we are not home so we do not have to listen to her whine and snivel and then ask me for money and cry when I say no. That woman stinks of sadness. Sometimes I am home joking and laughing with relatives and she comes and tries to make us all sad the way she is. "Oh, Chino beat me again last night! Oh, his head was full of hashish and he tried to cut me with his knife! Oh, he insults and beats the children! Oh, he never gives me money for food! Oh, nobody in the family cares if he kills me! Oh, my brothers don't care if my children and I starve to death!" That woman could make a wedding seem like a funeral. May God forgive me for speaking badly of my sister.

13. *Fatima Zohra on her cousin Zohra*

WHEN ZOHRA AND I WERE CHILDREN growing up in the cobblestone quarter, she was very mean. She would beat us up if we did not listen to her. I was afraid of her. Then when she grew older, she started going with men and my aunt Shama was very sad. The old women in the family say that Zohra's bad luck is the effect of her mother's curse upon her because she did not obey her. But my aunt Shama, may God have mercy upon her, was a good woman and she would not have cursed any of her children. It is bad to say such things.

Zohra is two years older than I am. According to my passport, I am now twenty-nine, but my mother says I am twenty-eight. So Zohra is now thirty or thirty-one. But she looks much older. Sometimes she complains that I look so much younger than she does. She says that I have had an easy life, always driving around in my own car while she has to walk with her children on her back and in her arms because she never has enough money even for the bus. Everyone in the family thinks I have had an easy life because I have had a car since I was seventeen and because I live in the States. But I have always worked hard. I bought my first car with money I saved working in a Belgian department store—although my father helped a little. And in the States, I was working at two jobs, as a bank teller and as a waitress, before my husband graduated. Zohra has never worked. She has always lived on the money her mother or her sister Habiba gave her. Habiba has worked hard all her life. But not Zohra.

It is true that Zohra has not had a happy life. But nobody forced Zohra to start going with bums when she was only thirteen or fourteen. Nobody is forcing her to stay with Chino.

She always went with the bums with honey in their mouths and no money in their pockets. You can see them walking along the *bulivar* with their white shirts unbuttoned almost down to their belly buttons. And they wear tight bell-bottom pants that are perfectly pressed. And they wear shiny shoes with high thick heels. Seeing them stroll along the *bulivar*, you would think they worked for the king and had just parked their Mercedes. But the truth is that they don't have enough money in their pockets to buy a glass of tea! They walk up and down the *bulivar* hoping to meet a Christian woman yearning for a hot Moroccan lover. All day and all evening, they walk up and down the *bulivar*, their eyes darting from face to face looking for lonely Christian women, or even for lonely Christian homosexuals. In one way or another, all Moroccans spend their lives selling themselves to the Christians. Anyway, these young men just keep walking up and down the *bulivar* dreaming of a rich Christian woman who will marry them and take them to Europe and the States. That's all my cousin Malika's husband Abd as-Slam ever talks about. He works in a bazaar in the old city. And he is always telling us how he met some German or French lady who took his address and is going to take him to Europe. In the meantime, his wife and baby are lucky to eat meat once a year. That's the kind of man who would go with Zohra. Instead of the beautiful rich Frenchwoman of their dreams—Catherine Deneuve—they have to settle for a poor Jibliyya whose front teeth are missing.

Or else her men have been day laborers with charcoal dust still in their ears from the hills—bums like Chino. At the wedding of my cousin Abd Allah in the village of the streams in August 1976, the only times Chino put down his *sibsi* (hashish pipe with a clay bowl) were to eat and to drag one of the dancing girls away from the light of the oil lamps into the darkness of a field. And Zohra was there and she knew he was going with the dancing girls. And she did nothing except complain to the family. If she had any self-respect, she would have divorced him right away. But then she would have had nothing to complain about. And she wouldn't have anything to say. If I ever heard her laugh from her heart or say "Praise be to God" (*al-hamdu li Illah*), I think I'd faint. God forgive me for speaking badly of that poor woman. She has had a hard life.

Zohra always complains that my mother and I often go to the quarter of the little mosque to visit Fatima, but we never go to visit *her*—and she lives next door to Fatima. We always say *la bas,* but we hardly ever enter her house because then we are in her clutches and we have to sit and listen to her tell us how Chino beats her and so on. Fatima, on the other hand, is always laughing and teasing me. God bless that woman. When she starts to laugh, it is impossible not to laugh with her. Her life with Mshish has not been easy, yet she never complains. Like al-Hajj Muhammad, she finds something funny in everything. She teases me because I am always with my husband while most Moroccan wives are hardly ever with their husbands except in bed. If she sees that I am tired or have bags under my eyes, she says, "Aha! I see your man didn't let you sleep last night!" And she laughs that wonderful big laugh of hers. What a sweet woman Fatima is. May God grant her a better life than she has had so far.

Zohra is lucky to have a sister like Habiba. They are the only two children that my aunt Shama had with Si Muhammad A. And Habiba is very good to Zohra. Zohra lives in a house Habiba owns, without paying rent. And Habiba sends her money from Belgium. When Habiba leaves Tangier at the end of August to go back to Belgium, Zohra sobs hysterically and her whole body shakes. And she makes a strange sound in her throat. She gets very thirsty and drinks a whole bucket of water. She clutches Habiba and sobs on her shoulder. The men have to pry her arms from around Habiba, who always sobs too, and they drag Zohra away from the car and into al-Hajj Muhammad's house. Everyone cries when Habiba and Ahmad and his children leave for Belgium at the end of August. Even al-Hajj Muhammad and Ahmad.

Not only does Habiba provide Zohra with the house she lives in and with the food she eats, she also took her son Muhsin to live with her in Belgium. Zohra always used to beat and insult the boy whenever Chino would beat and insult her. Muhsin used to flinch every time she moved her hand, thinking that she was going to hit him. So Habiba took him to Belgium in 1976 and enrolled him in a Belgian school and bought him nice clothes. Habiba loves him as if he were her own son. And she can never have a son of her own. She brings him back to Tangier every August. And when the month is over and the cars are loaded and ready to leave, Zohra holds the boy in her arms and they both sob. And she begs God to forgive her for beating him. And Habiba takes the boy and puts him in the car that will take them to Belgium and bring them back the following August. God willing.

View looking down into the valley. (Photo: Daniel Blaise.)

Orchard in the
village of the streams.
(Photo: Daniel Blaise.)

The house in the village of the streams where the eight children of Si Abd Allah were born, now used as a stable. (Photo: Daniel Blaise.)

Hired laborers hoeing the fields. (Photo: Daniel Blaise.)

Stream and sluice above the village mill. (Photo: Daniel Blaise.)

Grindstone of the village
watermill.
(Photo: Daniel Blaise.)

A peasant winnowing wheat.
(Photo: Jacques Vignet-Zunz.)

Threshing the wheat. (Photo: Jacques Vignet-Zunz.)

A house in the village of the streams. (Photo: Daniel Blaise.)

Children in the village of the streams. (Photo: Daniel Blaise.)

A mountain woman baking bread in a traditional oven. (Photo: George Joffe.)

Siesta in a Jbalan village. (Photo: George Joffe.)

Mound of roots ready to be covered with dirt
and slowly burned into charcoal. (Photos:
Daniel Blaise.)

Charcoal mound covered with dirt but not yet
burning.

Charcoal mound after burning and removal of
dirt.

Jbalan village wedding procession with covered bride being transported by mule to her new home. (Photo: Jacques Vignet-Zunz.)

Jbalan village wedding procession showing gifts for the bride being taken to her new home on muleback. (Photo: Jacques Vignet-Zunz.)

Lowland Jbalan village. The tile roofs are a sign of wealth; thatched roofs, a sign of poverty; and tin roofs represent an intermediate level of income. (Photo: Jacques Vignet-Zunz.)

High-rise apartment buildings as seen from a hillside tin shack in
Tangier. (Photo: R. Bernikho.)

The old city of Tangier. (Photo: Jacques Vignet-Zunz.)

Women in jillabas walking to the
principal mosque of Tangier.
(Photo: Jacques Vignet-Zunz.)

Men in jillabas going to Friday prayers in Tangier. (Photo: Jacques
Vignet-Zunz.)

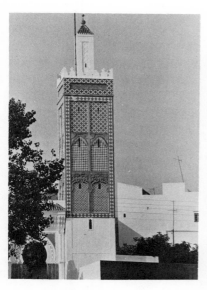

The minaret of the
mosque of the Marshan
quarter of Tangier.
(Photo: Jacques Vignet-
Zunz.)

A mother waiting for her child
to come out of a *msid*, or
Quranic school. (Photo:
R. Bernikho.)

Student at a Quranic school (*msid*) washing the wooden *luh* on
which he has written verses of the Quran. (Photo: R. Bernikho.)

Entrance to the Jutiyya market of Tangier. The squatting Jbalan woman in the hat is selling onions. (Photo: Jacques Vignet-Zunz.)

Three women buying melons in Tangier. The one on the left is wearing the striped *mindil* and shawl of mountain women; the middle one, a jillaba and a shawl tied around her to hold her baby; and the one on the right, a hayyik. (Photo: Jacques Vignet-Zunz.)

Bus stop in Tangier. (Photo: Jacques Vignet-Zunz.)

The *muqaf,* or "standing place," where poor women wait to be hired for menial labor, usually washing clothes. (Photo: Jacques Vignet-Zunz.)

A shantytown in Tangier. (Photo: R. Bernikho.)

Old woman and boy at the public fountain in a popular quarter of
Tangier. (Photo: R. Bernikho.)

An alley in a shantytown of Tangier. (Photo: R. Bernikho.)

Women at a public fountain in a shantytown of Tangier. (Photo: R. Bernikho.)

Muslim cemetery in the Marshan quarter of Tangier.
(Photo: R. Bernikho.)

The *qubba* of a saint's tomb in Tangier.
(Photo: Jacques Vignet-Zunz.)

III

Amina,
Daughter of
Si Abd Allah

(1919–)

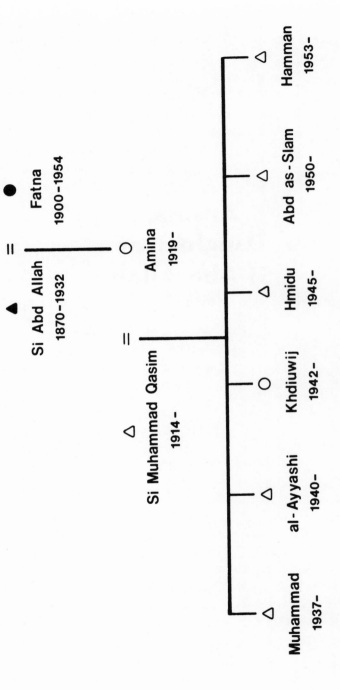

Genealogical Diagram III: Amina and Her Six Children

1. Al-Hajj Muhammad on his aunt Amina and her husband Si Muhammad Qasim (1914–), the wealthiest peasant in the village of the streams

MY AUNT AMINA WAS BORN IN ABOUT 1919, a year after my mother Shama. She was married to Si Muhammad Qasim of the Sons of Y. in about 1935, when she was about sixteen years old. When a Jbalan girl is not married by the time she is seventeen, usually something is wrong with her. When my aunt Amina married Si Muhammad Qasim, he had nothing (*ma kan andu hatta haja*). And now he is the richest man in the village of the streams. But he has sold his place in the hereafter for the goods of this world.

Si Muhammad Qasim's father, Luhsin Y., was a poor peasant who made his living by slash-and-burn cultivation on village land as well as by making charcoal, carving wooden utensils, and collecting and selling the honey from his beehives. I don't think he owned any plow land in the valley. Si Muhammad Qasim never studied the Quran at all. Nor did any of his sons. He is the richest man in the village and yet he never sent any of his five sons to study the holy book! What kind of Muslim is that?

When he married my aunt Amina, Si Muhammad Qasim was

just a poor Jibli. But then he started selling partridges, hares, and the polluted meat of the wild boar (al-halluf) to the Spanish in Dar Shawi and to a Spanish butcher in Tangier. Like all rich Muslims, he made his wealth by serving the Christians.

But he also grew rich by cheating, lying, and stealing. One day, when the Spanish still ruled the north, my uncle Hmid asked Si Muhammad Qasim to lend him some money. And he offered to put up the still undivided valley land bequeathed by Si Abd Allah to his children as collateral. He had no right to do this. That land belonged to all the children of Si Abd Allah, including my mother Shama, may God have mercy upon her. But my uncle Hmid paid a notary (adil) to write a fake deed saying that the land was his. Everyone in the village, including Si Muhammad Qasim, knew that this deed was a fake. But he pretended not to. And Si Muhammad Qasim lent my uncle Hmid the money—ten or twenty thousand francs I think. Then, a few months later, after harvesting his wheat and barley in early June, my uncle Hmid returned to Si Muhammad Qasim and told him, "Here is your money. Now give me back my deed." But Si Muhammad Qasim said that it was too late and now the land was his.

My uncle Hmid was furious. As was my mother and as were all the other children of Si Abd Allah. They took Si Muhammad Qasim to court, but he paid the judge to rule in his favor. If you have money, you can buy any judge in Morocco. If you have no money, you are just wasting your time going to court—unless the person you take to court is as poor as you are. Thus it was that Si Muhammad Qasim stole the valley land of Si Abd Allah. Now he is the only man in the village of the streams who eats only bread baked from wheat grown on his own land. The children of Si Abd Allah must buy their wheat, except for my aunt Amina of course, and except for my uncle Mhammad who rents hbus valley land. Everyone will be hung by his leg (Kull wahid ghadi ikun mallaq min rijlu).

Si Muhammad Qasim also makes a lot of money from his beehives. He sells over three hundred liters of honey a year to Swilah, a merchant in a nearby village, and to a Susi grocer in

Tetuan. Swilah sometimes brings caravans of ten to fifteen mules, with big barrels of honey on both sides of each mule, down from the village to Dar Shawi. There he has the barrels loaded onto the roof of the bus to Tangier.

Oh the sweetness of the honey of the hills! Hot, sweet mint tea. Hot wheat bread fresh from the bread oven. Sweet butter. And the thick sweet honey of the village of the streams. Praise be to God for all the bounty he has given us!

Sometimes my aunt Amina gives me a little honey when I visit the village. But usually I have to buy it even though she is my mother's sister. Si Muhammad Qasim is tight, very tight. I think he is even tighter and greedier than my brother Ahmad. That Jew and a half would not give a drop of his honey to his own brothers!

One day, Si Muhammad Qasim was staying with my aunt Khadduj in Tangier. And he noticed the clothesline on her terrace. It was a tough cord that he could use to tie down the panniers on both sides of a mule's packsaddle. So he just took out his knife and cut down the clothesline and hid it under his *jillaba*. His hair is white and soon he shall return to God. And yet he continues to steal from his wife's siblings.

> as for the miser
> who thinks only
> of riches
> and denies the good
> We shall smooth
> his path
> to eternal pain
> and his riches
> will be
> of no avail
> as he plunges
> down to hell   [XCII : 8–11]

Si Muhammad Qasim owns many gardens and orchards in the village, in addition to a small forest of cork oak (he used to sell the cork bark to the Spanish) and the copse of heather where he has his

147

beehives. He also owns the only water mill in the village, along with his son Hmidu. There is nothing left of Si Abd Allah's old mill except the rocks of its foundations. People say that Si Muhammad Qasim has millions of francs (one million francs = $2,222) hidden somewhere in his big two-story house with a tile roof and carpets in the guest room. They say the old bills are rotting into dirt because they have been there so long. Nobody knows exactly where they are. If anybody did know, he would have stolen the money a long time ago. Hmidu is trying to get Si Muhammad Qasim to buy a tractor with Abd ar-Rahman. Hmidu would drive it. And they could hire the tractor out by the hour, the way Si Allal does in Jbil Hbib. Si Muhammad Qasim could make a lot of money this way. But an old monkey cannot be taught to dance (*al-qard ash-sharif ma itallim ash-shitha*). He would sooner let his millions rot than risk losing them. He was thinking of buying a house in Tangier with my aunt Khadduj in 1977. But it was the same story. He was afraid to lose his money. He was afraid she would cheat him. And she was afraid he would cheat her. I told her she was crazy to think of buying anything with that infidel (*kafir*). Sooner or later, he would find a way of tricking her out of her share of the house.

Like all rich Jbala, Si Muhammad Qasim used to serve the Spanish. During the last four years of the Protectorate (1952–56), he was the *nayyib* (representative) of the village of the streams in the *junta de fraccion* of the Upper Wall of Bni Msawwar. This was like the *majlis al-qarawi*, or rural council, that has existed since independence. It is just a group of rich peasants who meet a few times a year to listen to the *qayyid* tell them what to do. Today, as in the past, the *qayyid* still rules like a little sultan in the hills. These rural councils are just a joke. But all rich Jbala try to get elected to them.

Si Muhammad Qasim used to have a lot of Spanish friends. They bought his pork—may God punish him for dealing in this polluted meat—and his honey. And they would come and stay in his house in the village and they would hunt wild boar amd jackals together. Partridges and hares too. He was not ashamed to pollute his house and his village by the presence of infidels. It is not enough

148

that they pollute our cities. He had to pollute the very house that he, his wife, and his children lived in. I think he even took them to the holy tomb of Sidi Hbib (Saint Hbib). Everyone will be hung by his leg.

Everyone in the village of the streams hates Si Muhammad Qasim. Even his own sons hate him—not just because he is a miser, but because of the way he has always treated their mother, my aunt Amina.

One evening when my aunt Amina was pregnant with Hamman in about 1953, my aunt Khadduj and her husband al-Hajj M.B. were sitting in Si Muhammad Qasim's house. They were talking and drinking tea. At this time, Si Muhammad Qasim was having an affair with the wife of the *fqih* Si Ahmad the Cripple (*al-Arij*). Si Ahmad lived in the village of the streams, but he was the *fqih* of the village of the slopes in Jbil Hbib. So he was away from the village of the streams five or six days a week, leaving his wife alone during this time. And Si Muhammad Qasim would lie with her almost every night the *fqih* was gone. He would sneak to her house at night, but everyone knew about it. However, no one ever dared to mention it to Si Muhammad Qasim.

That evening al-Hajj M.B., the husband of my aunt Khadduj, asked Si Muhammad Qasim to lend him a mule to ride down to Dar Shawi. In those days, Si Muhammad Qasim had only one mule. Now he has two. But Si Muhammad Qasim told al-Hajj that he had lent his mule to Si Ahmad the Cripple (*al-Arij*). So al-Hajj M.B. said, with his eyes twinkling, "Ah Si Muhammad, you have the mule only for the wife of the cripple!" He meant that Si Muhammad Qasim had lent the limping *fqih* his mule in order to have fun with the *fqih*'s wife. Si Muhammad Qasim's face turned red and he looked like he had just sat on a brazier full of hot charcoal. My aunt Amina laughed, but then she saw her husband's angry face and she covered her mouth with her hand to stifle her laughter. Si Muhammad Qasim's eyes bulged in rage, but he said nothing. He kept on talking with my aunt Khadduj and her husband al-Hajj M.B. until they left to go to my uncle Mhammad's house. After they left, Si

Muhammad Qasim exploded and said Amina had been laughing at him and he said that she had told my aunt Khadduj and her husband about the wife of the *fqih*. He started beating her with a big leather belt. And she was pregnant with Hamman at this time. My aunt Amina was screaming. But her sons Muhammad, Hmidu, and Abd al-Slam did not dare to stop their father, who was possessed by *jnun*. So Muhammad ran to my uncle Mhammad's house, which is only twenty meters downhill from Si Muhammad Qasim's house. And he begged my uncle, who was very strong in those days, to come up to their house and save their mother.

My uncle Mhammad jumped up and ran right to Si Muhammad Qasim's house, followed by my aunt Khadduj and al-Hajj M.B., who had been drinking tea with him and his wife. When he reached the house, Amina's face was all bloody. He picked up a log and started beating Si Muhammad Qasim with it. Now *he* was possessed by the *jnun* and he would not stop beating him. He was beating Si Muhammad Qasim for beating his sister, who was pregnant. But he was also beating him because he had stolen the land of the children of Si Abd Allah. And because Si Muhammad Qasim was already rich and powerful while my uncle Mhammad was poor and without power. He would have killed Si Muhammad Qasim if al-Hajj M.B. and at-Tayyib Y., may God have mercy upon him, had not pulled him away. And it was a long time before they could stop him because he was as strong as a bull in those days. Si Muhammad Qasim was drenched with his own blood. And his right arm was broken in several places.

Ever since that night, Si Muhammad Qasim has been unable to use his right arm. He always hides it under his *jillaba*. When people ask him what happened to his right arm, he tells them he fell off a mule. But nobody in the family or in the village would ask such a question because they all know how my uncle Mhammad broke his arm. So now he has to eat with his left hand. This is bad. It is said that the *jnun* eat with those who eat with their left hand. The good Muslim uses his right hand for all that is pure and clean: eating, giving alms, greeting a fellow Muslim and counting the beads of the rosary (*tasbih*). The left hand is just for washing your ass hole after you shit. People who eat with their left hand bring bad luck.

After al-Hajj M.B. and at-Tayyib managed to pull my uncle from Si Muhammad Qasim, he shouted at the latter: "You are not a man. You hit the mother of your children!" (*Ntina mashi rajil. Katdrab yimma diyal awawil diyalik!*) Then they dragged him back to his house.

Si Muhammad Qasim was afraid Zillal the *qayyid* would put him in jail so he sent him some large jars of his sweetest and purest honey. Zillal just scolded him and told him not to beat his wife when she was with child. And Zillal did not punish my uncle Mhammad for beating Si Muhammad Qasim because he was just protecting his sister.

My aunt Khadduj and al-Hajj M.B. took my aunt Amina down to Tangier. And she stayed two months with them in their house in the cobblestone quarter. Her whole body was bruised. But after two months, she said she wanted to return to the village. So my aunt Khadduj took her on the bus to the Tuesday market of Jbil Hbib. And my aunt Amina walked back up to the village with my uncle Mhammad after he finished his marketing. But once she arrived in the village, she went straight to the house of Si Muhammad Qasim, instead of staying with her brother. And about five months later, she gave birth to Hamman, her youngest child. Maybe she went back to Si Muhammad Qasim because he was already rich and powerful while her brother was poor. God knows best.

Not long after this, Si Ahmad the Cripple died, may God have mercy upon him. And Si Muhammad Qasim asked my aunt Amina if he could take the *fqih*'s widow as his second wife so that he wouldn't have to sneak over to her house in the darkness any more. She agreed on condition that he sign over half of all his property to her on a paper signed by a notary (*adil*). He agreed. Most people say that the *fqih*'s widow had given him a magic potion to make him love her like a crazy man. He winces in pain every time he has to take a coin out of his pocket, so it is hard to picture him signing over half of everything he owned to Amina. But he did it. And her sons say she still has the paper in a safe place in their house where Si Muhammad Qasim can't find it. But she has never actually claimed her share. If she did, he would find some way to outsmart her. He'd have another notary write up another document canceling the other one. And he'd have the notary forge her X. She can't write her name any more than Si Muhammad Qasim can. You can't trick Si Muhammad Qasim. And you can't stop him from tricking you.

Anyway the *fqih*'s widow came to live in the little house that Si Muhammad Qasim now uses as a stable for his mules. But Amina and her children hated her and they did everything they could to chase her away. After about a year, Si Muhammad Qasim divorced her. Maybe Amina got a charm from a *fqih* to make him stop wanting the *fiqh*'s widow. Or maybe weaving with her was not so much fun now that he didn't have to sneak in the dark to get to her. Or maybe he was just tired of the arguments between Amina and his new wife. Anyway, he divorced her. And I don't think he has had any other women besides my aunt Amina since then. Now, of course, he is too old to think of women.

Now he prays every prayer at its time, hoping that his prayers will wash away all the evil that he has done. But his prayers will not save him from the wrath of God. He is still as tight as ever. He has dozens of chickens, but when he visits the tomb of Sidi Hbib, he does not even bring *one*. My uncle Mhammad says that he does not pay the tithe (*al-ashur*) on his crops and he stole most of his land from the children of Si Abd Allah! And on the day of reckoning, the angels will bring forth the records of all that he has done, all the evil and all the good, if any. And he will pay.

> the competition
> for the accumulation
> of the goods
> of this world
> diverts you
> until you visit
> the grave
> oh but you shall know
> oh but you shall know   [CII : 1–4]

2. Al-Hajj Muhammad on his cousin Muhammad, son of Si Muhammad Qasim (1937–), peasant and charcoalmaker

MY AUNT AMINA and Si Muhammad Qasim have six children: (1) Muhammad, born in about 1937; (2) al-Ayyashi, born in about 1940; (3) Khdiuwij, born in about 1942; (4) Hmidu, born in about 1945; (5) Abd as-Slam, born in about 1950; and (6) Hamman, born in about 1953.

Muhammad lives in a little house near his father's big house. His father owns it. He is about forty-three years old. His front teeth are crooked and chipped. And his head is usually full of *kif* and hashish. He is a bum. He makes charcoal and honey and grows mint. But most of the time he is sitting on the front porch of the village mosque (*aj-jama*) talking and playing checkers. In the evening, he usually smokes *kif* and plays cards in the grain mill on the stream of Maymun with his brother al-Ayyashi and the other men who go there every night. He steals from his father all the time. People say that he has raped many women and young boys. He once worked in Tangier for about eight months—as a laborer in construction. But he decided that stealing from his father was easier.

In about 1962, Muhammad married Slama daughter of Abd al-Malik D. from the village of the weavers in Jbil Hbib. She looks even more like a mule than my wife. May God forgive me for saying so. She used to look better before she had all those nine children. She used to go with Ahmad son of at-Tayyib, the carpenter. Now he has his own carpenter's shop in Tangier and he is rich. He would not even look at her now. What does he want with a Jibliyya who smells of goat shit and charcoal? But in those days, he still lived in the village and he was just a poor Jibli himself. Abd as-Slam, Muhammad's younger brother, says Muhammad knew all about it but didn't do anything! What kind of a man would let his wife lie with another man? Now Ahmad son of at-Tayyib has bought some cows. And Muhammad takes care of one of them. Muhammad gets all the cow's milk and half the calves. So now he is working for the man who used to enter his wife and the mother of his children when he was not at home. That is the kind of man Muhammad is. God forgive me for speaking badly of the son of my mother's sister. But everyone in the village and everyone in the family knows that what I am saying is true.

3. *Fatima Zohra on the silver spoons*

MY COUSIN MUHAMMAD and his wife Slama have nine children not counting the ones that died in infancy. Their oldest child is named Rahma. She was born in about 1963 and I think she is seventeen years old now. When I was in Morocco in 1976, my sister Zubida was thinking of hiring her as a maid (*khaddama*). So Rahma came down to Tangier and stayed three days at my mother's apartment near the *bulivar*. My mother was very nice to her and took her to see everyone in the family in Tangier. But Zubida decided not to hire her. She hired another Jibliyya who was not a cousin. I think the reason that Zubida did not hire Rahma the daugher of my cousin Muhammad is that Rahma the wife of my cousin Mustafa told her that she was a thief. Rahma the wife of Mustafa said that Rahma the daughter of my cousin Muhammad once stole two of her gold bracelets when she was at Mustafa's house for dinner. "Her hand is so fast she can steal your eyes (*kattiyyar al-aynin*) before you know it," she warned us. Oh, Rahma of Mustafa was upset about those gold bracelets! A woman's gold bracelets are her savings and her security in Morocco. Most peasant and working women would never keep their money in a bank. They think the people in the bank would just steal it. So they carry their savings on their arms. Year after year, Rahma scrimps and saves out of the money Mustafa gives her for food in order to buy those gold bracelets. And she was very angry when Rahma the daughter of my cousin Muhammad (the son of my aunt Amina) stole two of them. But Rahma the daughter of Muhammad and her mother Slama say that she never stole the bracelets. God knows best. Anyway, Zubida didn't hire her to work for her as a maid.

A few months after this, my mother and I were in the village of the streams. And one day we visited the shrine of Sidi Hbib with about ten other women of the family from the village of the streams. This is the custom in the hills (fi aj-jbil). Sometimes all the women of the village (aj-jmaa) spend a day at Sidi Hbib's tomb. Everyone bakes bread, boils eggs, and makes butter the day before they go. Then they all go together early in the morning, before the sun is too hot. It is about an hour's walk from the village to the tomb of Sidi Hbib. And the path up the mountain is steep and rocky. But once you get up there, it is like paradise. There is always a cool breeze from the valley. And the water from the spring of Sidi Hbib is sweet and cold, sweeter and colder even than the springs of the village of the streams.

High up there on the mountain, you can see the blue water of the ocean far to the west and the little town of Arzila and its big beautiful beaches and even Tangier. And far down in the valley, you can see the whitewashed buildings and walls of the Tuesday market of Jbil Hbib. The qubba (shrine) of the saint and the mosque are also whitewashed. You are high above the world. High above the men harvesting the wheat on the valley floor and on the barren, rocky slopes. High above the smoking mounds of charcoal in the forests and scrub forests of the hills. High above the village which looks so peaceful and quiet far below. High above all the people in the world who are working from morning to night to fill their stomachs and the stomachs of their children. High up there on the mountain of Sidi Hbib, you feel close to God. There is a wonderful fig tree near the tomb of Sidi Hbib. Because the air is so cold way up there on the mountain, its figs don't ripen until long after all the figs in the village have been picked. Sometimes those figs don't ripen until just before the winter rains start to fall in October. And the pure cold air of the mountain gives those figs a sweetness like no other figs in the world.

Anyway, about twelve of us climbed up to Sidi Hbib that day. And we sang on the way and our voices echoed in the hills. And we were all very happy. Everyone brought something for the saint. It is said that a visit to a saint is not accepted (*az-ziyara mashi maqbula*) unless you bring something for the saint. We all brought candles which we lit next to the tomb. And my mother and several other women brought chickens—some for the saint and some for us to eat. The *muqaddim* (guardian) of the saint's tomb and al-Wazzani sacrificed them for us. And we gave them some chicken, some stew of tomatoes, potatoes, green peppers, and olive oil, and some bread and tea. The round loaves of wheat bread had just been baked the day before. So the bread was wonderful. And the water of the spring was sweet, as was the wild mint we picked on the way, so the tea was also wonderful. We were all laughing and teasing the women who had tied rags to the olive tree so that Sidi Hbib would bring them a child. Laughing and singing together, we were all very happy. It was like the times I used to come up to Sidi Hbib with the women when I was a little girl.

But then my mother noticed that Rahma daughter of my cousin Muhammad was stirring the tea in her glass with a beautiful silver spoon. "Where did you get that spoon?," my mother asked Rahma. "Oh, my father bought it in Tangier," she answered. My mother and I looked at each other. But, we didn't say anything. But we both knew that I had bought that spoon in the States. And we both knew that a number of silver spoons that I had brought to Tangier from the States had been missing from my mother's apartment in Tangier ever since Rahma stayed there. I didn't care so much about the spoons. But I was mad because Rahma had stolen them from us. And I was mad because she ruined that wonderful day for me. But I said nothing. And just before the sunset prayer, we started walking back down to the village.

The next day, I sent a boy to tell Slama, Rahma's mother, to come and speak to me at the house of my grandmother (*ad-dar d al-aziza*), where my husband and I were staying. She came. I said, "Slama, you know that silver spoon that your daughter Rahma was using to stir her tea on the mountain of Sidi Hbib?" She looked shocked. "That's my spoon, Slama. Your daughter took that spoon, and some other spoons, from my mother's house when she stayed there." I thought her eyes were going to pop right out of her head. She was furious. Then she said, "My daughter did that?" "Yes," I said. I told her I didn't care about the spoons. But she shouldn't let her daughter do such things or she would get into trouble. I tried to soften the insult by saying that all children steal. I told her that I too had stolen as a child. But Rahma was now a young woman who would soon be married, God willing. And I told her that I didn't want to insult her. I just wanted to help her teach her daughter not to steal. Her face was bright red and she looked so mad I thought she was going to hit me. But she just said, "My daughter would not do anything like that." And she turned and started walking up the hill to her house.

Slama is a good woman and I like her. She always used to send her children to bring me apples, figs, and walnuts when we stayed in the village. Or maybe my aunt Amina told her to send her children with these things. Because my aunt Amina is very good. But Slama is good too, even though everyone knows she steals from my aunt Amina all the time. And I think she knew that her daughter had stolen those spoons. In fact, I think maybe that she told her daughter to steal from my mother. People in the family think my mother is rich. And they often try to cheat her, and even steal from her. This is a terrible thing in Morocco—kinsmen stealing from kinsmen. But it happens often.

Well, Slama went straight to her mother-in-law, my aunt Amina, and complained about the way I had talked to her. And both my aunt Amina and my mother told me that I should not have spoken that way to Slama. They said I should have spoken to them. My mother was very mad about the stolen spoons too. But she said I was wrong to insult Slama that way. But I told my mother and my aunt that I was very mad and that I just couldn't relax until I had "cooled my *jnun*" (*birridt jnuni*).

One thing I like about the States is that there you can speak directly. In Morocco, you always have to zigzag and make circles around what you are trying to say.

After that day, whenever I went to my aunt Amina's house in the village, Slama would never come to greet me, although she lives right next door. And if we saw each other at a wedding or at a *saba* on the seventh day after a child is born, she would not talk to me. But after a few months, she started to speak to me again. And I was glad because, despite everything, I like her. I knitted some socks for her youngest baby and she was very happy.

4. *Al-Hajj Muhammad on his cousin al-Ayyashi,* *son of Si Muhammad Qasim (1940–), miller,* *peasant, and charcoalmaker*

SOME PEOPLE SAY THAT my cousin al-Ayyashi has the face of a rat. I would never say such a thing about the son of my mother's sister. But his front teeth certainly are big and sharp. And he certainly is afraid of places where there are many people. He spends most of his time up in the water mill on the stream of Maymun. He runs the mill for his father and his brother Hmidu, who own it. They split the money they make three ways. In the rainy season from October through April, when the stream is full and fast, that mill brings in as much as ten thousand francs ($22.22) a week, or 3,333 francs ($7.41) for each of them. That is more than they spend each week at the Tuesday market of Jbil Hbib. But in the summer, the stream slows down and the mill does not bring in more than two or three thousand francs ($4.44–$6.67) a week.

Al-Ayyashi is at the mill almost every evening with a few of the other men of the village. It is a wonderful place. You can hear the water of the stream splashing and the old grindstone creaking. And at night, you sometimes see the tiny white headlights of cars moving far down in the valley. And you can see the glow of the lights of Tangier behind the black silhouetted hills to the west. The men drink tea and smoke *kif*. And they play cards by the light of an oil lamp in the little mill. Or else they just sit and talk and look at the stars outside. It is a nice place just above the village. Al-Ayyashi hardly ever comes to Tangier. He says it is full of impure Christians and Jews. But I think he is afraid of all the noise and the crowds. He used to smuggle *kif* and tobacco into Tangier by mule when it was an International Zone. And he would buy radios, watches, and cigarettes from Spain. He would bring them back by mule through the hills at night, so the police at the border wouldn't see him. And he would sell these things to merchants in Tetuan, Dar Shawi, or the Tuesday market of Jbil Hbib. But I don't think he ever sold anything in a market himself. He is too afraid of people. And his teeth would scare people away.

Maybe the reason he keeps away from people is that he is bald. He is not old. He was born in about 1940. But he has been bald (*qra*) ever since he was a young man. And he is ashamed of this so he always wears the hood of his *jillaba* over his head, even inside his own house and the house of his father. One day we were eating together with some relatives at Hmidu's house and I pulled down his hood. We all laughed, but al-Ayyashi was very mad. I thought he was going to kill me. But he just got up and left the house. I didn't want to make him feel bad. I just thought it would be funny to see that hairless head that he has been hiding from us all these years. Al-Ayyashi is a little strange, but he is good.

In addition to running the water mill (the only one in the village because nothing is left of Si Abd Allah's mill except the rocks of its foundations), al-Ayyashi also makes charcoal and grows a little wheat and barley in a field he cleared on village land (*ard d aj-jmaa*) near Hmidu's vegetable garden. He used to do most of the plowing and harvesting on his father's fields (which his father stole from the children of Si Abd Allah) in the valley. But in 1977, he revolted and told his father that it was not fair that he spent weeks sleeping on hay and working from morning till night in the valley, but received hardly any more wheat than his brothers did. Now Si Muhammad Qasim has his fields plowed by tractor. It is the tractor of the agricultural cooperative (*Jamaiyya*), the one driven by the drunken Rifi.

That Rifi could be the richest man in Bni Msawwar, but his brains are always soggy by the time the sunset prayer is called. He used to be the boss of the Spanish factory in Dar Shawi where they used to crush the leaves of the dwarf-palm. The Spanish owner lived in Tetuan, and he let the Rifi run the factory. He was the boss of the sixty men and seventy women who used to work there. And the Spaniard paid him a fortune. But he just wasted his money on whiskey. Now the factory is closed because the government said that the Spaniard had to have a Muslim partner. And the Christian shut the factory down rather than have a Muslim partner. But that Rifi still makes a fortune driving that tractor. Now everybody in Bni Msawwar hires him to plow the valley land! Of course, most people don't own any valley land. But still, in October when people who do own valley land sow their wheat and barley, and in the spring when they sow their sorghum (*ad-dra*), he is on that tractor from dawn until after the sunset prayer. He doesn't drink during plowing. But when plowing is over, he just wastes all his money on whiskey. He could be the richest man in Bni Msawwar. Richer even than al-Hajj Muhammad Zillal, who was *qayyid* after his father. And richer even than al-Hajj T., the charcoal merchant who buys all the charcoal made in Bni Msawwar and sells it in Tangier. But he is just a drunk. There is nothing more disgusting than a drunken Muslim. We Muslims don't need the whiskey of the Christians. We have *kif* and hashish to make our heads fly.

> oh you who believe
> wine and games of chance
> idols of stone
> and divination
> are an abomination
> wrought by Satan
> turn away from them
> so that you may prosper   [V : 93]

As for the harvest, Si Muhammad Qasim now hires *at-Talib*

Muhammad, the son of as-Sfiyya, to do most of the reaping. *At-Talib* Muhammad is the father of al-Ayyashi's wife Zohra. He is of the B. clan (*irq* or *darat al-umumiyya*), but he is not one of the family. In June of 1977, Si Muhammad Qasim paid him 11,000 francs ($24.44) to reap his wheat, barley, and broad beans. It took him eighteen days, so his daily wage was only about 611 francs ($1.36). Most Jbala pay their workers at least 700 francs ($1.56) a day. And Hmidu pays his men 750 francs ($1.67) a day. But Si Muhammad Qasim is the tightest miser in all of Bni Msawwar.

Al-Ayyashi married *at-Talib* Muhammad's daughter Zohra when he was thirty-two (1972) and she was fifteen or sixteen. She is a good woman, may God bless her. She is young and pretty like a Dutch girl, with white skin and rosy cheeks and light brown hair. I think she is one of the few women in the village who don't cheat on their husbands. And who could blame her for cheating a man with the face of a rat? But she is a very good woman. She never talks with men. And whenever we all get together for dinner at Si Muhammad Qasim's house or at Hmidu's house, she hardly talks. She sits quietly. She is beautiful and she is good. She is the kind of woman every Muslim dreams of marrying. But for every such woman there are a thousand whores! Oh how I wish I had married such a woman! But it was not God's will.

Al-Ayyashi and Zohra live next door to Hmidu. Si Muhammad Qasim built houses for both al-Ayyashi and Hmidu. And they live just up the hill from *at-Talib* Muhammad, Zohra's father. She always goes down to sit and talk with her mother. But her parents never come to al-Ayyashi's house. Nor to the house of Si Muhammad Qasim. *At-Talib* Muhammad is poor and Si Muhammad Qasim is rich.

I remember one day we drove to Dar Shawi in my cousin Fatima Zohra's husband's car. We left the car by the mosque, and Fatima Zohra and her husband, my aunt Khadduj, and I walked out to the field by the olive trees where the women of the sons of Si Muhammad Qasim were gleaning the wheat left after *at-Talib* Muhammad had reaped it. Zohra the wife of al-Ayyashi was there.

As was Malika the wife of Abd as-Slam and Rahma the daughter of Muhammad (the one who stole the spoons Fatima Zohra brought back from America). And as was Rahma the daughter of Luhsin son of Qasim. She is fifteen or sixteen and she still makes pee pee in her pants at night. They call her the pee pee girl (*al-buwwala*). And there were some other girls from the village too. Both Malika wife of Abd as-Slam and Zohra wife of al-Ayyashi tied both ends of their *hayyiks* (white outer garments) to branches of an olive tree, so that they were like little hammocks. And their babies slept there in the shade while their mothers gleaned the wheat in the sun with the other women.

Actually, that year they pulled out the wheat roots and all, because the heavy winter rains and drought in the spring had ruined the wheat crop. People were lucky to get back the seeds they had sown in the fall. Si Muhammad Qasim had all the wheat he would need for the year. But his sons would have to buy some.

Anyway, the women were in the field gleaning and singing and laughing, even though the sun was very hot. My aunt Khadduj and even my cousin Fatima Zohra joined them. That was funny! Fatima Zohra, who has lived much of her life in Belgium and America driving her own car, was out there gleaning wheat with women who were lucky to come down from the village once a year. But Fatima Zohra is not proud like her sisters. She likes her relatives in the village even though she is in some ways more like a Christian than a Muslim.

Al-Talib Muhammad cooked a *tajin* of fish with tomatoes, potatoes, green peppers, and olive oil. Oh what a wonderful *tajin* it was! And we boiled mint tea on a brazier full of charcoal. All the women came and ate with us in the shade of the olive trees. It was a *twaza*. That is, Si Muhammad Qasim was giving them this meal in return for gleaning his wheat. Usually, women get one-fourth of all the wheat they glean. But this day, they got a meal instead. It was delicious. But usually, you give people meat, at least chicken, in their stew when you have a *twaza*. But these women were mostly the wives and daughters of Si Muhammad Qasim's sons. So they have to do what he says. And he is too cheap to give them meat.

We were all sitting and eating the *tajin* and Zohra called out to her father *at-Talib* Muhammad to come and eat with us. But he said no and he ate with another man who was working for wages as a harvester. He felt ashamed to eat with us. Maybe because he is poor and just Si Muhammad Qasim's hired harvester working for wages, even though his daughter is married to Si Muhammad Qasim's son al-Ayyashi. And al-Ayyashi was there. So was Abd as-Slam. They had brought the mules down from the village for threshing. But *at-Talib* Muhammad doesn't like al-Ayyashi. He says al-Ayyashi beats Zohra. But he is afraid to complain to the *qayyid* because Si Muhammad Qasim is rich and could bribe the *muqaddim* and the *shaykh* and even the *qayyid* himself.

At-Talib* Muhammad is a good Muslim who prays every prayer at its time. He doesn't even smoke *kif.* May God grant him sustenance. He has had a hard life and he says that he soon may come down to Tangier like his brothers. He has a little store in the village where he sells cigarettes, flour, vegetable oil, olive oil, bottled gas for Butagaz burners, and batteries for flashlights. But he says he hardly makes any profit on what he sells because the government (*al-makhzan*) makes him sell everything at set prices. For example, he has to sell a pack of CASA cigarettes at 120 francs ($.27), the same price you pay in Tangier. He only makes five francs profit on each pack. And he has to spend hours riding that skinny old mule of his down to Dar Shawi and back to buy those cigarettes. Moreover, he says, when he's not home, his wife sells people things on credit. But she can't write, not even numbers. And she forgets who bought what and who paid by money and who paid by credit (*bi ad-din*). Most people buy on credit. And the women often buy oil and flour with the eggs from their chickens. So he has to load dozens of eggs in the panniers on his mule to take them down to Dar Shawi where he sells them to a *sbaybi* (peddler) who will sell them in Tangier or Tetuan. Everybody has chickens in the hills, so no one will buy eggs there. So he has to wrap up all those eggs in paper and leaves and pray that he does not have one big omelette by the time he and his mule get down to Dar Shawi.

Sooner or later, *at-Talib* Muhammad will have to move to

Tangier. Like almost everyone in the village, he makes charcoal. And he makes a little money chanting the Quran on the seventh day after births and at circumcisions, weddings, and funerals. But he says he cannot hold out much longer. When the ranger catches him making charcoal, he will probably follow his two brothers to Tangier. His oldest son is already there working with a shovel and a pick. That is the life of the poor Jibli: charcoal in the hills and a shovel and a pick in the city.

I don't blame *at-Talib* Muhammad for not being too happy with al-Ayyashi as a son-in-law, even though he will inherit some of Si Muhammad Qasim's land, God willing. Al-Ayyashi is really strange, may God forgive me for saying so. Maybe the reason Luhsin the village idiot likes al-Ayyashi so much is that al-Ayyashi is a little crazy too.

Luhsin the idiot goes to the water mill every evening after the call to the sunset prayer. Al-Ayyashi gives him tea and cigarettes and a few pieces of stale bread. That's all poor Luhsin needs. He just wanders around the woods in the daytime in that ragged *jillaba* that the dirtiest beggar of Tangier would not wear. He looks at you with those big eyes of his—like the eyes of a fish. Once, a woman from a nearby village was walking along a path, and she saw him squatting high up on some rocks, watching her. The poor woman was terrified. She thought he was a *jinn* and she was afraid he was going to jump on her and enter her by force. But Luhsin never hurt anyone. He is a scary sight when you see him for the first time with those big fish eyes staring out from his dirty matted hair and beard. But he is harmless. They say that such idiots (*buhala*) are really blessed, for their minds are in heaven while their bodies remain in this world. And God rewards those who are good to them. And al-Ayyashi is good to Luhsin.

Al-Ayyashi is good to al-Wazzani too. Al-Wazzani hides up at the tomb of Sidi Hbib. He's been up there for years, I think. He committed some crime in al-Wazzan. Some say he stole a fortune from the man he worked for. Others say he killed a man. God knows best. Anyway, he hides up there at the saint's tomb because that is sacred ground. The police cannot touch a man at a saint's tomb. Al-Wazzani looks a little savage too, but not as bad as Luhsin. His black hair is dirty and matted and he always has several days' black stubble on his face. And his *jillaba* is dirty. But not as dirty as Luhsin's. And it is not ragged and torn like Luhsin's.

Usually, al-Wazzani lives on the chickens, eggs, and bread people bring to the saint. The *muqaddim* of the saint's tomb doesn't like having al-Wazzani there, because it means less food for him. But he lets him stay. I don't know how they survive during the winter rains. Because then the mule paths become swift-flowing streams and people don't go up into the hills unless they have to. Hardly anybody visits the saint then. And the *muqaddaim* and al-Wazzani do not stay at the tomb of Sidi Hbib during this time.

Anyway, sometimes al-Wazzani comes down from the mountain of Sidi Hbib, down to the water mill where he passes the time talking with al-Ayyashi. Al-Ayyashi gives him food, cigarettes, tea, and *kif*.

Al-Ayyashi likes al-Wazzani and Luhsin because they are like him—all three of them are afraid of noisy, crowded places. And afraid of strangers. Some people think al-Ayyashi is an idiot (*buhali*) like Luhsin. That is not true. He is really just like any other man. He is just afraid of people. That's all. Maybe it is just because he is bald. God knows best.

5. *Fatima Zohra on her cousin al-Ayyashi*

AL-AYYASHI IS LIKE A LITTLE BOY or a dog that flinches at every sudden movement because he has been beaten so often. He is always hiding from the world up there in the water mill. In his heart he is good. But even when people are good in their hearts, sometimes they can be cruel.

165

I couldn't believe it when al-Ayyashi finally got married. What woman would lie with such a man? But in the hills, a girl marries the man her parents pick for her. So Zohra married al-Ayyashi. They had a baby girl in 1973. The baby was sickly and Zohra would get charms (*hjuba*) from the village *fqih* to ward off the *jnun*. And she would ask the saint of the Tuesday market of Jbil Hbib to protect the child. She wanted to take her to see a doctor in Tangier but al-Ayyashi said doctors were no good.

One day when the little girl was three years old, she was crying and crying. And al-Ayyashi became angry and told her to stop crying or he would burn her hand. But the little girl kept crying. So al-Ayyashi lit a match and burned his little daughter's hand! Zohra screamed and grabbed the girl away from him. About a year later, the little girl died. May God have mercy upon her. For many months after she died, Zohra walked around without talking to anyone. Even when people spoke to her, she just smiled like an idiot. But whenever she saw a little girl, she would stare at her and sob hysterically. Later, she had a baby boy and she was well again. She is still with al-Ayyashi.

6. Al-Hajj Muhammad on his cousin Khdiuwij, daughter of Si Muhammad Qasim (1942–), wife of a peasant and charcoalmaker

MY COUSIN KHDIUWIJ used to be very pretty. Like Zohra the wife of al-Ayyashi, she has milky white skin and pink cheeks and light brown hair. Even now, with her oldest boy about fifteen, she is still very pretty. May God bless her. Her blood is light and she loves to talk and laugh. I think she has always been a good faithful wife to her husband, Si

Muhammad son of Abd as-Slam M. Of course, all wives cheat their husbands. But she is better than most.

Si Muhammad married my cousin Khdiuwij in about 1959 and they have four children that did not die. He is about eleven years older than she is. He is poor, but not so poor. He lives in the village of the two springs. Like most Jbala in the highland villages where the woods still cover the hills, he makes charcoal. If you see a Jibli with no charcoal dust in his ears, you know that he is either rich or from a low-lying village where the forest has disappeared.

I don't think he owns any plow land in the valley. But he always rents about two hectares of *hbus*. The man from the Ministry of *al-ahbas* in Tetuan comes out to auction off the right to plow *hbus* land in Dar Shawi every September, before the start of the winter rains and the winter plowing. The right to plow *hbus* land is auctioned off for two years at a time so that a man can grow the winter crops of wheat, barley, and broad beans one year and the summer crop of sorghum the next.

Si Muhammad son of Abd as-Slam al-M. also owns a nice mint garden as well as a vegetable garden near his house. And he owns a cow and two heifers, about thirty goats, fifteen chickens, and a mule. Now a Jibli with thirty goats is not starving. And he also takes care of several goats that belong to my uncle Hmid, who lives in Tangier now. He gets to keep their milk and one of every three kids. Maybe some of those thirty goats also belong to other people and he is just taking care of them. I don't know. But I know he doesn't own any land to speak of except for those two gardens of his. If it weren't for the charcoal, he'd be down here in Tangier working with a shovel and a pick for wages. That is what he says anyway.

Si Muhammad is a good man. He does not chase after other men's wives. But he does not pray. However he is getting older. He must be about forty-five I would say. Soon he will start to fear the grave and start to pray as God has commanded us to—God willing (*in sha' Allah*). May God guide him.

7. Fatima Zohra on her cousin Khdiuwij

MY COUSIN (*bint khalti*) Khdiuwij is a wonderful person. May God grant her a long and happy life. Unlike many Jbalan women, I think she loves her husband. I remember one day I was visiting her in the village of the two springs. We were talking and laughing when her husband Si Muhammad came home from making charcoal in the woods. Khdiuwij teased him because his face was grimy with sweat and charcoal dust. And she caressed his cheek with the back of her hand. He laughed but he was shy because I was there. Four children, including a boy of fifteen, and she still caresses him on the cheek! That is wonderful. Usually Jbalan men and women do not touch each other except in bed. So it was nice.

8. Al-Hajj Muhammad on his cousin Hmidu, son of Si Muhammad Qasim (1945–), peasant and charcoalmaker

MY COUSIN HMIDU works hard and he does not lie or cheat like his father Si Muhammad Qasim. It is true that my brother Ahmad once lent him fifty thousand francs ($111.11) to start his big vegetable garden and he never paid him back. I don't know what happened there. That is between Ahmad and Hmidu. But Hmidu is a good man. May God bless him. He never talks about people. And his word is good. If he says he will do something, he will do it, if God wills.

Sometimes people think Hmidu is stupid because he doesn't talk much. But it is said that silence is wisdom and wisdom spreads from it (*as-sumt hikma was minnu tfarrqat al-hkayim*). Hmidu is not at all stupid. He used to collect roots which he would sell to a pipe factory in Tetuan. And he saved his money and built the water mill. His father also put up some money for the mill, and they became partners. Hmidu built it along with some other men. Now, during the winter rains from October through April, he often makes as much as three thousand francs ($6.67) a week from that mill without doing any work at all. A man can live on less than that in the hills.

And now Hmidu has that big vegetable garden, the biggest in the hills. It is over half a hectare in size. Most Jbala grow their tomatoes, potatoes, green peppers, cucumbers, and watermelons just to feed themselves. But Hmidu decided he was going to start a big garden and sell vegetables and melons at the Tuesday market of Jbil Hbib, the Monday market of Bni Harshan, and even in Tangier, God willing. Everyone thought he was crazy! Nobody thought he could turn that scrub forest into a big garden like that. His father Si Muhammad Qasim said it was a crazy idea and he refused to lend him any money to hire laborers and buy seed. So Hmidu asked Abd ar-Rahman, Mustafa's friend with the ice cream parlor in Tangier. And Abd ar-Rahman said yes.

Hmidu worked clearing the brush and building a scrub fence and he used mules to pull out the rocks. He had six or seven men working for him, for 750 francs ($1.67) a day. And he worked alongside them. The sons of Sidi K. al-Baqqali and the old son of al-Ayyashi F. would sit on their butts on the front porch of the village mosque and they would laugh at him. They kept saying that he was just wasting Abd ar-Rahman's money. But they were all envious because Abd ar-Rahman was lending him all that money, about 450,000 francs ($1,000) altogether, they say. And Hmidu would stop off at the mosque about the time of the sunset prayer, after working all day on the garden, and they would all tease him. "When are you going to start planting anything up there in that garden of yours, Hmidu?" "When are you going to start selling all those vegetables at the Tuesday market of Jbil Hbib?" And he would smile. He wouldn't get angry even though he is strong. His brothers Muhammad, al-Ayyashi, Abd as-Slam, and Hamman would always help him in a fight, so those Baqqali snakes wouldn't want to make him too angry. And they know that Si Muhammad Qasim is the richest man in the village and could always bribe the *muqaddim*, the *shaykh*, or even the *qayyid*. So they are careful, like rats hiding in rotting hay. But their hearts burn with envy because Si Muhammad Qasim and his sons are rich and they are poor. They are envious of Hmidu because he was smart enough to think of growing vegetables for the market and had a friend who would lend him enough money to do it. And they envy him because everyone respects him and no one respects them. People know that the sons of Sidi K. al-Baqqali are nothing but thieves and beggars, even if they are *shurfa*. God forgive me for saying so.

Sidi Muhammad and Sidi Mustafa, sons of Sidi K. al-Baqqali, would like to work for Hmidu up in that garden of his high above the village. They know he pays better and treats his men better than any other Muslim in the hills. But they are too proud. It would be admitting that he is better than they are to accept wages from him. So they just sit on the front porch of the mosque yapping about how stupid Hmidu is and hoping that no vegetables ever ripen in that garden. Anyway, they haven't worked enough to sweat for years. Their younger brother Luhsin makes charcoal and grows mint. They grow a little mint too. But mostly, they live off the sweat of their younger brother. And every year they bring up big sacks of wheat from the valley on their mules. People say they beg in the lowlands. Or maybe they steal. God knows best. But I never saw either one of them do anything but sit on the front porch of the mosque insulting people behind their backs. And the old son of al-Ayyashi F. joins them too, because Hmidu and Si Muhammad Qasim used to give him one-third of the money from the water mill to take care of it. Then Hmidu found out that he had been grinding more flour than he had told them. So Hmidu fired the old son of al-Ayyashi F. and hired his brother al-Ayyashi instead. Now the old man joins the Baqqali snakes in making fun of Hmidu when Hmidu is not there. And the *fqih* Si Abd al-Ali, he just sits there on the porch sewing his *jillabas*. His heart burns with envy too. But he is better than the Baqqalis and the old son of al-Ayyashi F.

And my uncle Mhammad, he is full of envy too. He wishes he had a good son like Hmidu instead of those bums of his always having trouble with their women in Tangier. And of course his head is crazy with envy because Si Muhammad Qasim is rich and has many powerful friends, whereas he is poor and has no friends at all. I remember one day at the Tuesday market of Jbil Hbib, Hmidu and Abd as-Slam were talking with Si Allal, who has his own tractor and plows most of the valley land in Jbil Hbib. He is one of the richest men in Jbil Hbib and he is a good friend of Si Muhammad Qasim's, and of Hmidu's and Abd as-Slam's. My uncle Mhammad was tethering his mule and saw Si Allal talking with Hmidu and Abd as-Slam about two meters from him. So he shouted, "Peace be upon you Si Allal" (as-salamu alaykum ya Si Allal), as if Si Allal were his friend. Si Allal looked at him as if he were crazy, mumbled "Upon you be peace" without smiling, and then kept on talking with Hmidu and Abd as-Slam. My uncle's face turned red. He was ashamed because Si Allal had answered his greeting coldly and quickly, without respect. For most of his life, my uncle Mhammad has been eaten by envy and hatred because Si Muhammad Qasim has everything and he has nothing. Si Muhammad Qasim stole the land of the children of Si Abd Allah in the valley and made millions from his honey and pork while my uncle has hardly more than a couple of footsteps of land in the valley and no beehives. Moreover, Si Muhammad Qasim has a good son like Hmidu, the kind of son every Jibli dreams of having. And even his other sons have at least stayed in the village and helped their father, whereas all of my uncle Mhammad's sons except young Abd as-Slam have gone to Tangier. That's natural. The sons of a rich man stay close to him because they want his money and his land. The sons of a poor man have no reason to stay with their father.

So there are many people in the village who hoped that Hmidu would never be able to grow anything in that garden. And they were angry when Hmidu came down from the garden one evening and stopped off at the mosque long enough to tell them that he had found a little spring in the garden, big enough to water it. They couldn't believe it. And the next day they all went up to the garden themselves. And they saw it themselves. Then, for the first time, they all knew that Hmidu was not crazy. The soil was rocky and crumbly, but with water he could do it. But he would need to strengthen the soil. And he did. Si Allal sold him a little mountain of mule manure. And Hmidu hired about fifteen mules to carry all that manure from the valley. By the late spring of 1977, that field was green with cucumbers, tomatoes, potatoes, and watermelons. And he was selling at the Tuesday market of Jbil Hbib and the Monday market of Bni Harshan. He was starting to pay Abd ar-Rahman back his money. And nobody was calling him crazy any more. Even Si Muhammad Qasim himself, who had refused to give him any money even though he has millions rotting somewhere in that house, was proud of Hmidu. He would rant on and on about how Hmidu pays his men too much and doesn't work them enough. But he was proud. He knows that Hmidu is smart like him when it comes to making money. But Hmidu is different. He doesn't lie, cheat, or steal. Everything he does, he does straight. Si Muhammad Qasim can't understand how Hmidu manages to make money that way! But he is proud. Oh, is he proud! But of course he never praises Hmidu and he doesn't like it when other people do either because he is afraid of the evil eye. The evil eye (al-ayn) caused Hmidu's prob-lems, he says.

Hmidu's problems started with the parliamentary elections on June 3, 1977. The qayyid had told all the shaykhs and muqaddi-miyya to tell everyone to vote for the "independent" candidate for parliament. The slogan of the independents is "God, Country, and King" (Allah, al-Watan, wa al-Malik). But Hmidu supported Si Allal's brother, who was the candidate of the Istiqlal (Independence) party. Hmidu is a good friend of Si Allal's, as is his father Si Muhammad Qasim and his brother Abd as-Slam. Moreover, he wanted Si Allal to use his tractor to clear a road up to his vegetable garden so he could take his vegetables to Tangier by truck. Now he has to bring them down by mule. And Si Allal had sold him all that mule manure at a low price. So Hmidu had to support Si Allal's brother. And he didn't think the qayyid would mind. Maybe he didn't even know that everyone was supposed to vote for the independent. And it was not as if Si Allal's brother were from the Socialist Union of Popular Forces. He was the Istiqlal candidate, and the Istiqlal party has never been illegal since independence. Anyway, Hmidu urged everyone in the village of the streams and the neighboring villages to vote for Si Allal's brother.

Hmidu himself had run in the local elections on November 12, 1976, as a candidate for the district council (*al-majlis al-qarawi*). He lost by a couple of votes because Swilah the grocer told everyone he would stop letting people buy on credit unless they voted for *him*. And the Baqqali snakes and the other envious ones didn't want to see Hmidu win. So they voted for Swilah the grocer too. But Hmidu would have won if the election had been honest. He is a good leader. Whenever the mule paths to the valley have to be cleared, he leads the men of the village when they clear them. If it weren't for him, nobody would clear those paths. As for the Baqqali brothers and the old son of al-Ayyashi F., they never help to clear those paths. They always pretend they are too sick or too busy to clear them. But they use them every time they go down to the valley.

Hmidu got many people to vote for Si Allal's brother. But the independent candidate won, according to the *qayyid*. As the old son of al-Arbi says, the government just wastes money having elections because everyone knows that only one man's vote counts, and that's the *qayyid*'s. And the *qayyid* just follows the orders they send him from Rabat. But the *qayyid* was mad because many people had voted for Si Allal's brother.

And not too long after the election, the head of the district council, Si Umar, told Hmidu that several men from the village of the streams had complained that his garden was on village communal land. They wanted to use that land to graze their goats. And Si Umar said he was going to tear down the scrub fence around the garden and let the village goats eat it up in the day while the wild boars and rabbits would eat it up at night.

Hmidu had been working on that garden every day, from shortly after the call to the dawn prayer until the call to the sunset prayer, for about two years. And he had spent over 450,000 francs

($1,000) hiring men to work for him and buying seed. And now that he was just starting to see the fruits of all that labor and money, Si Umar was going to bring up some *mkhazniyya* to destroy his garden!

Who had complained? The Baqqalis and the old son of al-Ayyashi F. denied that they were the ones. They were afraid of Hmidu and his father and brothers. But they are snakes that only slither out from under a rock when they are sure there is no danger. When Hmidu and his brothers were sitting on the front porch of the mosque complaining about Si Umar, their mouths were full of honey. The kept telling Hmidu that they would never do anything like that. And the *fqih* just sat there sewing his *jillaba*, listening to the others speak. But after Hmidu and his brothers left, they all started laughing and making jokes about Hmidu. Even the *fqih*, Si Abd al-Ali, who is supposed to teach the boys of the village the path of righteousness! He too is jealous. He doesn't even have a mule, just a little donkey. So he is full of envy like the others.

Nobody knows who complained about Hmidu's garden. It could have been the Baqqalis, the old son of al-Ayyashi F., the *fqih* Si Abd al-Ali, or my uncle Mhammad. But maybe nobody complained. None of those snakes would have the courage to complain to the *qayyid* about Hmidu on their own. I think the *qayyid* called Si Umar and the other rich peasants on the district council (*al-majlis al-qarawi*), as well as the *shaykhs* and *muqaddimiyya*, and asked them who had been telling people to vote for Si Allal's brother. And they told him about Hmidu. Then the *qayyid* probably asked them how he could punish Hmidu without looking like he was punishing him for voting for the Istiqlal candidate. Then Si Abd al-Latif the *muqaddim* or Si Hasan the *shaykh* probably told him about Hmidu's garden that was on village communal land. And Si Abd al-Latif the *muqaddim* probably knew that he could get the envious snakes of the village of the streams to complain about this garden and say that the village council (*aj-jmaa*) had never allowed Hmidu to clear a garden there.

In the old days, a man would request the permission of the village council to clear a piece of village communal land and it became his after he had worked it for ten years. The village council includes all the grown men in the village. But, really, Si Muhammad Qasim and Hmidu have controlled the council of the village of the streams for many years. Hmidu says he *did* ask for the permission of the village council when he cleared his garden. But the snakes say he didn't. Maybe he just assumed it was all right because his father and he really *were* the village council, which doesn't have any real power anymore anyway. Or maybe he did ask the permission of the council and the snakes are just saying that he didn't because that is what Si Umar, the *muqaddim,* and the *shaykh* told them to say. And they were happy to oblige. They probably didn't mind him clearing a garden up there in that scrub when he started because they all thought he was just going to make a fool of himself. And they wanted to see that. But now that he is making money out of that big garden, they want some of that money too. He is going to have to pay them all if he wants them to allow him to transform that village land into his own private property *(mulk)*. He should have had the papers taken care of when he started because then they would not have asked for much money at all. Now they will squeeze him dry, especially because they know that Abd ar-Rahman could lend Hmidu even more money.

Anyway, Hmidu was scared and for weeks he could hardly sleep at night worrying about his garden. He went down to Tangier and asked Abd ar-Rahman to help him turn the land into their private property or just Hmidu's private property. Abd ar-Rahman said he would try to help him but he didn't want to get involved in politics. No man with a brain in his head gets involved in politics in Morocco.

But Hmidu was lucky because not too long after the parliamentary elections of 1977, a couple of weeks I think, the Istiqlal party joined the government and Bu Sitta (Boucetta) became Minister of Foreign Affairs. And I guess the *qayyid* forgave Hmidu for supporting Si Allal's brother the Istiqlal candidate, because Si Umar never said another word about the garden. Neither did the *muqaddim* or the *shaykh.*

175

Some people say that maybe Si Umar threatened Hmidu on his own, without orders from the *qayyid*. That is nonsense. Si Umar is the *qayyid*'s errand boy. He has no power of his own. On market day he walks around the *qayyid*'s headquarters (*al-qiyada*) trying to look like one of the king's ministers. If you try to talk to him, he says he is too busy and he rushes into some office where he will probably sit and smoke a *sibsi* pipe of *kif* and drink tea with the *shaykh* and the *muqaddimiyya*. If you want to talk with him, you have to pay him, just like you have to pay the *shaykh* and the *muqaddimiyya* to get a birth certificate or any other paper. And he strolls through the market with his hands behind his back, trying to look as though he controlled the whole market. But when the *qayyid* calls him, he scurries to him like a slave to his master. And whatever the *qayyid* says, he answers, "Yes sir. Yes sir. Yes sir." (*Naam ya sidi. Naam ya sidi. Naam ya sidi.*) The *qayyid* could shit on his face and he would say, "God bless you, sir" (*baraka Allahu fik ya sidi*). That is why I say that the *qayyid* told Si Umar to threaten Hmidu. Si Umar wouldn't do something like that on his own. Si Muhammad Qasim is too rich. And Si Allal is too rich. Si Umar would not fight such men unless the *qayyid* told him to. Anyway, what does he care about the parliamentary elections? What do any Jbala care about any election unless their brother or cousin is a candidate? Or unless someone pays them to vote for someone. What do elections change? Nothing. Will the government stop arresting Jbala for trying to eke out a livelihood in the hills by making charcoal? No. Will the government allow Jbala to cultivate the hillsides by slash-and-burn? No. Will the government take land from rich peasants like al-Hajj Muhammad Zillal and distribute it to the poor Jbala who own no valley land at all? No. Will the government give them regular jobs so that they don't have to make charcoal to feed their families? No. So why should the Jbala care about the elections? And the story is really pretty much the same in the city. At election time, all the candidates are full of words about how they will make Morocco a wonderful place to live in. But these are just empty words. The elections change nothing.

Anyway, Hmidu learned his lesson. He will never get involved in politics again. No one is bothering him about the garden now. But he is trying to change it into his own private property in case the snakes ever come out from under their rocks again.

Hmidu works hard. But he also likes to have fun. When he was younger, before he started that garden, he had many women. And he also liked *kif*, hashish, and even whiskey. May God forgive him. Sometimes he and his brother Abd as-Slam would take a couple of divorcees or widows from the village down to Tangier. They would spend a week or two in a room in the city, just weaving (i.e., "screwing"), smoking *kif*, and drinking whiskey. I am not sure they drank whiskey, but that is what people say. Two of those women have since married other husbands in Tangier.

Hmidu would also go with other women in the hills. He would sometimes go with the dancing girls at weddings. Then, in about 1969, he married Zohra daughter of Si Abd as-Slam M. from the *qbila* of Bni Yidir. She's a spunky little lady and pretty too. They say she is very hot. Maybe that is why he has not divorced her although she has not borne him any children. He still goes with other women, and they say that she has fooled around with many men, including two of Hmidu's brothers! God knows best. She certainly talks a lot. Whenever I eat with Hmidu and al-Ayyashi, Hmidu's Zohra is busy chattering away while al-Ayyashi's Zohra just sits quietly. And she is funny. And, oh, she knows how to tease! I would never cheat Hmidu and go with his woman behind his back. But that little lady has a body that would set any man on fire. May God forgive me for thinking this way about the wife of the son of my mother's sister!

9. *Fatima Zohra on her cousin Hmidu*

HMIDU IS SMART. He's probably the smartest man in the village of the streams. When everyone else in the village could think only of mint and charcoal, he thought of clearing a big vegetable garden in the scrub brush up above the village and selling vegetables in the local markets and in Tangier.

But he still thinks like the Jbala in most ways. One night we were having dinner with him and his brothers and all their wives and we started talking about the American astronauts who landed on the moon. He said it was just a trick. No man could ever go the moon, he said. He even saw them on the moon on the television in Mustafa's house in Tangier. But he still says it was just a trick. And all his brothers agreed. I told them it was real and they said that I shouldn't believe everything the Christians say. I gave up trying to convince them. Al-Hajj Muhammad was there too that night. He was trying to show everyone how modern and intelligent he was, so he was saying that it *was* possible that the astronauts really did go to the moon. But I am not sure that he really believes they did.

10. *Al-Hajj Muhammad on his cousin Abd as-Slam, son of Si Muhammad Qasim (1950–), peasant and charcoalmaker*

MY COUSIN ABD AS-SLAM grows mint in a big garden just below Si Muhammad Qasim's house. Si Muhammad Qasim lets him do whatever he wants with this garden. And he will probably leave it to him when he dies, God willing. It is a good garden that gives sweet mint leaves. In 1977, it yielded 270,000 francs ($600). That is about what my uncle Muhammad made from *both* his mint gardens put together, although he says he only made 100,000 ($222.22). My uncle is afraid of the evil eye so he pretends he is poorer than he really is. But he *is* poor compared to Si Muhammad Qasim and his sons. He looks up the hill at Abd as-Slam's beautiful green mint garden and his heart burns with envy!

The mint of Bni Msawwar is famous all over the north. In the markets of Tangier, you can hear vendors shouting "Mint from Bni Msawwar! Mint from Bni Msawwar!" (*Nana d Bni Msawwar! Nana d Bni Msawwar!*) And the village of the streams has some of the best mint gardens in all of Bni Msawwar because of the streams from which little ditches water the mint bushes even in the driest, hottest days of summer. Every morning after the dawn prayer is called, you can see eight to ten mules loaded with freshly cut mint winding their way down to Dar Shawi. Hmid son of *al-fqih* Muhammad and the other mint traders load the sacks of fresh mint on the roof of the 8:30 bus to Tangier.

The brothers of Abd as-Slam's wife Malika not only grow their own mint in the village of the shoemakers, they also sell it themselves in their own stall at the Casa Barrata market in Tangier. That's what brothers can do when they trust each other!

Abd as-Slam also makes charcoal. Actually he hires his father's half-brother Luhsin son of Qasim to make charcoal. When Si Muhammad Qasim's father Luhsin Y. died, may God have mercy upon him, his mother married Luhsin Y.'s brother Qasim Y. And Luhsin son of Qasim was their son. So he is Si Muhammad Qasim's brother on his mother's side. And she raised them together. But today Si Muhammad Qasim is the richest man in the village and Luhsin son of Qasim is one of the poorest. Poor Luhsin, may God help him. He used to work for Abd as-Slam for 700 francs ($1.56) a day plus lunch. He was the one that hoed that beautiful mint garden of Abd as-Slam's! He would come to Si Muhammad Qasim's house early in the morning to meet Abd as-Slam. He would never come in. He would never step through the front door. He would just sit on the threshold of the door and my aunt Amina would give him a glass of mint tea and a piece of bread. He had to sit on the threshold of his own brother's house and he had to work for wages for his brother's son who is young enough to be his. So much as you possess, so much you are worth! (*Qadd ma andak qadd ma tiswa!*).

Luhsin has nothing (*ma andu hatta haja*). He doesn't even have a mule, so he has to carry heavy sacks of wheat up from the Tuesday market of Jbil Hbib on his back! And he is not young any more. Si Muhammad Qasim has two strong mules, the best mules in the village. But he would never lend one of them to his own brother to bring God's bounty up from the valley to feed his wife and children. Luhsin and his wife and children could starve to death and all Si Muhammad Qasim would think about would be the cost of the bread and figs for the funeral. That man has a rock where other people have a heart!

Luhsin wanted to send his oldest daughter to work as a maid for my cousin Zubida in Tangier. Zubida pays her maids 5,000 francs ($11.11) a month and that money would help Luhsin. And he wouldn't have to feed her any more. But people in the village warned my aunt Khadduj that his daughter still wet her pants even though she was fifteen or sixteen years old. So Zubida didn't hire her.

Abd as-Slam used to work Luhsin hard. But he treated him well. He would lend him money when he needed it. Abd as-Slam, like Hmidu, is a better man than his father. But they had an argument about something. I think Luhsin wanted to go to the Tuesday market of Jbil Hbib and Abd as-Slam wanted him to mind their charcoal mound (*kusha*). Anyway, Luhsin stopped working for him. Now he is living by the mercy of God (*ayish bi rahmat Allah*). He can, of course, make charcoal like any other poor Jibli. But without a mule, he cannot bring the charcoal down to Dar Shawi to sell it to al-Hajj T. He could carry some on his back, maybe forty kilos. But he is getting old. He must be about forty-five. And the path down to Dar Shawi is long and rocky. Two hours on that path with forty kilos of charcoal on his back and poor Luhsin would be dead. May God preserve him. He's bound to come down to Tangier any time now, if he hasn't come down already. There's no way a man can survive in the hills without a mule. May God assist him.

Si Muhammad Qasim has millions of old rotting franc notes hidden in that big house of his with the tile roof and his own brother is going to have to go down to Tangier and live in a *barraka* (tin shack) and send his little girls to work in a rug factory for 350 francs ($.78) a day! Si Muhammad Qasim can't sleep at night because he worries that someone will sneak into his big house and steal all that money that has been rotting away all these years. But his brother can't sleep because he doesn't know how he is going to feed his wife and children the next day! Not even a Christian would treat his brother the way Si Muhammad Qasim treats Luhsin!

Abd as-Slam's heart is white but sometimes he is like his father. I remember the wedding of Abd Allah, the son of my uncle Mhammad, in August of 1976. That was before I went to the east (Mecca). It was the night that the men of the groom's family were to go to the village of the spring of as-Snad across the valley to bring back the bride. Most of the men of the village were on their mules, their faces lit by the lanterns in their hands. I thought Abd as-Slam was going to let me ride one of his father's mules. But then I saw my brother Ahmad mounting it with Hamman's help. Ahmad was home from Belgium for his August vacation. And Hamman, Abd as-Slam's younger brother, told me they didn't have a spare mule for me. I punched that young whiskey-drinking bastard in the face. Then Abd as-Slam ran toward me and tried to hit me, but the other men grabbed him. And some other men held me. Oh, I was mad! I could have beaten them both. They have a mule for my younger brother but they think I am going to walk all the way to the spring of as-Snad! Abd as-Slam was screaming: "You are nothing!" (*Ntina walu!*) "You own nothing!" (*Ma andak hatta haja!*) "You live in the house of your brother! You are getting old and you do not even own your own house!" His words were like boiling water being poured upon me and scalding my skin. Five or six of them had to hold me or I would have killed him. I was crazy with rage. But they dragged me away from there and splashed cold water in my face. And I calmed down. And then Abd as-Slam left with the others on the mules. I watched the lanterns winding down the mountain in the darkness. Then I saw the long string of lanterns cross the valley floor and wind its way up to the spring of as-Snad far across the valley. And I was sad.

Sometimes I feel sad because people in the family respect my brother Ahmad because he is rich. And they do not respect me because I am poor. They love to listen to my jokes and my songs and my stories. But when it is time for a wedding, only Ahmad gets a mule.

And sometimes I am sad because I have no son. When a man has a son, even when he dies, he still lives in his son. When a man has a son, he is not alone. A wife may leave her husband. But a son can never stop being a son. When you are old and the flesh is sagging from your bones and you are too feeble to seek God's bounty, your son will feed you and clothe you and take you into his home. But what happens to a man with no son to sustain him when he can no longer sustain himself? What will happen to me when I can no longer sell the garbage of the Christians? My brother Ahmad will not help me. He is like Si Muhammad Qasim. Like a Christian. When I die, he will worry about the cost of the bread and figs. God forgive me for saying so!

Sometimes I awake in the morning and the sadness is heavy upon me. I don't want to get out of bed. I just want to sleep. Then Rahma grabs my shoulder and shakes me and shouts, "Wake up you lazy good-for-nothing bum! We cannot even heat the tea because there is no gas left in the Butagaz burner and there is no charcoal for the brazier. And we have no money and the grocer won't give us any more credit! Go sell in the market or work for wages with a shovel and a pick! But get up and make some money!" And I mumble, "Trust in God!" (*Tawakkil ala Allah!*). And I try to go back to sleep. I don't blame Rahma, my wife. But when the sadness is heavy upon me, I cannot do anything. I get up and wash for the morning prayer. Then I leave the house so I won't hear her braying in my ear. I drink tea in Abd ar-Rahman's café. And I just walk and walk.

But after a while, the sadness lifts. Often I hear the chant of the call to prayer and this makes the sadness disappear.

Allahu akbar	God is greater
Allahu akbar	God is greater
Ashhadu al-la ilaha illa Allah	I bear witness that there is no god but God
Ashhadu al-la ilaha illa Allah	I bear witness that there is no god but God

Ashhadu anna Muhammadan
    rasulu Allah
	I bear witness that Muhammad
	    is the messenger of God

Ashhadu anna Muhammadan
    rasulu Allah
	I bear witness that Muhammad
	    is the messenger of God

Hayya ala as-sala	Come alive to prayer
Hayya ala as-sala	Come alive to prayer
Hayya ala al-falah	Come alive to success
Hayya ala al-falah	Come alive to success
Allahu akbar	God is greater
Allahu akbar	God is greater
La ilaha illa Allah	There is no god but God

When I hear the call to prayer, I go to the mosque by the stream. And there I feel happy and clean. The whitewashed walls and the chanting of the Quran wash away the sadness and all the worries of this world. I chant the Quran with the *tulba*. And then we pray. Prayer at its time is better than the world and what is in it (*as-sla fi waqta hsin min ad-dunya wa ma fiha*). And prayer in a mosque is better than prayer alone.

The greatest part of the prayer is the touching of the floor with the forehead. The *imam* intones *Allahu akbar*, "God is greater." Then all the Muslims in the mosque respond *Allahu akbar* and prostrate themselves with their foreheads and palms on the floor, whispering *Subhana Rabbi al-ala*, "My Lord the most high be praised." The whole mosque is silent but for these whispered words of praise and supplication. It is then, when the Muslim touches his forehead to the ground in utter submission and humility before God, that he is closest to Him. This is the best time for supplication, when the Muslim is lowest to the ground and closest to God the most high. This is the moment when the Muslim is purest and happiest and safest from the temptations of Satan. And it is then, with my forehead and my palms upon the floor and the praise of God upon my lips, that I forget that I am a poor peddler with no house and no son and with a wife who looks like a mule.

11. *Fatima Zohra on her cousin Abd as-Slam, son of Si Muhammad Qasim*

M Y COUSIN ABD AS-SLAM'S TEETH are all black and decayed at the edges. He looks better when he doesn't open his mouth. Almost all Jbala do, because they do not brush their teeth and they put mountains of sugar in their mint tea. They do scrub their teeth with *as-swak*, the bark of the walnut tree, but that does not clean between the teeth as well as a brush. It is a serious problem. Sometimes you see very handsome men and beautiful women in the hills, but when they open their mouths, you see the rotting black edges of their teeth and the empty holes where teeth used to be.

Abd as-Slam married Malika daughter of Muhammad B. from the village of the shoemakers in 1976. His father helped him pay the *sdaq* of 60,000 francs ($133.33). His older brother Muhammad paid only 22,500 francs ($50) for his wife Slama in 1962. And his father slaughtered a young bull at his wedding. Only very rich peasants do that in the hills. And everyone was surprised that Si Muhammad Qasim did it, because he only slaughtered goats and sheep for the marriages of his other children.

Abd as-Slam refused to perform the traditional custom of placing a white cloth under the bride on her wedding night so that her blood could be shown the following morning as proof that she had remained a virgin until she married. He said this was a shameful old custom and people shouldn't follow it any more. He is right of course. But the old people said that he was afraid to let people know that she was not a virgin.

Abd as-Slam and his wife live on the ground floor of Si Muhammad Qasim's big house. But Abd as-Slam wants to have his own house as soon as possible. He wants to get a work contract to work in northern Europe and save enough money to buy a tractor. He dreams about that tractor, but it is hard to get work contracts now in Belgium and Holland because they are trying to stop Moroccans from going there. But he might be able to get a contract to work in Libya. The young man who used to live on the ground floor of Mustafa's house has been working there for a couple of years now.

12. Al-Hajj Muhammad on his cousin Hamman, son of Si Muhammad Qasim (1953–), ladies' man and loafer

THE TOMCAT THAT HAS ITS MOTHER will not hunt (*al-qatt bi yimmah ma isad*). That is what people say about my cousin Hamman. He sleeps late in the morning, long after Si Muhammad Qasim and Abd as-Slam have gone out to graze the cows or hoe a garden. His mother sells honey and eggs to give him money which he spends on cigarettes and *kif*, and even whiskey. Getting up in the morning is the hardest work he usually does in a day. He is spoiled (*mfishish*). His father lets him be because he was born a few months after he beat my aunt Amina with Hamman still inside her. And my aunt Amina spoils him because she is glad he didn't die when Si Muhammad Qasim beat her that night. But she would probably spoil him anyway because he is the youngest. He is the only one of their children not yet married. He has gone with almost all the pretty women in the village, but he doesn't even think of marriage. He is a good-looking boy and women like him. He never prays. But none of his brothers does either. May God guide them.

13. Fatima Zohra on her cousin Hamman

MY COUSIN HAMMAN IS A BUM. But he is young and I hope he will change. Right now, he spends all his time sleeping with the pretty wives of the village while their men are working far from their homes. His head is usually full of hashish. He tried to work as a waiter in a café in Tangier a few times. But each time he went back up to the village after a few months because in the village his mother gives him all the money and food that he needs. I hope he will change, God willing.

185

IV

Suudiyya, Daughter of Si Abd Allah

(1920–)

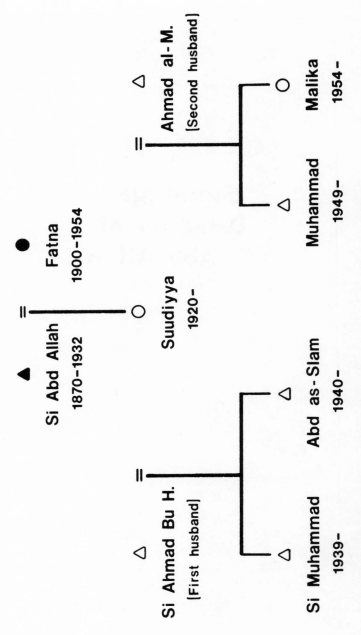

Genealogical Diagram IV: Suudiyya and Her Four Children

1. *Al-Hajj Muhammad on his aunt Suudiyya and her first husband, a fqih (teacher of the Quran) in the village of the springs, and her second husband, a night watchman in Tangier*

MY AUNT SUUDIYYA looks like a frail little old lady, but sometimes she is younger in her heart than her own children. I remember one night the whole family was together on the terrace on the roof of Mustafa's house in the cobblestone quarter. It was in August and Habiba and Ahmad were there on their summer vacation. Habiba and I were singing Jbalan songs and beating the rhythm with a tambourine and a *darbuga* (oblong tambourine without jingles). And we were dancing around, with Habiba in back of me holding my hips with her hands. Then my aunt Suudiyya joined us, placing her hands on Habiba's hips. And when she was tired, she beat the rhythm with her palm on the tambourine. And she sang with us, even though some of the songs were about men wanting women and women wanting men. Her son Abd as-Slam kept telling her it was late and they had to go home. And she kept telling him to wait a little longer. She was singing, dancing, and laughing with us until two or three in the morning. May God grant her a long life.

My aunt Suudiyya was married to the *fqih* Si Ahmad Bu H. of the village of the two springs when she was about sixteen or seventeen, that is, in about 1937. The *fqih*, may God have mercy

189

upon him, was many years older than she was. God granted them two sons: Si Muhammad, who was born in about 1939, and Abd as-Slam, who was born in about 1940. The *fqih* died when they were still boys. May God have mercy upon him. She then married Ahmad al-M., a poor peasant and charcoalmaker in the village of the two springs. In 1973, they came down to Tangier where he found a job as a night watchman (*assas*). He still works as a night watchman in the same place and makes 28,800 francs ($64) a month. He works every night from the sunset prayer to the dawn prayer. But like most night watchmen, he probably sleeps on the job. He is lucky to be paid for sitting on his butt and sleeping! At most, he just walks around a little. All old Jbala dream of getting such a job. But not many do. So Ahmad al-M. is lucky, even though he does not make much money. He and my aunt Suudiyya have two children: Muhammad, born in about 1949, and Malika, born in about 1954. Muhammad and his wife and children, and Malika and her husband and baby, live with them in the Marshan quarter, near the cobblestone quarter. Ahmad al-M. pays 10,000 francs ($22.22) a month for the room he and Suudiyya live in, and their son Muhammad and Malika's husband Abd as-Slam pay 5,000 francs ($11.11) a month each for the rooms they live in. They all share a little terrace where the women cook and wash clothes and hang them on a cord to dry.

Ahmad al-M. always complains that Muhammad and Malika's husband Abd as-Slam waste money on cigarettes, *kif*, and clothes. They often ask to borrow money from him. But they are young and strong and earn more money than he does.

2. *Fatima Zohra on her aunt Suudiyya*

WHEN MY MOTHER CAME BACK from Belgium in November 1977, my husband and I took her to my aunt Suudiyya's house in Marshan—the poor part of Marshan where the Muslims live, not where the Christians have their villas overlooking the Straits of Gibraltar. Malika let us in. My aunt was upstairs sitting on the floor carding wool. We told my mother to stay behind and hide. Then we entered my aunt's room and greeted my aunt. I told her we had a surprise for her. Someone was with us she would be very happy to see. "Who? Who?" she asked. Then my mother walked in and my aunt shouted, "My sister!" And they embraced and wept. Both of them are wrinkled old ladies with grandchildren and yet my aunt kept saying, "Oh my sister! Oh my sister!" as if they were both still little girls running barefoot in the village of the streams. And I thought that someday, perhaps in forty or fifty years, I might be embracing one of my sisters and we would be wrinkled old ladies too.

3. *Al-Hajj Muhammad on his cousin Si Muhammad, son of the* fqih *Bu H. (1939–),* talib *(reciter of the Quran), peasant, and charcoalmaker in the village of the two springs*

MY COUSIN SI MUHAMMAD is a *talib*. He memorized the holy Quran in the mosque of the village of the two springs, which is right next to the village of the streams. He is a good Muslim who prays every prayer at its time. He does not go with women other than his wife. And he does not smoke *kif* or even cigarettes. He makes a little money chanting the holy book on the seventh day after births and at circumcisions, weddings, and funerals.

Si Muhammad has six goats and about a dozen chickens. Sometimes, he works for the government public works program (*al-Inash al-Watani*) for 750 francs ($1.67) a day. And he has a little mint garden. But mostly he depends on charcoal (*al-fham*). He was caught by the ranger (*al-wardiyya*) for a second time in 1977. And the judge in Tetuan made him pay 10,000 francs ($22.22). That is a fortune in the hills, where many Jbala do not see that much money in a month. Al-Hajj T. only pays thirty-five or forty francs a kilo for the charcoal he buys in Dar Shawi, even though he sells it for as much as 120 francs ($.27) a kilo in Tangier in the winter, when people use a lot of charcoal to heat their homes as well as to cook their food. Tangier is cold and damp during the winter rains and a brazier (*mijmar*) full of glowing charcoal burns away the cold and the dampness, especially if you sit right next to it. But making charcoal in the winter is hard because of the heavy rains.

When you make charcoal, you pile up roots and sometimes branches and then you cover them with leafy branches, which you then cover with dirt, leaving a hole at the top of the mound (*al-kusha*). You set fire to the leafy branches under the dirt so that gradually the fire will burn the roots and big branches into charcoal. But when the roots, the leafy branches and the dirt are all wet, it is hard to light a fire. If the rains *do* hold off long enough for you to make a mound of charcoal, you still have to bring it down to Dar Shawi by mule. And the paths are all muddy and slippery when they are not in fact fast-flowing streams. So a mule has a hard time making it down to the valley without breaking a leg. God preserve us. Moreover, you have to bring your charcoal down early in the morning or at dusk after the sunset prayer so that the forest rangers won't see you and confiscate that charcoal you spent ten days making and which will feed your family until you make some more, God willing. Usually, Jbala bring their charcoal down about the time of the sunset prayer. Every evening mules come down from the hills loaded with charcoal, just as in the morning they come down loaded with freshly cut mint for the 8:30 bus to Tangier. Mint and charcoal—that's all that's keeping people in the high hill villages, where only one man out of fifty has any plow land in the valley. Si Muhammad Qasim is the only man in the village of the streams who owns any plow land in the valley except for my uncle Mhammad, who has a few footsteps near Dar Shawi.

In the summer, charcoal is cheaper than in the winter. It only costs about seventy or eighty francs ($.16–.18) a kilo because people don't need it to heat their homes and many people cook with Butagaz burners instead since they don't give off as much heat. And charcoal is easier to bring down from the hills in the summer. It is also easier to make then. But you have to make it early in the morning or in the late afternoon, not just because of the rangers, but also because the summer sun is blazing hot. And a smoldering mound of charcoal is hot enough by itself. Trying to work on a charcoal mound in the heat of the midday summer sun is a sure way to die fast. Verily, God is with those who patiently endure (*Inna Allaha maa as-sabirin*) (II : 153).

4. Al-Hajj Muhammad on his cousin Abd as-Slam, son of the fqih Bu H. (1940–), fruit and vegetable transporter in Tangier

MY COUSIN ABD AS-SLAM, the son of my aunt Suudiyya and of the *fqih* Bu H., is in his late thirties or early forties. He only studied the holy Quran for a few months in the mosque of the village of the two springs. But even though he is not a *talib* like his brother Si Muhammad, he is a good Muslim just like his brother. He prays every prayer at its time.

Abd as-Slam used to grow mint and make charcoal in the village of the two springs. Then he bought a used motorbike with a pushcart in front of it. And he moved to Tangier and started carrying vegetables from the wholesale market in as-Swani to the market of the big tree. All day long he drives back and forth with that cart full of vegetables. He brought his wife and children down from the hills and they rented an apartment in the quarter of the lemon tree.

But after about six years, he decided to move his wife and children back up to the village of the two springs. He said there was too much rottenness (*fsad*) in the city. Muslim girls were wearing bikinis at the beach like Christian girls. And Muslims drank whiskey and neglected their prayers and didn't fast during Ramadan. He said he wanted his children to grow up as good Muslims in the hills far from the corrupting influence of the Christians and Jews of Tangier.

But Abd as-Slam's wife, La Slama, and his seven children, especially the older ones, were very sad to leave Tangier. La Slama would shout and scream and insult him. But they went back to the village in 1976. Abd as-Slam kept carrying vegetables from as-Swani to the market of the big tree six days a week. And he would ride his motorbike pushcart to Dar Shawi on Thursday afternoon and spend Friday in the village with his family and at the mosque. He also grew a little mint. But his wife La Slama kept ranting and raving like a wounded boar. She wanted to go back to the city and she was making him suffer in the village. And traveling back and forth each week was tiring. So in 1977 he brought them back down to Tangier, where they still live in the quarter of the lemon tree. His oldest daughter married one of his wife's nephews in 1977.

Abd as-Slam's wife La Slama is a Baqqaliyya, a *sharifa*. She is the daughter of La Ftuma the dancing girl (*ash-shaykha*). La Ftuma's mother, La Shama, was a dancing girl too. But La Slama never was. La Ftuma's father, Sidi al-Ayyashi the elder, was born in the village of Fijj Hanun in the *qbila* of Bni Yidir, east of Bni Msawwar. He was a shoemaker. He lived in the village of the weavers in the *qbila* of Jbil Hbib for a few years. Then he moved to the village of the streams in about 1916 and married La Shama daughter of Sidi Muhammad al-Baqqali. They were both of the Baqqali clan but they were not really cousins.

La Ftuma was born in the village of the streams in about 1920. She's an old woman now, yet she still dances at weddings in late summer. She is a big woman with plenty of meat on her bones. That's the kind of woman a man wants. She was first married in about 1935 to a poor peasant from the village of the weavers in Jbil Hbib. He was a Baqqali but not a real cousin. He divorced her after a few years. Maybe because she bore him no children. Maybe because she was already going with many men in those days. Then she married another Baqqali, Sidi Abd Allah al-Baqqali from the village of Zawiya al-Fuqiyya in Bni Yidir. This man, may God have mercy upon him, was the father of La Slama, Abd as-Slam's wife. He divorced La Ftuma after a few years too. Then she married Muhammad M. from the village of the Sons of Yaqub in Bni Msawwar. He was a bum who lived on the money La Ftuma made dancing and going with men at weddings. It was when she was married to this man that La Ftuma stole some bracelets from Rahma, the wife of my brother Mustafa. Since then, most of the family refuses to let her in their homes for fear that she will steal something else.

After being divorced by her second husband and before marrying her third one, La Ftuma worked for my aunt Khadduj in the cobblestone quarter. She helped her make the bread which she had baked at the public oven (*farran*) of the Rifi and which Sidi Mahdi al-Baqqali sold in the old city.

5. *Al-Hajj Muhammad on his cousin Muhammad, son of Ahmad al-M. (1949–), shoemaker in Tangier*

MY COUSIN MUHAMMAD is the only son my aunt Suudiyya had with Ahmad al-M. He memorized the holy Quran at the mosque of the village of the two springs when he was a young boy. Then he went to study at the Religious Institute (*Mahad ad-dini*) in Tetuan. He lived in a dormitory there. He was a very good student and his mother thought that he would become a schoolteacher or some other kind of white-collar civil servant (*mwaddaf*). But when he was in his late teens, he started going with prostitutes. He wasted most of his money on *kif*, hashish, and whiskey. And he had to leave the Religious Institute.

Then Ahmad al-M. married Muhammad to a girl from the *qbila* of Bni Yidir. Her name is Zohra. Al-M. wanted to keep Muhammad near him, as he is his only son. And he and my aunt Suudiyya hoped that having a wife would make Muhammad stop going with whores and filling his head with *kif*, hashish, and whiskey. This was in about 1971 when Muhammad was about twenty-one. But Muhammad kept leaving the village and going to Tangier and Tetuan to waste his money as before. He would often go to Tangier with Hmidu. They were good friends when Muhammad still lived in the hills. They still are. But now Muhammad is in the city and Hmidu is very busy in the village of the streams with his big vegetable garden.

In 1973, after a big argument with his wife Zohra and his parents, Muhammad left the village and took a bus to Casablanca. He told them he would never come back. My aunt Suudiyya, Ahmad al-M., their daughter Malika, and Muhammad's wife Zohra and her little daughter Layla then moved down to Tangier and rented an apartment near Sabila aj-Jmaa (the fountain of the village), which is really part of the cobblestone quarter. Al-M. started to work as a night watchman and my aunt Suudiyya started to make a little extra money carding and spinning wool in her home. And they all waited for Muhammad to return home.

Muhammad came back from Casablanca after about six months. He went back to his wife Zohra even though she is a dimwit and words ooze out of her mouth slowly, like honey from a jar. I'd go crazy with that woman even though she is pretty—even now after three children that are still alive (Layla, Yusif, and Abd al-Wahhab), and two that have returned to God. May God have mercy upon them. Muhammad and his wife and children live in a room near the room of my aunt Suudiyya. They live downstairs and my aunt and al-M. live upstairs. Muhammad makes about 30,000 francs a month ($66.67) as a shoemaker. If he hadn't left the Religious Institute, he could be making 80,000 or 90,000 ($117.78–$200) a month as a schoolteacher. Everything is in the hands of God.

Muhammad is a *talib*. He knows the holy book by heart. And yet he never prays and he still wastes his money on whiskey. All those years spent memorizing the word of God and he is no better than a Christian! He even tried to enter my brother Mustafa's daughter Latifa by force, when she was about thirteen. Mustafa caught him and threw him out of the house. But he didn't take him to court because he didn't want to harm his daughter's reputation.

Si Muhammad and Abd as-Slam, the sons of my aunt Suudiyya and the *fqih* Bu H., do not get along with their half-brother Muhammad, the son of my aunt Suudiyya and Ahmad al-M. They see him when they come down to the city and stay with their mother and when he comes up to the village. But they try not to see him any more than they have to. They are both God-fearing and hardworking Muslims. But Muhammad is a bum. It is hard to believe they are the sons of the same mother. My aunt Suudiyya keeps saying that he will change as he grows older. Of course he will, when he is a frail old man about to be buried and judged by our Lord. But a few years of righteousness from an old man too old to do much evil anyway cannot wash away all the sins of a lifetime.

6. Fatima Zohra on her cousin Muhammad, son of Ahmad al-M. (1949–)

ON HIS DAY OFF, my cousin Muhammad goes to the beach to look at the girls in bikinis. He wears sunglasses that look like two round silver mirrors from the outside, but he can see through them. And he just sits on the sand in his bathing suit, with music blaring from his big battery radio, and he watches the women through those two little round mirrors that hide his eyes. And he smokes *kif* and cigarettes. Then at night, he visits the whores in the Bni Yidir quarter. I don't know how his wife and three children survive on the little money he gives her.

He makes only about thirty thousand francs a month as a shoemaker in the Belgian quarter (*al-Hawma d Bergika*), but he dresses as if he made a hundred thousand francs ($222.22) a month. He wears a shiny black leather sports coat with a belt, tight shirts that he leaves unbuttoned down to his belly button, tight bell bottoms and fancy shoes with high, thick heels. Like most young Moroccan men, he does not care if his wife and children have nothing to eat but *baysar* and stale bread, so long as he can walk the streets in flashy clothes.

7. Al-Hajj Muhammad on his cousin Malika, daughter of Ahmad al-M. (1954–), wife of bazaar salesclerk in Tangier

Y COUSIN MALIKA is a beautiful young woman with skin that is white like milk and hair that is black like charcoal. She and her mother, my aunt Suudiyya, are always together. They live in the same house and they almost never leave it except with each other. They go to the market together, to the public steam bath (*al-hammam*) together, and they are always together when they visit anyone in the family.

Malika's husband, Abd as-Slam Q., came to Tangier as a boy from the *qbila* of Anjra. They were married in 1974. He works as a salesman in a bazaar in the old city. He started working there for fifteen thousand francs ($33.33) a month, but by 1977 he was making about twenty-six thousand ($57.78) a month. He works six days a week from nine in the morning until ten-thirty at night. He talks big, as if he worked for the king, but he has nothing (*ma andu hatta haja*).

8. Fatima Zohra on her cousin Malika

Y COUSIN MALIKA is a wonderful person. May God grant her a long life. She lived most of her life in the village of the two springs. Then, in 1973, she came down to Tangier with her parents when her brother Muhammad ran off to Casablanca. She was always beautiful and many men wanted to marry her. But not long after arriving in Tangier she met Abd as-Slam Q., a young man who had come to Tangier from the hills several years earlier. He was standing in front of the bazaar where he works in the old city and he saw her walking by in her dark blue *jillaba*. They looked at each other. And he found out who she was and his brother asked her father if he could marry her. Her father said yes and they were married in 1974. They had a baby girl, Rhimu, in 1975. May God bless her. They still live with Malika's parents.

Abd as-Slam, Malika's husband, is young and handsome. Like most young Moroccan men in Tangier, he dreams of finding a rich Christian woman who will take him to Europe or the States and make him a rich man. His brother actually realized his dream, to some extent. His older brother Muhammad used to work in a bazaar just as *he* does now. And he met an American woman who married him and took him to Rockford, Illinois, many years ago. Then, after a few years, Abd as-Slam's family received a letter from the American woman stating that Muhammad had died in a car accident. But Abd as-Slam does not believe this. He thinks the Christian woman just wanted to cut all ties between her husband and his Moroccan family. But I think the brother really is dead because he has not written his family for many, many years.

Anyway, Abd as-Slam dreams of doing what his brother did. One day I was visiting Malika and my aunt Suudiyya, and Abd as-Slam rushed in, his face bright red. "I'm going to Germany! I'm going to Germany!", he kept shouting. And he showed us a postcard he had received from a German woman to whom he had sold a rug when she was in Morocco. I read him the card, which was written in English. The German lady simply thanked him for showing her around Tangier. But Abd as-Slam was jumping around shouting, "She's going to take me to Germany and I'll come back in my own Mercedes with millions in my bank account!" Malika just laughed and told him he was an idiot. But my aunt Suudiyya was worried because she thought he was going to divorce Malika. I told her not to worry because Abd as-Slam was just dreaming. And even if he did divorce Malika to marry a Christian woman, Malika could take care of herself. She is beautiful and she is smart. She could find another man easily. But Moroccan women all live in fear of being divorced. People think of a divorced woman as being little better than a prostitute. This is because people think of a woman as a brainless bundle of desire who will give herself to any man unless she is strictly controlled by a husband or a father. This is particularly true of a woman who is no longer a virgin, as in the case of a divorcee or a widow.

I am sure that Abd as-Slam *would* go to Europe or the States with a Christian woman if he had the chance. And he probably would even divorce Malika if he had to. He enjoys sleeping with Malika and eating the food she cooks. But like most Moroccan men, he does not really love his wife.

Malika and I have always gotten along very well. But we live in different worlds. I remember I once gave her a lightweight aluminum and canvas backpack from the States to carry her baby in. She had never seen such a thing and was pleased. But my aunt Suudiyya told her not to wear it because the neighbors "will give you the evil eye" (*ghadi ayyinuk*). So she never used it. It is true that the neighbors would have made fun of her because Moroccan women do not use such things. I should have known better than to give it to her.

I remember another time when I told Malika that she should not wear the veil any more. My aunt Suudiyya was horrified, even though she herself does not wear the veil. This is because my aunt still wears the clothes peasant women wear in the hills, where women do not wear *jillabas* and veils. But in the city, all but highly modern women and women who have recently come from the hills wear a *jillaba* and usually a veil (*ltam*). Young unmarried women are permitted to wear a *jillaba* without a veil. But it is considered shameful (*hshuma*) for a married woman to leave her home without one—at least by traditional standards. I *never* wear a veil in Morocco. And even my mother, who is really very traditional in most ways, has not worn a veil since returning from the States. The family expects such "Christian" behavior from me, but most of our relatives are shocked because my mother, who has visited the holy places of Islam in Mecca, walks the streets of Tangier with her face naked. I am proud of her because she does not care what they say and she refuses to wear a veil. And many women whose children are well educated and modern have stopped wearing the veil. My mother's good friend al-Wadrasiyya, who used to live next to us in the cobblestone quarter, never wears the veil. And she is an old lady like my mother. Her sons all have well-paid jobs as bureaucrats (*mwaddfin*).

But in the traditional neighborhoods of Tangier, most married women still wear the veil. And my aunt Suudiyya told Malika that she had to wear it. And Malika's husband Abd as-Slam said the same thing. So Malika still wears the veil.

I don't think the veil in itself is such a terrible thing. But what I hate is the idea that a woman has to wear it and that she is "loose" if she doesn't. And this is the way most Moroccans still think even though more and more young Moroccan women no longer wear the veil and even wear western dresses and skirts and blouses. Some of our relatives condemn my sisters and me because we wear western clothes. They say we have apostatized (*kfarna*) and become Christians because we wear western clothes! But most rich and well-educated young Moroccans now wear western clothes, and since we are rich and well-educated compared to most of our relatives, they are not terribly surprised that we wear western clothes. But Malika is poor and never attended a day of school in her life. And she lives in a traditional neighborhood. Her neighbors would ridicule her if she were to stop wearing the veil, let alone wear western clothes.

I remember another incident that also shows how Malika and I live in different worlds, even though she is one of my favorite cousins. One day I invited her to go to the beach with me in my car. And she brought along a friend of hers, the daughter of the landlord of the building where she and my aunt Suudiyya live. This was in 1977. When we got to the beach of the bay of Tangier, I took off my clothes and wore only my bikini. Malika's eyes almost popped out of her head! She couldn't believe I would dare appear almost naked in public. She took off her *jillaba* and wore the traditional bloomers (*sarwal*) down to her knees, and a skirt and blouse. The daughter of the landlord wore a bathing suit.

As we were sitting on the beach, a lifeguard came along and started to flirt with us. I insulted him and told him to go away before I called the police. And I was also very angry with Malika's friend, the landlord's daughter, because she was flirting like a slut with the lifeguard, who of course had only one thing on his mind. The lifeguard was angry when I insulted him. And he said Malika could not stay on the beach because she was not wearing a bathing suit. Everyone on the beach had to wear a bathing suit, he said, so that those who were clothed would not stare at those who were not. And it is true that this is the rule on the beach of Tangier. Once my sister Rhimu had a terrible argument with a policeman who wouldn't let my mother on the beach because she was wearing a *jillaba*. My mother did own a bathing suit at one time and I remember she used to wear it at the Marqala beach near the cobblestone quarter when we were young. But we would go to the beach early in the morning when there were hardly ever any men there.

My mother would never wear a bathing suit at the beach of Tangier, where there are always men watching the women. And this is true of most of the Muslim women in Tangier. So it is very difficult for a Muslim family to spend time together at the beach of Tangier. Of course, a Muslim family with a car can drive to any beach in northwest Morocco. But most Muslim families do not have cars. So despite the fact that some of the most beautiful beaches in the world are on the bay of Tangier, most Moroccan families cannot enjoy them. And the beach of Tangier is used primarily by Christian tourists and young Moroccan men. The Moroccan men play soccer and watch the beautiful blonde European women with bronze skin and tiny bikinis who stay in the big hotels on the bay. Many people think that the rule that everyone must wear a bathing suit at the beach is just a trick to reserve the beach for Christian tourists. I think this is true. It is shameful that my mother cannot accompany her daughters to the beach of Tangier. Shameful.

Anyway, I insulted that lifeguard, who told Malika, her friend, and me that we had to leave, or that Malika had to leave, because she wasn't wearing a bathing suit. And I insulted him for trying to flirt with us. Then he insulted us because the landlord's daughter and I were wearing bathing suits—in my case a bikini. He said, "You have no shame" (*ma kathashmu shi*). He said it was shameful for a Muslim woman to bare her body. I told him that he was an imbecile and that the world had changed. Malika and her friend were terrified and did not say a word. They were used to obeying anyone connected with the government. And they were even more scared when the lifeguard called a policeman, who also told us that Malika could not stay because she was dressed. Finally, I stopped arguing, because when Rhimu had argued with the policeman who wouldn't let my mother on the beach in a *jillaba*, he took her to the *kumisaria* (police station). So we picked up our things and walked off the beach. And I drove them back to Sabila aj-Jmaa (the village fountain). And I swore I would never take any of my relatives to the beach of Tangier again.

In those days, my husband and I would take our children and drive to beaches outside the city, usually the beach of Sidi Qanqush or the beach near the cave of Hercules, where there are mostly European tourists and westernized Moroccans. There you can wear a bikini without being bothered by anyone. I also love the big, beautiful beach north of Arzila. There are hardly any people there and the waves are huge. And you can swim naked if you want! Every time I think of that damn lifeguard telling us to leave the beach of Tangier, I become angry. But I don't really blame him, because most Moroccans think the same way he does.

Men have landed on the moon. Doctors transplant hearts and lungs from one body to another. Satellites transmit images from one side of the earth to another instantaneously. And yet most Moroccans and most Arabs in general still think that a woman should be covered from the top of her head to the soles of her feet! They think that if she uncovers her body, she will arouse the lust of all the men who see her and will give herself to them all. This conception of the woman as a lust-driven animal that must be kept under lock and key is one of the sickest and most disgusting aspects of Arab culture. More and more young Arabs, men and women, are rejecting this traditional idea. But they are still a tiny minority. God willing, things will change.

V

Hmid,
Son of
Si Abd Allah

(1923–)

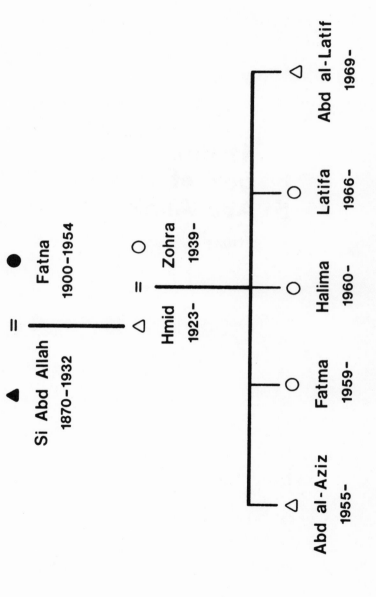

Genealogical Diagram V: Hmid and His Five Children
[Hmid had no children by his first wife.]

1. Al-Hajj Muhammad on his uncle Hmid

MY UNCLE HMID IS A DOUR OLD MAN. He is always complaining about his son Abd al-Aziz because he doesn't work and hardly ever gives him any money. He is always whining about how hard he works and how his bones ache, especially during the winter rains. The good Muslim never complains. Whatever befalls us befalls us because it was God's will that it befall us. We must always trust in God (*ntawakkilu ala Allah*) and submit to His will. Those who complain have been led astray by Satan.

My uncle Hmid criticizes me for joking and singing and teasing the women when the family gets together for an evening (*milli kanqassru*). But I don't do anything wrong. I make everyone happy, while he makes people sad with his whining.

When he was still a young man in the village of the streams, my uncle Hmid married his father's brother's daughter Aysha. He divorced her after two and a half months. Later, he married his present wife Zohra daughter of Si Tuhami F., the sister of the *fqih* of the village of the streams. They have five children: Abd al-Aziz, born in about 1955; Fatma, born in about 1959; Halima, born in about 1960; Latifa, born in about 1966, and Abd al-Latif, born in about 1969. May God bless them.

My uncle Hmid used to plow the valley land of his father, Si

Abd Allah, along with my uncle Mhammad. But then, in about 1950, he paid a notary to forge a deed saying that the land of the children of Si Abd Allah, may God have mercy upon him, was his alone. He put up this land as collateral to borrow some money from Si Muhammad Qasim. And when he tried to repay him, Si Muhammad Qasim said it was too late. In this way, the children of Si Abd Allah lost their plow land. When he is called before our Lord on the day of reckoning, my uncle Hmid will have to pay for the suffering he has caused his brothers and sisters. In fact, God has already punished him in this world—in part. When he complains about how hard he works making tiles while his son spends his time sitting in cafés doing nothing, I think to myself that he deserves much worse than this. It is true that he is old and he collapses on his bed when he comes home from work. But he does not think of all the pain he has caused his brothers and sisters by allowing Si Muhammad Qasim to take their valley land!

After Si Muhammad Qasim stole the land, my uncle Hmid depended upon charcoal to feed his wife and children. He lived in Si Abd Allah's old house, which we call Grandmother's house (*dar d al-aziza*). And he grew a little mint and he had some goats. But mostly he made charcoal. Then, in 1968, he was caught by the forest ranger (*al-wardiyya*) for the second or third time. The fine was too much for him and he brought his family down to Tangier, where he started to work with a shovel and a pick.

My aunt Khadduj let him and his family live in a tin shack (*barraka*) she owned near her house by the stream of the Jews in the cobblestone quarter. She let him live there without paying any rent. But after about a year she decided to sell her house to a grocer from Ahl Srif. My uncle demanded "his share" (*haqqu*) of the money the Srifi paid for the house and the land and the two *barrakas* on it! "We invited him to spend the night and he became one of the owners of the house!" (*Aradnah ibat wa rja min mwalin ad-dar!*). Instead of thanking his sister for her generosity, he tried to cheat her out of her money, just as he cheated all his brothers and sisters out of their land many years before. Everyone shall be hung by his leg (*Kull wahid ghadi ikun mallaq min rijlu*).

After my aunt Khadduj sold her house and the land and the two *barrakas* by the stream of the Jews, my uncle Hmid took his family back up to the village of the streams. He wasn't going to stay in the city if he had to pay rent. And he was very angry because my aunt Khadduj refused to give him a single peseta of the money the Srifi paid her.

So he returned to Grandmother's house and he started making charcoal again. But he was very poor and life in the hills was too hard for him, so he came back down to Tangier after a year or two. He rented a little apartment in the quarter of the lemon tree for 6,500 francs ($14.44) a month. And he went back to work as a laborer. But after a while, he decided that life in the city was too hard, and he returned to the village of the streams once again.

He went back to making charcoal. And the forest ranger caught him and fined him once again. He was back down in the city in less than a year. Now he lives here in the city, in the quarter of the lemon tree, and he works for wages for the tilemaker on the Road of the Mountain in the cobblestone quarter. He makes 1,000 francs ($2.22) a day or about 26,000 ($57.78) a month. He pays 8,000 francs ($17.78) a month for rent. His daughters Fatma and Halima work in a lingerie factory (*mamal nilun*) and they give him most of what they earn. But Abd al-Aziz, who is a strong young man, never gives him money. My Lord has punished him (*Rabbi khalsu*). Sometimes when I see him struggling to push a big heavy wheelbarrow full of sand on the Road of the Mountain, I feel sorry for him. Then I remember all the evil that he has done and I wish there were even more sand in the wheelbarrow.

2. *Fatima Zohra on her uncle Hmid*

LIKE ALL OLD MOROCCAN MEN, my uncle Hmid is always talking about how Muslims must pray the five daily prayers (dawn, noon, mid-afternoon, sunset, and evening) at their proper times. And he is always talking about the day of reckoning and the hereafter. But even though he prays every prayer at its time, he does bad things sometimes. He caused my mother and all her brothers and sisters to lose their land in the valley. And after my mother let him live rent-free in a shack she owned, he demanded a share of the money she received when she sold this shack along with another one and the house and land she used to own by the stream of the Jews! Everyone is always cheating everybody in Morocco. Brothers even cheat brothers. This is terrible.

When we were in Morocco in 1977, my mother sold my uncle Hmid a bed for three thousand francs ($6.67). He paid her a thousand francs as deposit and said he would pay the rest in instalments, a thousand francs a month. But one month passed. Then two months. Then three months. And he paid nothing, although he had the bed in his house and was sleeping on it. So my mother spoke to him and asked where were the two thousand francs. Then he started saying how poor he was and how my mother was rich with two daughters married to men with automobiles. And he said my mother should be generous to her poor brother. And so on. My mother realized that he had never intended to pay more than a thousand francs ($2.22) for the bed. So she called him a liar. And she asked my husband to go get the bed and bring it back to our apartment on top of our car. And he did. My uncle Hmid complained to everyone in the family that my mother had the heart of a Christian. But he was really mad because she had not let him cheat her.

3. Al-Hajj Muhammad on his cousin Abd al-Aziz, son of Hmid (1955–), housepainter in Tangier

ABD AL-AZIZ WAS ABOUT twenty-two years old in 1977. He is tall and handsome with black hair and a black mustache. He could be a movie star. But he is lazy. He is a house painter. But he does not work very often. I have painted a few houses with him and he is a fairly good worker once he is working. But trying to get him to work is hard. He never studied the Quran and he never went to school.

He used to have a motorcycle. He would spend most of his time riding that machine all over the city. But he didn't have enough money for gas and insurance and he sold it to Mshish, my sister Fatima's husband. He spends a lot of money on flashy clothes and cigarettes and *kif*. I see him sometimes on the *bulivar* strolling with a friend, trying to look like a rich man. He stays out late at night at cafés with his friends, and he sleeps late in the morning, long after his old father starts working for the tilemaker. His father starts work at eight-thirty in the morning, but Abd al-Aziz is sometimes still asleep when the noon prayer is called! His father insults him because he is so lazy and never gives him money, and also because he never prays. But his mother always defends him. She says that he looks for work but there is no work to be had. That is what Abd al-Aziz says too. And it is true that it is hard to find work. But it is not impossible. Every time a house is built, someone has to paint it. Of course, there are many house painters because any idiot can paint. Abd al-Aziz did have a steady job working for a contractor in September 1977, and he was earning 1,500 francs ($3.33) a day, which is good money. But he kept coming to work late, so the boss fired him even though they were friends.

Abd al-Aziz, like most men in Morocco, has always dreamed of working in Europe. Everybody thinks that if he goes to Belgium or Germany he will come back rich like my brother Ahmad. But look at me. I spent years in Belgium and I have nothing. Everything is in the hands of God. Anyway, Abd al-Aziz even married my sister Habiba so that she could get him a passport and papers to work in Belgium. But it was just a temporary marriage for a few days. He didn't touch her. It was just for the papers. It is hard to get a passport in Morocco, very hard. But after many years of waiting, he finally received a passport in May 1977. Soon after that he went to look for work in Spain, but he came back broke after a few weeks. Then, in 1978, he went to work in Belgium, without papers. Who knows? Maybe someday he will be as rich as Ahmad, God willing. But I don't think so. He does not work the way Ahmad works. And he does not save his money the way Ahmad does.

4. Al-Hajj Muhammad on his cousins Fatma and Halima, daughters of Hmid (1959– and 1960–), seamstresses in a lingerie factory in Tangier

MY COUSINS FATMA AND HALIMA are both beautiful girls, especially Halima. Her skin is creamy and soft and her face is so pretty that I try not to look at it too much. Because once I start looking at her, I cannot stop. Oh, what a lovely girl! May God bless her! Fatma is pretty too and has a wonderful firm young body. But she is not as soft as Halima. Fatma has been working for many years at a lingerie factory (*mamal nilun*), but Halima only started working there a few years ago, when she was fourteen or fifteen. And when girls work in such places, they lose their softness and their innocence. They become tough. They talk like women of the street! No father should send his daughter to work in such a place! They are usually crowded rooms with about twenty or so girls and a boss who is a man, usually a Rifi! They work all together like that ten hours a day, from eight in the morning until one in the afternoon, and then from two in the afternoon until seven at night! The only day they don't work is Sunday. Why Sunday? Because it is the Christian day of rest. Even though we are Muslims who pray on Friday, Sunday is still the day of rest because the Christians still control Morocco!

Anyway, imagine one man, or sometimes two, spending ten hours a day, six days a week, in a crowded little shop with twenty beautiful young girls. And he is the boss. He pays them for their work. Without his money, they earn nothing. And often their families depend upon what these girls earn to live. My uncle Hmid could not feed his family if Fatma and Halima did not bring home money. Fatma makes about 19,000 francs ($42.22) a month. And Halima makes about 15,000 ($33.33) a month. But I think they tell their father they earn less so they can keep some of the money for themselves.

What would any man do in a little shop with twenty or thirty beautiful girls sewing bras and panties? How can any of these girls say no? If they refuse to lie with their boss, they lose their jobs and their father will beat them because he needs their money. Men with daughters sewing in such lingerie factories say that nothing happens and that the bosses respect the girls who work for them. They never touch them! Who would believe such nonsense? I say that the man who lets his daughter work in a lingerie factory has no self-respect. He is not a Muslim. He might as well send her to work as a whore in a bar!

My uncle Hmid is always talking about being a good Muslim. He criticizes me for laughing and joking. He cannot read one word of the holy book, which I know most of by heart! And yet he thinks he can preach to me about Islam. And what right has he to speak of being a good Muslim—a man who sends his beautiful young daughters to work for strange men far from their families? Who knows what Fatma and Halima do at work with their Rifi boss? Young girls are full of desire. When you let them work for strange men like that, you are selling their virginity! My uncle Hmid is without shame (*ma kayhishim shi*). He is without shame.

5. Fatima Zohra on her cousins Fatma and Halima

MY UNCLE HMID used to tell my mother that she shouldn't let my sisters and me wear Christian dresses and skirts and blouses. He would say that it was forbidden (*hram*) for a Muslim girl to bare her arms, her legs, and her hair like Christian women. But now his daughters Fatma and Halima often wear Western clothes at work. I have seen them wearing tight blue jeans and blouses in downtown Tangier. But they put on their *jillabas* when they return to their house in the quarter of the lemon tree.

Many young girls have to work in Morocco. Little girls only six or seven years old often work in the rug factories (*maamil az-zrabi*). Salesmen in the bazaars tell tourists from Europe and America that the rugs in the bazaar were made by peasants in some beautiful mountain village. But really most Moroccan rugs are made in sweatshops near the shantytowns (*bidonvilles*) of Moroccan cities. People build rug factories near the shantytowns because they know that the families there are poor and need the 350 francs ($.78) a day that their little daughters can earn weaving rugs.

And there are many girls like Fatma and Halima in the lingerie factories, too. People are ashamed to send their daughters to work in such a place. But many parents have no choice. Some people say that such girls are forced to lie with the men they work for. Other people say that the bosses do not touch the girls because they are afraid their parents will call the police. God knows best. But it is very sad that so many young Moroccan girls have to spend their youth weaving rugs or sewing clothes in dimly lit sweatshops instead of going to school.

6. *Fatima Zohra on her cousins Latifa and Abd al-Latif, daughter and son of Hmid (1966– and 1969–), elementary school students*

MY LITTLE COUSIN LATIFA was in the fourth year of elementary school at "the school of the stream" (*madrasa d al-wad*) when I last saw her in 1977. She is a sweet little girl. She is very smart and does very well in school, but by now my uncle Hmid has probably put her to work as an apprentice (*mitallma*) in a rug or lingerie factory. And she is a sickly little girl. She cannot stand long hours of work. May God preserve her.

Latifa's younger brother, Abd al-Latif, was in the second year of elementary school in 1977. He is a wonderful little boy, very sweet and very shy. I remember sometimes when we would drive to their house in Ayn al-Hayyani, he would chase away the children who would gather to stare at us and our car. And sometimes he would come to our house and draw with my children. He is a very sweet little boy.

VI

Mhammad,
Son of
Si Abd Allah

(1925–)

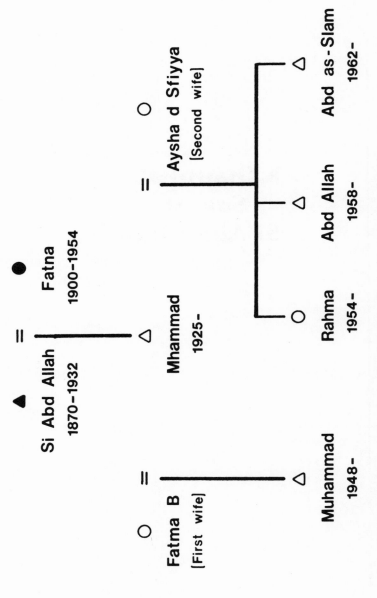

Genealogical Diagram VI: Mhammad and His Four Children

1. Al-Hajj Muhammad on his uncle Mhammad

MY UNCLE MHAMMAD was very strong when he was young. Everyone was afraid of him. But now he is growing old and weak. And ever since he was a young man he has been eaten by envy and hatred for Si Muhammad Qasim, who is rich while he is poor. He loves to talk about the night he broke Si Muhammad Qasim's right arm. That was the only time he ever beat him at anything. Si Muhammad Qasim always wins and he always loses. He lives only about ten meters from Si Muhammad Qasim and my aunt Amina, but they hardly ever see each other except at the mosque. When my uncle goes to sleep at night, I am sure he always dreams about beating Si Muhammad Qasim.

My uncle Mhammad always condemns Si Muhammad Qasim for being a miser and a cheat. But he is no better. A few years ago, I bought a goat (*jdi*) for my daughter and I left it with my uncle in the village. And he killed it to feed the guests at the wedding of his son Abd as-Slam. It was my goat and he killed it without even asking me. I was very angry and I warned him that I would complain to the *qayyid* and take him to court. So he finally agreed to pay me for my goat—but only because he was afraid.

Moreover, my uncle Mhammad tried to trick his brothers and sisters out of their share of the property of Si Abd Allah, may God have mercy upon him. That is, out of their share of what was left of this property after Si Muhammad Qasim took the best valley land, thanks to my uncle Hmid's forged deed. Even the house my uncle Mhammad lives in is not his alone. It belongs to all the children of Si Abd Allah. And the same is true of Grandmother's house (*dar d al-Aziza*). He was mad when Fatima Zohra and her husband went up to the village and lived in that house for a few months. He had been using it as a stable and intended to have his son Abd as-Slam and his wife live there. But Fatima Zohra's mother, my aunt Khadduj, and my brothers and sisters and I, and all my mother's other brothers and sisters have shares in that house. He has no right to use it only for himself. He thinks because we have all moved to Tangier that he can steal from us. But he is wrong. He should send all of us mint from the mint gardens, and figs, pears, and plums from the orchards. But he is tight, very tight. He is no less a miser than Si Muhammad Qasim. But Si Muhammad Qasim is smarter and luckier. Like Si Muhammad Qasim, he prays every prayer at its time now that he is old. But they will both have much to answer for on the day of reckoning.

My uncle Mhammad was first married to Fatima B., of the B. clan but not a kinswoman. She was from the village of al-Hrisha in Bni Msawwar. They had a son, Muhammad, born in about 1948. Then after a few years, my uncle divorced Fatima and married Aysha d Sfiyya. She is the sister of *at-Talib* Muhammad, whose daughter is married to al-Ayyashi the son of Si Muhammad Qasim. People call her *at-Tirrum*, "the Butt," because her butt is very big. But no one calls her this to her face. She is a short old woman who looks a little like a mushroom. But she is a good woman. She and my uncle have had three children that lived: (1) Rahma, a daughter born in about 1954; (2) Abd Allah, a son born in about 1958; and (3) Abd as-Slam, a son born in about 1962.

Sometimes my uncle Mhammad insults the sons of Si Muhammad Qasim (who are also the sons of his sister Amina) because they never pray. But *his* sons never pray either, except maybe for Abd as-Slam, who is still just a boy.

2. *Fatima Zohra on her cousin Muhammad, son of Mhammad (1948–), housepainter and smuggler in Tangier*

MY COUSIN MUHAMMAD has always been unlucky (*miluq*) just like his father, my uncle Mhammad. He is tall, skinny, and has prickly black hair. We used to call him Broomhead (*ar-ras d ash-shattaba*) because his hair is stiff and sharp like the straw of the head of a broom. He was always afraid. He used to hide whenever there was a fight. He came down to Tangier when he was a little boy. His mother married another man in Tangier and this new husband didn't want him. And my uncle's new wife at-Tirrum didn't want him because he was not her son. So he stayed with us at our house by the stream of the Jews (*Wad al-Ihud*) in the cobblestone quarter. He would go to see his mother in the Msalla quarter sometimes, but only for short visits of half an hour or so. So my mother was like his mother for a few years. During Ramadan, when my mother would bake the pan bread (*khubz d al-maqla*) of Ramadan, he would help Sidi al-Mahdi al-Baqqali sell it in the city. And when it was not Ramadan, she would bake *al-ghayf* cakes, which are like pancakes. Muhammad would help Sidi al-Mahdi sell the *ghayf* too. People say that both Sidi al-Mahdi and Muhammad are kind of stupid, like idiots (*bu-hala*). Such people are said to be blessed by God. But Muhammad is not really an idiot. He is just afraid.

Even my uncle Mhammad says that Muhammad is simple-minded. And he makes fun of him, as do most people. That is terrible. A father should protect his children, not insult them. If my uncle had been a good father to Muhammad perhaps he would have been stronger and smarter. The only people in the family who ever treated Muhammad with kindness and respect were my mother and my cousin Ahmad. People say that Ahmad is a miser, but he is good in many ways. He always tries to help Muhammad, as does my mother.

As he grew older, Muhammad started painting houses for people. This is a simple job anyone can do. And he saved some money and bought an old decrepit Volkswagen minibus. People couldn't believe it when they saw him driving because they think he is an idiot and they think driving is a very difficult thing to do. Anyway, he started smuggling watches, radios, blankets, and many other things from Sibta (Ceuta), the Spanish duty-free port about seventy kilometers northeast of Tangier. Many people make a living smuggling from Sibta, just as they used to make a living smuggling from Tangier when it used to be a duty-free port. Muhammad made a lot of money this way, and he saved enough to get married.

Muhammad married a beautiful black woman named Najjat. People in northern Morocco are usually quite light-skinned and they make fun of black people (al-azziyyus). And many people in the family made fun of Muhammad because he married a black woman. But they are stupid. She is a beautiful woman. If she were in Europe or the States, she could be a fashion model. And she earns about 20,000 francs ($44.44) a month sewing clothes for women in her own home. They have one child. She and Muhammad argue sometimes. And he beats her. He is crazy to mistreat such a wonderful woman. And in 1977, he was arrested for smuggling and his minibus was impounded. Then he had to depend on the money she made as a seamstress. He is lucky to have such a wife who is both beautiful and who brings in money every month. But men are stupid sometimes. And he even forced her to leave their house for a while. But then they were reconciled and now they are back together again. I feel sorry for Muhammad because he grew up feeling that his parents didn't want him. But he should treat Najjat better than he does.

3. Fatima Zohra on her cousin Rahma, daughter of Mhammad (1954–), wife of a factory worker in Tangier

Y COUSIN RAHMA is said to have gone with many young men in the village of the streams and the nearby villages too. In 1975, when she was about twenty or maybe a little younger, my uncle discovered that she was pregnant. The father could have been any of a dozen or so young men, according to village gossip. But it was decided that a young man from a nearby village was the father, and they were hurriedly married. The baby was born the day of the wedding. My mother says that you could hear the baby crying from inside my uncle's house on the night that the groom was supposed to enter the bride for the first time. Rahma refused to give her breast to the baby, perhaps at my uncle's command, and the baby starved to death within days.

Rahma and her husband moved down to Tangier a few days later. They live near the Qasba. The women in the family insult her when she is not there, but she comes to the celebrations of births, circumcisions, and weddings in the family and she is welcome in all the houses of the family. The women know that she is not the only woman in the family to have been with men before being married. She is just one of the unfortunate ones to have conceived a child out of wedlock.

If you ask many of the men in the family about birth control, they will tell you that it is murder and contrary to Islamic law. But if you ask what they think of killing a baby because it was conceived out of wedlock, most of them will say that this is God's will.

4. Fatima Zohra on her cousin Abd Allah,
son of Mhammad (1958–), housepainter in Tangier

ABD ALLAH RAN AWAY from home when he was still a young boy. He left the village of the streams and came down to Tangier. He would stay with relatives and he would beg and steal from Christian tourists. Sometimes he would sleep in the street, on pieces of carton in dimly lit alleys where few people walked. He was always close to his half-brother Muhammad. And as he grew older, he started painting houses with him. Then, in 1976, he got a steady job as the painter and repair man at a little one-star hotel near the beach of Tangier. Over eighty years ago, it was one of the best hotels in Tangier, I think, but now it is mostly for Europeans without much money. Anyway, Abd Allah was earning 52,000 francs ($115.56) a month there, which is more than most of the men in the family make. The Spanish owner of the hotel (almost all hotels in Tangier are owned by Christians) liked him. So Abd Allah was no longer a street urchin. He was one of the most successful men of the family.

In August of 1976, Abd Allah was married to Latifa G., the daughter of a peasant from the village of the spring of as-Snad who rented *hbus* valley land with my uncle Mhammad. It was at this wedding that al-Hajj Muhammad got into a fight with the sons of Si Muhammad Qasim because they wouldn't lend him a mule to join the men who went to fetch the bride from her village.

But after six or seven months, Abd Allah grew tired of his bride. He is smart and he grew up mostly in the streets of Tangier. His bride was a rather simple Jibliyya who was not very pretty. And he became infatuated with a pretty cousin of his in Tangier, the daughter of his mother's brother. This girl was not only very pretty, she also earned over 16,000 francs ($35.56) a month as a seamstress in a lingerie factory. Abd Allah would walk her home from the factory. And this was a great scandal. It would have been scandalous even if he hadn't been married, but it was doubly scandalous because he was. He divorced his wife in order to marry his pretty cousin, but his uncle (his mother's brother) refused to let him marry her because he was mad at Abd Allah for walking his daughter home and thus ruining her reputation. And the pretty cousin married another man. And Abd Allah married another homely Jibliyya in August 1977. And about this time, he lost his job at the Spanish hotel. "God punished him" (*Rabbi khalsu*) said the old women in the family. They could have forgiven him for sleeping with his pretty cousin in secrecy, but walking her home in public was unforgivable.

5. *Fatima Zohra on her cousin Abd as-Slam, son of Mhammad (1962–), goatherd in the village of the streams*

MY COUSIN ABD AS-SLAM is still a boy. He still grazes my uncle's goats. And this is the work of a boy not a man. Nonetheless, Abd as-Slam is married. He married Ftuma, daughter of his mother's sister, in March 1977. Many people joked about this wedding for two reasons. For one thing, weddings usually take place in August, after the winter wheat and barley have been harvested and when Ahmad and Habiba are home from Belgium. Relatives who work in Europe are relatively rich and are expected to give a lot of money at weddings. And their presence makes the wedding seem more important. Also, there is no rain in August and that is important because many of the wedding activities take place outdoors. No one marries his children in March, unless there is an urgent need to do so when the girl is pregnant, because this is the end of the rainy season. Rain could fall and ruin the wedding. So everyone assumed that Abd as-Slam and Ftuma were married in March because Ftuma was with child. The other reason everyone joked about this wedding was that Abd as-Slam was still just a boy tending his father's goats. Once again, it was assumed that Ftuma had to find a husband fast. All the old women of the family wondered if young Abd as-Slam were really the father of the unborn child. God knows best. The child was born the following October.

For the first few months they were married, Abd as-Slam and Ftuma lived in my uncle Mhammad's house. Then they moved into the old house of Si Abd Allah, which we call Grandmother's house. Before they moved out of my uncle's house, which is just a few meters away, my uncle and his wife, "the Butt" (*at-Tirrum*) had a terrible argument. My uncle, who had once beaten Si Muhammad Qasim for beating my aunt Amina, now beat his own wife. Some say he was mad at her for giving too much mint and butter to their daughter Rahma, who had come up to the village for a week. But most people say that my uncle had been forcing his son's young wife Ftuma to have sex with him, and his wife caught him and started screaming. So he beat her. She went to the house of her brother *at-Talib* Muhammad, who took her to the *qayyid* at the Tuesday market of Jbil Hbib. The *qayyid* made my uncle go to the Tuesday market. But he only scolded him and told him not to beat his wife again. Two days later, his wife came back home. A few days later Abd as-Slam and his young bride moved to Grandmother's house.

I think my uncle did force Abd as-Slam's young bride to lie with him. I have heard rumors that he used to do the same thing with the wives of his other sons. This is a terrible thing.

When you talk with my uncle, he seems like the perfect Muslim. He speaks only of God and the day of reckoning. He never tires of condemning the young people in Tangier "who have become Christians." I know he condemns my sisters and me for being like Christians. Sometimes when he talks, he sounds almost like a saint. But when you learn about all that he has done, you realize that he has done much evil. This is also true of Si Muhammad Qasim, who also looks and sounds like a saint unless you know the story of his life. In fact, this is probably true of most old men in Morocco. Their words of piety hide a lifetime of cheating, stealing, and abusing women. There are some old men whose lives have been as good as their words. But they are rare.

There is a great difference between what people say and what people do in Morocco. This is true everywhere. But sometimes I cannot believe how true it is in Morocco.

VII

Al-Hajja Khadduj, Daughter of Si Abd Allah

(1926–)

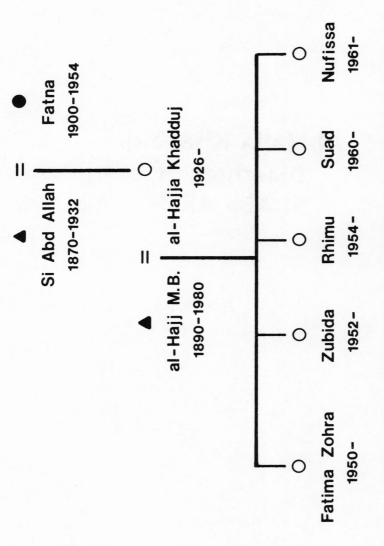

Genealogical Diagram VII: Al-Hajja Khadduj and Her Five Children

1. Al-Hajj Muhammad on his aunt al-Hajja Khadduj and her husband, al-Hajj M.B. (1890–1980)

Y AUNT KHADDUJ is the youngest child of Si Abd Allah. When my brothers and sisters and I were young, she used to take care of us for my mother (Shama). She has always been like a second mother to me and I would do anything for her. She is getting old now and she does not always know what she is saying. But she is good, very good. May God grant her a long life.

When my aunt Khadduj was still a young girl, my mother arranged for her to marry al-Hajj M.B., who was over fifty years old at that time. This was during the war of the Christians (WW II). My aunt Khadduj hid in a tree on the day of the wedding in the village of the streams because she didn't want to marry al-Hajj. And she never forgave my mother, may God have mercy upon her, for making her marry him.

Al-Hajj M.B. was born in Marrakesh. His parents sent him to memorize the holy Quran in a mountain village when he was a boy. He came to Tangier as a young man before the Christians occupied Morocco in 1912. He sold souvenirs to the Christian tourists. When he grew older, he owned several bazaars of his own in the old city. Oh, he was rich in those days! Even today there are old men in the cobblestone quarter and in the old city who remember when al-Hajj M.B. was one of the richest merchants in Tangier. But he had a partner who cheated him out of his share of the biggest bazaar, and after that he had many problems, although he had some other stores and good jobs even after that. He also used to work as a cook on a ship that took pilgrims to the east (Mecca). He made the pilgrimage eleven times this way. And each time he would buy goods in the east and sell them for great profit here in Tangier.

At the time he married my aunt Khadduj, al-Hajj M.B. had a general store at the Monday market of Bni Harshan in Bni Msaw-war. The store still stands even though it is not his any more. He would bring his merchandise to this store by mule from Tetuan and sometimes from Tangier. Now trucks go to this market, but only in the summer, because the dirt road is just a muddy stream during the winter rains.

Then, not long after he married my aunt Khadduj, al-Hajj M.B. moved back to Tangier. For a while, they lived in the Bni Yidir quarter in the old city, then they moved to Sabila aj-Jmaa (the Village Fountain), and then later they moved to the house by the stream of the Jews in the cobblestone quarter. He had a tobacco stand (*stanku*) in the Inner Market (*as-Suq ad-Dakhil*) for a few years. Later he worked as a watchman on a boat in the harbor of Tangier. Then he was in charge of loading and unloading cargo at one of the piers in the harbor. He was once again very rich at this time. Then he worked in the Dar al-Barud hospital in the old city. He was in charge of buying the food for the hospital's kitchen. Later he was transferred to al-Qurtubi hospital in the Marshan quarter, where he did the same kind of work. Then after some years, his boss decided that he was getting too old for this job, and he was made a watchman and an orderly at the hospital. But even then he was making about 50,000 francs ($111) a month, which was more than anyone else in the family was making in those days—except for the *qadi* Muhammad B., of course. But after some years, the boss said that he was too old and had to stop working. He had worked in the two hospitals for about fifteen years altogether, and all those years

232

money had been taken out of his salary each month for his old age pension (*as-sunduq*). But when he tried to get his pension, they told him that officially he had never been a permanent employee. So they wouldn't give him one franc. He went to many government offices in Tangier and Rabat. But no one would help him. When he was rich, he had many important friends. But now that he was old and poor, he no longer had any friends. So my aunt Khadduj was stuck with five daughters and an old husband who could not work! Verily, God is with those who patiently endure (*Inna Allaha maa as-sabirin*).

My aunt started baking bread and *al-ghayf* pancakes to earn some money. Sidi al-Mahdi al-Baqqali, La Ftuma, and my cousin Muhammad worked for her in those days. And she bought the house by the stream of the Jews from an Italian barber. In those days before independence there were Christians and Jews in the cobblestone quarter. But now the cobblestone quarter is a clean neighborhood: there are no Christians or Jews in it (*ma fiha shi la Nsara wa la Ihud*). It was a nice house with a little garden and a little wooden shack and a *barraka* next to it. My uncle Hmid lived in the *barraka* and al-Ghmariyya lived in the wooden shack.

Later, my aunt moved to a Christian building near the *bulivar*. Most of the people in her building used to be Christians and Jews, but since independence more and more Muslims have started living there. It is a big building with six floors and an elevator. Until 1976, she paid 10,000 francs ($22.22) a month in rent. Since 1976, she has paid 20,000 francs a month. She is the only one in the family who has ever lived in such a building with an elevator, except for Fatima Zohra of course.

Many people in the family say that my aunt has become like a Christian since she moved to that building. And her daughters are all more like Christian girls than Muslim girls. After she went to America, my aunt even stopped wearing the veil. But even though she is a little strange, she is a good Muslim. She went with me on the pilgrimage to Mecca. She is like my own mother. May God grant her a long life.

2. *Fatima Zohra on her mother, al-Hajja Khadduj*

M Y MOTHER HAS HAD A HARD LIFE. She was married to my father when she was still a young girl and he was already an old man. He was my aunt Shama's lover. And it was my aunt Shama who forced my mother to marry him. My mother often says that God will make my aunt pay for this on the day when all the dead will arise to be judged (*yawm al-qiyama*).

When we lived in the old city of Tangier, my father used to lock the door so that my mother could not leave. My mother hated this because she was used to being free and playing in the fields and woods in the village of the streams. She was not used to the life of a city-woman locked up in her own home. So she was very sad. Then one day she was talking with a Jewish lady who lived next door. They would talk to each other from windows in their houses. And she complained to the Jewish lady about the way my father locked her up at home. The Jewish lady told her that *she* would see to it that my father stopped locking the door if my mother would just hide that night when he came home. So that night, when she heard his key in the lock, my mother hid under a *jillaba* lying in a corner. My father entered the house and started talking to my mother as usual even though he did not see her. He thought she was in the kitchen. So he started telling her everything that had happened at the bazaar during the day. In those days, he still owned one of the biggest bazaars in Tangier with a Fassi partner who later cheated him out of his share. And he described the Christians who had bought rugs and furniture. And he talked and talked until finally he noticed that my mother had not said anything. He looked everywhere and could not find her. And he kept calling, "Khadduj! Khadduj!" but my mother, who was still a young girl, just remained hidden under the *jillaba* and didn't say anything. By now my father was extremely upset. Then he called to the Jewish lady and asked her if she had seen my mother. The Jewish lady said she hadn't seen her but that maybe the rakish young men who had an apartment across the street had managed to get into the house and taken her away with them for an orgy. When my father heard her say this, he was almost out of his mind. Then my mother stepped out from under the *jillaba* in the corner and my father saw her. "You have killed me!" (*qtiltini*), he moaned, and he fell to the floor exhausted. He was very, very happy to see her. And he promised that he would never lock my mother in the house again. But after my older sister Zohra, may God have mercy upon her, was born, my father did start locking my mother in the house again. Like many Moroccan women even today, my mother spent much of her life locked up in her own home.

My father always treated my mother as a child, which she was when she married him. Then when he grew old and his mind and body became weak, she began treating *him* like a child. She would often complain to us about him before he died, may God have mercy upon him (*Allah irahmu*). She tried to leave him once when she was still young, but he sent *tulba* and sacrificed a calf in front of the house she was in so as to compel her to return to him by the *ar*. The idea of the *ar* is that when someone sacrifices a calf and sends *tulba* to plead with you to do something, if you don't do what is asked of you, the person whose request you refuse will bring down a terrible curse upon you. And it is said that the curse of the husband is as strong as that of the parents. So my mother was afraid of my father's curse and she returned to him.

Later, when my father was very old and poor and like a little child that needs its mother, she wanted to divorce him again. But I told her that that would be shameful. I don't blame her for resenting him. What young girl would want to spend her life with an old man who locks her up every day, turning her home into a prison? And this is what marriage is for many Moroccan women even today. And my mother was right to condemn my father for wasting his money. Once he was one of the richest merchants in Tangier, but he was penniless when he was old.

In Morocco, it is considered very important to own your own home. And my mother is ashamed that she still lives in a rented apartment. She often condemns my father for selling a wonderful piece of land he used to own in the Marshan quarter overlooking the Straits of Gibraltar. He sold this land for two million francs ($4,444), and he spent most of the money to make his twelfth pilgrimage to Mecca. My mother says that God will not accept this pilgrimage because my father left his wife and children homeless to make it. In 1977, this same piece of land was worth five million francs ($11,111). God knows how much it is worth now.

It is true that my father was wrong not to save his money and think of the future of his wife and children. But it was not all his fault. His partner in the big bazaar cheated him. And later, after he had worked about fifteen years for the hospitals, the government refused to give him his pension. This is justice in Morocco.

My father was good in his heart, may God have mercy upon him. When I was a little girl and he was still rich, he would have my mother bring me down to a café by the beach (*al-playa*) of Tangier. And we would drink café au lait and eat *churros* (fritters). He would smile and watch me eat. I used to love those mornings more than anything else.

And even my mother admits that he was very good to my sister Zohra, who died when she was about four years old. May God have mercy upon her. She was my mother's first child, the first of twelve children, and the first of my seven brothers and sisters who died in the first years of their lives. Only five of us are still alive. Anyway, my sister Zohra had a terrible disease. My father took her to Bennis, the best doctor in Tangier. But he said that there was no way to cure her. And the other doctors he took her to said the same thing. So my father knew from the beginning that she would only live a few years, becoming sicker each year. So he tried to make her as happy as possible in the short time she had in this world. He would take her in a stroller and walk her by the beach. And he bought her beautiful little dresses and toys and chocolates from Spain. And he was very sad when she died. She is buried in the cemetery of Sidi Bu Araqiyya. May God have mercy upon her.

When Tangier was still an International Zone (until 1956) and my father still owned his bazaar, he was rich and very proud. Even for many years after independence in 1956 he remained like the king of our house. My mother's family feared and envied him. In-laws (*an-nsab*) always fight in Morocco, even if they are relatives. And my father would often make fun of my mother's family. He made fun of all *Jbala,* which word means "mountain people," but also means "hillbillies." Like most Moroccans in the cities, he would say that Jbala are stupid. Once he insulted my uncle Hmid in front of other people by saying to him "*Ya Jibli!*"—that is, "Oh, you dumb hillbilly!" My uncle Hmid says he wanted to kill my father that day. But my father did get my uncle Hmid a job in Tangier. Everyone in my mother's family was always asking him for money or for a job. They would smile to his face although they insulted him behind his back.

My mother would often argue with my father because she always wanted to be with her mother. She wanted to bring her mother down from the village of the streams and have her live with them in Tangier. But my father did not like that idea at all. Not at all! I guess that is natural. My husband feels the same way about the idea of my mother living with us, although she once did. That is why parents pray for sons rather than daughters. A son will take care of his parents in their old age. But a daughter cannot force her husband to take care of her parents in their old age. Nonetheless, my mother's mother would come down to Tangier and stay with them for short visits—which my father hated because all my mother's relatives in the city would come to the house to see her mother. "The house stinks of goat shit and charcoal!," my father would say. And my mother's relatives hated him because they knew how he made fun of them. But they would always smile and speak to him like fawning dogs in the hope of squeezing some of his money from him. This is how Moroccans always act with the rich even when they hate them.

But then my father lost all his money. And he grew old and senile. And my mother no longer feared him and would constantly insult him, trying to take revenge for all the years when he had been

237

her master. I don't blame her. But I felt sorry for him. Once he had been powerful and proud, and now he was like an old beggar dependent on his wife and daughters for the food he ate. Once he had terrorized my mother. And now she terrorized him.

During the last years of his life, he spent most of his time in a dingy café overlooking the harbor of Tangier. Every morning my mother would give him a little money to buy a glass of mint tea, a bowl of *baysar* for lunch, and a pack of CASA cigarettes. I would often buy him cigars, which he loved. And he would sit in that café day after day and talk about the old days with other old men. And they would play dominoes for hours on end. Sitting in that café was all that he wanted to do during the last years of his life.

Sometimes my mother would lock him up in the apartment while she went out, just as he used to do to her. He would just sit there chanting the Quran to himself until she returned. Then he would ask her if he could go the café, as a little boy would ask his mother. May God have mercy upon him.

As I said, my mother was always very close to her mother, very close. And she was sick when her mother died. She would speak quickly without knowing what she was saying—just like al-Hajj Muhammad when he is sick. My father was on the pilgrimage to Mecca at this time, and my mother's brothers Hmid and Mhammad took her to the saint Sidi al-Arbi of Arzila. This was the saint she always visited when she was sick. And they had her chained to a tree near the saint's tomb, with an iron collar around her neck. There were many other people chained in the same way to the other trees near the saint's tomb. Most Moroccans believe that when people are sick or crazy they are possessed by the *jnun*. And they believe that the blessedness (*al-baraka*) of a saint can drive away the *jnun*. My father would not have let my uncles take my mother and chain her in this way. He would have taken her to see a doctor. But he was in Mecca and didn't even know that she was sick. And she remained chained like a mad dog for over a month. One day while she was still chained to that tree, she overheard my uncles Hmid and Mhammad talking while they visited her. My uncle Mhammad said that he was ashamed to have a sister possessed by the *jnun* and said that they should kill her. My mother swears that she heard him say this. But my uncle Hmid stopped my uncle Mhammad from killing her. My uncle Mhammad prays every prayer at its time and fasts during the month of Ramadan and pays the tithe on his crops. Yet he has raped his son's wife and tried to kill his sister. Everyone will be hung by his leg.

After about a month, my uncles brought my mother back to Tangier. She was not sick anymore and everyone said that Sidi al-Arbi had driven away the *jnun*. Every year my mother would return to visit Sidi al-Arbi, often several times a year—whenever she felt sick or depressed. And she would always take me with her. Just as Sidi al-Arbi was *her* saint, so I came to feel that he was also *my* saint. All Moroccans, except the rich westernized people, have a saint that they feel they belong to. People visit many different saints for many different things—some saints are famous for making sterile women fertile, such as Sidi Hbib. And others have other specialties. But usually there is one saint who is believed to have cured you or a relative of some sickness, and you always feel close to this saint. I always felt close to Sidi al-Arbi, as my mother did because she believed that he had driven away the *jnun* that possessed her after her mother died.

I was always terrified of all the crazy people chained to the trees by Sidi al-Arbi's tomb. They were all like mad dogs, with their eyes wide open staring at me as if they hated me because I was sane. The *muqaddim* (guardian) would flog them with bamboo canes. So although they all screamed when the *muqaddim* was not there, they would be absolutely silent when the *muqaddim* came. And they remained chained to those trees with iron collars around their necks all night and all day, and all year long, during the winter rains as well as the summer heat. Their clothes were ragged and dirty and they were all filthy and they stank of the feces that accumulated at their feet.

There was a young girl there, chained and filthy like the others. She would howl like a jackal. Her mother lived there and took care of her. The mother was poor and lived by begging from the people who visited the saint. She had no relatives. Every time my mother and I visited the saint, we would see her and give her a gift—sugar, tea, shoes, or clothes. She was always happy to see my mother, with whom she had become friends while my mother was chained like the others. And she was happy to see that Sidi al-Arbi had cured my mother. This gave her hope that he would also cure her daughter. But the years passed and her daughter remained like a wild animal. Some years ago, the king, Hasan II, made it illegal to chain crazy people near saints' tombs. And he said that such people had to be cared for in asylums. This is one of the few good things he has done. The insane asylums in Morocco are perhaps terrible places—I don't know—but at least the people in them are protected from the rain and the cold. However, this girl has remained at the tomb of Sidi al-Arbi, but in a room instead of chained to a tree. And her mother has remained with her, taking care of her for over twenty years. When I returned to Morocco in 1976, after many years in the States, I visited Sidi al-Arbi again with my mother for the first time since I was a young girl. And the old woman was still there caring for her daughter. But now she was blind. I shivered when I saw the emptiness of her eyes. But she was still the same sweet old woman. She was very happy to see me, that is, to touch me and talk with me, after all those years. And she was not at all bitter. She cited the Quranic verse: "Say nothing shall afflict us but what God has decreed for us" (*Qul lan yusibana illa ma kataba Allahu lana*; IX: 51). I was deeply moved by this beautiful old woman. And I thought to myself that if she did not have her faith in God and her hope that someday she and her daughter would be in heaven for all eternity, she probably would have gone mad herself many years ago.

Many young Moroccans dismiss religion as "the opium of the masses." In some ways they are right. But I think people need religion just as they need an anesthetic when a doctor cuts them open and removes something from their body.

Despite the terror I always felt because of the chained people nearby, I always felt cleansed and calm after I visited the tomb of Sidi al-Arbi in Arzila as a young girl. In some ways, I feel the same way after a sauna bath in the States. Maybe visiting a saint is like visiting a psychiatrist who just sits in a chair while you talk. Just as rich Americans tell their deepest secrets to their psychiatrist, so poor Moroccans tell their deepest secrets to their saint. Who knows if either the psychiatrists or the saints are really listening? It doesn't really matter, because just telling such secrets makes people feel better.

Saints' tombs are very beautiful. You kiss the pillars at the four corners of the sepulchre (*darbuz*) and you light a candle and place it next to the many candles flickering in a dark space in the wall above the tomb. And all around you old women whisper to the saint, pleading with him to intercede on their behalf before God. And pleading with him to heal their pains and the pains of the people they love. Perhaps the *ulama'* (religious scholars) are right to say that this is *shirk*—that is, the attribution of God's attributes to his creatures. But I don't know how many Moroccan women could bear their lives if they could not light candles for their saints.

3. *Fatima Zohra on herself (1950–)*

1 WAS BORN IN A BEAUTIFUL HOUSE near the mosque of the cobblestone quarter on the Road of the Mountain (*at-triq d aj-Jbil*). This is the main street in the cobblestone quarter. There is only one other street in the whole quarter where you can drive a car. The other streets are just winding cobblestone alleys and stairways. All of the cobblestone quarter is on a slope, so the alleys and stairways are usually quite steep. When I was a little girl, there were very few houses on the Road of the Mountain. Goats and cows grazed in the fields near our house. Now all the fields are covered by houses. Later we moved to another house near the village fountain (*Sabila aj-Jamaa*). And then my mother bought the house by the stream of the Jews, which was also on the Road of the Mountain. It was a wonderful little house built by a Christian. It had a beautiful garden and a little wooden shack and a little tin shack with it. My uncle Hmid lived in the tin shack without paying rent to my mother. And the Ghmariyya and her son and daughter lived in the wooden shack.

Al-Ghmariyya was a very good woman. Her husband was a clerk (*mwaddaf*) who always wore a suit and a tie. I think he worked for the city. For some reason he divorced her. And he never gave her money to raise their son and daughter. It was as though he forgot that he had a son and a daughter. So al-Ghmariyya, who was a beautiful woman with white skin and blonde hair like many people from the Ghmaran hills, began to carry firewood on her back. She would wake up every morning about an hour before the call to the dawn prayer. And she would walk up to the Big Mountain (*Jbil al-Kbir*) past the villas of the Christians and up to the woods near Sidi Amar. And she would cut firewood with a billhook and tie it up and carry it on her back. And she would carry this heavy load of firewood back down the mountain to a public oven (*farran*) in the cobblestone quarter. She also washed clothes for my mother. In this way, she earned enough money to feed her son and daughter.

Al-Ghmariyya sent her son to work as a *tarrah* carrying bread to and from the public oven when he was only about six years old. Then he went to work for a very good *fqih*. He helped the *fqih* make the woolen *jillabas* that men wear. And the *fqih* taught him the Quran and sent him to school and paid for his books. Al-Ghmariyya could not have afforded to do this. And when the son grew up, he became a *mwaddaf* (clerk) at city hall and he bought a house in the quarter of the lemon tree, where al-Ghmariyya lives today. I am happy that after working so hard for so many years she can now rest, thanks to her son.

And al-Ghmariyya's daughter has also been very lucky. When she was still a little girl, al-Ghmariyya sent her to work as a maid for the Guessous family. The Guessous family is a very rich Fassi family. And the son of this Guessous family fell in love with al-Ghmariyya's daughter and married her. And now she lives in a big villa and her husband is very good to her. So people say that God has rewarded al-Ghmariyya for her patient endurance (*as-sbar*) when her children were small and she had no husband.

When I was very young, my father was still rich and he would buy me beautiful dresses from Spain. And we often ate meat. But then he grew poorer and poorer, and my mother had to start baking bread and *al-ghayf* cakes to help support us. Several of my brothers and sisters were born before me. But they died. May God have mercy upon them. So I was the oldest and had to help my mother take care of my sisters: Zubida, who was born in about 1952; Rhimu, who was born in about 1954; Suad, who was born in about 1960; and Nufissa, who was born in 1961. And, as my mother says, my father was becoming like another child to care for.

I was not able to attend school for a long time because my mother needed me to watch my sisters while she made the bread and the *ghayf*. I did attend a *msid* (Quranic school) for a month or so as a little girl. But we were only three girls with about twenty-five boys, and they used to hit us. The *fqih* kept us right in front of him to protect us from the boys, but this meant that we were the first ones he hit when he was angry. My father was very angry one day when he found out that the *fqih* had hit me and he took me out of the *msid*. My father never hit my sisters or me. Never.

Then I attended the school of the stream (*mdrasa d al-wad*) in the cobblestone quarter for a few years before my mother forced me to stay home with my sisters. I loved school and I was sad when I had to stop going.

Those days were hard. We often ate *baysar*, which is what Moroccans eat when they cannot afford anything else. And my mother was often worried about how she was going to be able to feed us even *baysar*. As for me, I was always busy carrying my sisters on my back, feeding them, and washing them. Sometimes when I was in the garden, I would see cars going by. And I would dream that they were going to Casablanca or Rabat, which we all thought were like paradise in those days. And I would dream that someday I would marry a handsome army officer who would take me to live in a beautiful villa like the ones the Christians lived in on the Big Mountain (*Jbil al-Kbir*).

Then as I grew older, my mother started talking about marrying me to a young man. My parents tried to force me to get married when I was about twelve. But I refused. And some years later, I told my father that I wanted to go to work in Belgium, where my cousins al-Hajj Muhammad, Ahmad, and Habiba were. He allowed me to go.

When I arrived in Brussels, I stayed with my cousin Ahmad at first, but his wife Fatma insisted that I leave. So al-Hajj Muhammad, who was also staying with Ahmad, found me a room with a Belgian lady. And I got a job putting clothes on display in a big department store. The Belgian lady started to treat me as if I were her daughter. She was nice but too bossy. I liked to go out with some friends of mine—Italians and Belgians as well as Moroccans. And she didn't like that.

I hate the way the Belgians treat Moroccans—usually. As soon as they know you are Moroccan, they look at you and speak to you as if you were garbage.

And I hated the way Moroccans would speak to Belgians—like fawning slaves. "Oui, Monsieur. Oui, Madame. Oui, Monsieur. Oui, Madame." *They* were always "Monsieur" and "Madame." And we Muslims, we collected their garbage and mopped their floors. And no matter how much they insulted us, we had to smile politely and say, "Oui, Monsieur!" "Oui, Madame!".

But in some ways, I loved Belgium. I loved earning and saving money. I loved going out with my friends—especially to discotheques. I could not have done that in Morocco. And I had some very nice Belgian and Italian friends. Often, I preferred to be with them rather than with other Moroccans, because Moroccans are always trying to use each other or, as we say in Arabic, trying to eat each other. I remember one young Moroccan man who said he wanted to marry me. He was very handsome. And we would go for

244

walks together. But soon he started saying that I should give him the money I was earning each week as a cook in a Danish restaurant, where I worked after leaving the department store. I told him I never wanted to see him again. And even my own relatives in Belgium, except for al-Hajj Muhammad, often tried to use me. But I didn't let them.

Then one day I was talking with my best friend, an Italian girl. And she told me about America. She said it was a wonderful place where everyone could be free—and rich. And when my family came to stay in Belgium for a few months, I told them I wanted to go to the States to study and to work. And my parents said they would let me go with my sister Rhimu. I can't believe they let us go. But I insisted. My mother wanted me to go back to Tangier and get married. But I did not like the idea of a Moroccan husband locking me up at home and treating me like his concubine and cook. I could never live such a life. Never.

So my sister Rhimu and I took a Yugoslavian freighter to New York. I was eighteen and she was fourteen. And it was like a dream for both of us. Once we arrived in New York, we contacted some Americans we knew from Tangier. My sister Rhimu knew many Americans because she had studied at the American School in Tangier. In many ways, she was more American than Moroccan even before she came to the States. Anyway, we met many people and we traveled all over the States with Rhimu's friends. Then we returned to New York and rented an apartment. My parents sent us money, and once it ran out, we started working as waitresses in Greek restaurants and attended classes at night to get our high school diplomas.

Then, in 1971, I met and married my husband. My family came over to the States from Morocco and they lived near us, and even with us for a while. My husband was still a student then, and he taught French part-time at a private school. Later, we moved to another city in the States, and my mother started to make money baby-sitting for graduate students at my husband's university. She took care of many children and earned a great deal of money this way. In those days, my husband got along fairly well with my family. But later, the relations between them became tense, as is usually the case between in-laws.

In 1976 I returned to Tangier with my husband and two children for the first time in many years. And I was very happy to see all my relatives and friends again. The girls I had gone to school with and played with in the cobblestone quarter were now all married too. Sometimes I found it difficult to speak with them. I had changed and my friends had changed.

And by accident I saw an old friend of my mother's who used to live in a house next to ours in the cobblestone quarter. We always knew that this old woman worked as a maid for a Christian in Marshan, where many Christians have beautiful villas overlooking the Straits of Gibraltar. But we had never seen the villa where she worked. And I had not seen her for many years. Then, one day in 1976 or 1977, I went to Madame Porte's *Salon de Thé* in Tangier. This place is a relic of the colonial era when Muslims only entered it as employees and almost never as customers. When Tangier was an International Zone, all of *la ville nouvelle* was a European city which Muslims entered only to serve the Europeans and the Jews who lived there. But now Muslims sit in Madame Porte's *Salon de Thé* and drink tea or coffee and eat pastry and/or ice cream—but only westernized Muslims who can afford it. Many of the customers are still the old Europeans of Tangier who remember with nostalgia "the wonderful days" of the International Zone when Tangier was "their" city. I feel guilty about sitting in such a place. I always think how far it is from the cobblestone quarter and from the millions of Moroccans who could live for a week on what tea and pastry cost there. But I like the tea and I like the pastry. And it is clean and elegant in a way, and quiet. So I go there sometimes. And one day I was there and I noticed the girl selling pastry at a counter. I chose some pastries for my children and asked her to put them in a box. And I looked at her and suddenly knew who she was. She was the granddaughter of my mother's old friend who used to live near us in the cobblestone quarter. The last time I had seen her, I had probably been a young girl carrying one of my sisters on my back and she had been hardly more than a baby. She didn't recognize me at first in my Western clothes. But then she did. And she told me that her grandmother had sold their house in the cobblestone quarter and now lived in the basement of the Christian's villa where she worked as a maid. I wanted to ask her many questions, but she was nervous because her boss, a Frenchwoman, was looking at her. So I told her to give my best to her grandmother and to her parents.

Not long after this, my husband met an Englishman who invited us to dinner at his villa in Marshan. We drove to the villa and my husband knocked on the beautiful door. An old Moroccan woman opened it. My husband told her who we were and she said the Englishman was expecting us. Then as we entered, she stared at me and I stared at her. And she exclaimed in astonishment, "Aren't you the daughter of Khadduj?" And I said yes and she embraced me. Then she remembered my husband and the Englishman and she looked at my European dress. And she was surprised. I felt funny, especially during dinner when she served us as we ate with the Englishman. She was a close friend of my mother's and now she was the servant and I was the guest of her Christian master. I felt quite awkward.

Later, the Englishman showed us his beautiful garden, and from the front terrace of the house we saw the lights of Tarifa in Spain, across the darkness of the Straits of Gibraltar. And we saw the lights of the ships sailing through the Straits. And another time we were there in the daytime, and the garden and the Straits and the Atlantic Ocean to the west were even more beautiful. You hear the wind in the pines and the crashing surf far below the garden. And you think you have entered the gates of paradise.

But whenever we would go to this wonderful villa, I could not help but be angry. It is not right that such beautiful villas and gardens belong to foreigners. The old Englishman is a kind man. And I am sure that many of the other Europeans who own villas are also good people. But it is not right that all that is beautiful in Morocco should be in their hands.

It is, of course, true that Christians do not control Morocco today the way they did before independence. Now we can drink tea and eat pastry in Madame Porte's! And many rich Moroccans have moved into the villas vacated by Europeans after independence. But often these rich Moroccans are really worse than the Europeans. They think only of villas and cars and clothes from Paris. They often speak of "the oppressed masses" and of the injustices of neocolonialism. But this is just cocktail chatter for them. They do not know what it is to be poor in Morocco. And they scorn those who do.

After we returned to the States, I was in an elegant shoe store in Chicago one day hoping to find some shoes on sale. And I heard Moroccan Arabic! I was very happy to hear my language, but when I listened more carefully I knew that it was not really my language. It was a Moroccan woman in a stunning French dress and extraordinarily beautiful jewelry. And the two men with her wore elegantly tailored French suits. They were rich Fassis who sprinkled their Arabic with French. I thought to myself, "What do such people want with someone like me?" I am not from their class. I am not from their Morocco. And I did not speak to them.

4. Fatima Zohra on her sister Zubida (1952–), wife of a television repairman in Tangier

MY SISTER ZUBIDA was always different from my other sisters and me. She was always cruel to people. But this is because she often had bad luck and this made her angry. And her anger would make her mean. She was bitten three times by mad dogs when she was a young girl. And all three dogs died. People say that her *simm* (poison) was stronger than that of the dogs.

Zubida was always a very good student in school. She could have passed the *baccalauréat* exam but she had to leave high school to come to New York with my parents when I was married in 1971. Unlike Rhimu, Nufissa, and me, she did not continue her studies in the States. Shortly after she arrived in New York, she went to work as a salesclerk in a hardware store. Rhimu and I gave most of the money we earned as waitresses to my mother. But Zubida hardly ever gave my mother any money at all. And she and my mother would argue about this. She thought only about using the money to buy clothes and furniture for the apartment she would live in with her fiancé, Abd al-Aziz.

Zubida met Abd al-Aziz one summer in Tangier when they were both working in a television factory. He was as scrawny as a plucked chicken, but he was cute. And he is very funny. He knows almost as many jokes as al-Hajj Muhammad. Anyway, they fell in love and he wanted to marry her. So one day he asked me to meet him at Madame Porte's to talk to me about the marriage. This was after I had returned from Belgium but before I went to the States. He talked to me because my father was too senile to make much sense and he was ashamed to speak to my mother. I was, in a way, in charge of the family. So we talked and I said I would see what I could do. But I was against the marriage. I thought that Zubida needed a strong man who would control her terrible temper. And Abd al-Aziz seemed so skinny and so weak. And so short. Moreover, his mother had a bad reputation. People say that she had spent most of her youth as a prostitute in Spain and that Abd al-Aziz was a bastard whose father could have been any one of a thousand men, Christians as well as Muslims. She was originally from Tetuan. Then, after spending much of her life in Spain, she returned with a Moroccan she met there. And they were married and they opened a butcher shop in Sibta (Ceuta), the Spanish duty-free presidio about seventy kilometers northeast of Tangier. She owns a house in Tangier, and her husband runs the butcher shop in Sibta alone now, visiting her on weekends. She is a tough woman. Perhaps she is a good woman. But she is too tough and too coarse for me. And she controls Abd al-Aziz. And I didn't want Zubida to become part of such a family. But she was determined to marry him and nothing my mother or I could say would change her mind.

When Zubida was in New York, she met a handsome Palestinian named Ishaq. He was crazy about her and was dying to marry her. My mother and I encouraged him because he was a very good man. His family had been forced to leave Palestine after the Israelis occupied the West Bank in 1967. One of his brothers has been in an Israeli jail for over ten years now. But Ishaq and most of his family managed to come to the States. He had been a college student, but he was working full-time in a fruit store on Broadway when we knew him. Later he went back to college. He was quiet and shy except when he talked about what the Israelis have done to Palestine. He was sensible and would have been a wonderful husband for Zubida. But she just used him. She let him buy her gifts and take her to restaurants and movies. But she didn't care about him at all. She was still determined to marry that scrawny plucked chicken in Tangier. But I should not speak badly of Abd al-Aziz because he is really much better than I thought he was then.

In June 1972, my family flew back to Tangier from New York to prepare for Zubida's wedding. I stayed in the States with my husband. And Zubida became Abd al-Aziz's wife. Then, as the months passed, my mother became sick again because she missed me. She began speaking quickly without knowing what she was saying, as she had done after her mother died. My uncle Hmid and my cousin Mustafa tried to take advantage of her sickness. They ransacked her apartment looking for money. And they took whatever they wanted while she looked at them helplessly. My uncle Hmid had stopped my uncle Mhammad from killing my mother when she was sick after their mother died. But now he was stealing from her. And he and Mustafa took her back to Sidi al-Arbi in Arzila. And they wanted to leave her there again, but for some reason they didn't. Thank God. I think al-Hajj Muhammad was still in Belgium at this time, because he would not have let them treat her this way. It is true that al-Hajj Muhammad sometimes tried to cheat her out of her money, but he always protected her as if she were his own mother. In fact, my mother has always been more of a mother to him than his own mother ever was. He adores my mother just as she adores him. And I always thought that Mustafa, too, was too good a man to hurt her in any way. I would expect my mother's brothers to steal from her, but not Mustafa. I don't know what possessed him this time because usually he *is* good. But, thank God, my mother escaped from her brothers. And she and my father and my sisters Rhimu, Nufissa, and Suad returned to the States in 1973. Zubida stayed in Tangier with Abd al-Aziz.

Abd al-Aziz and Zubida lived with Abd al-Aziz's mother in Tangier. And his mother supported them for the first few years because he could not find a job. He is a skilled television repairman and speaks fluent Spanish and French. He graduated from a Spanish school. But he could not find a job in Tangier. So they wrote us asking us to get him a work contract in the States. And he almost got a contract to work in Kuweit. But finally he did get a good job working for a Spanish store in Tangier. He now makes well over 150,000 francs ($333.33) a month, including what he makes fixing televisions on his own. He is very sharp. He once told us how a wealthy Fassi brought him a television to be repaired. Abd al-Aziz looked inside the set and saw that all he had to do was change a little piece that only cost about forty cents. But he told the Fassi that the television was going to require a lot of work and that he would not be able to finish it in less than four days. And he made the Fassi pay him over fifty dollars!

In 1975, it seemed that Abd al-Aziz was going to divorce Zubida because of his mother. One day, Zubida had gone to see a doctor. And she had remained alone with the doctor for a long time, perhaps half an hour. Abd al-Aziz's mother accused Zubida of having sex with the doctor during this time! This was of course ridiculous. And Abd al-Aziz's mother was in no position to criticize any woman for being promiscuous. I think she just wanted an excuse to get rid of Zubida because she wanted to keep the money Abd al-Aziz earned for herself rather than let him spend it on his wife. The relations between a man's mother and his wife are always very tense in Morocco because they both want the man's love as well as his money.

So Abd al-Aziz told Zubida to leave their house! And she went to stay with my cousin Mustafa because my parents and other sisters were in the States and my mother had rented our apartment near the *bulivar* to a policeman. Zubida stayed with Mustafa and his wife Rahma for over a month. And Mustafa is poor. He barely manages to feed his own children. So an extra mouth was a burden. Al-Hajj Muhammad and the *qadi* Muhammad B. arranged for Abd al-Aziz to pay Mustafa 150 francs ($.33) a day for Zubida's food. It is not much money, but for a poor man like Mustafa it makes a difference.

Zubida kept writing my mother, who was in the States, complaining about her situation. And my mother was extremely upset and furious at Abd al-Aziz's mother. So my parents and my sisters Rhimu, Nufissa, and Suad flew back to Tangier to settle the problem in the spring of 1975. And thanks mostly to al-Hajj Muhammad, the problem was settled. Abd al-Aziz agreed to take Zubida back. And he agreed that they would have their own apartment and not live with his mother any more. So they were back together again.

I think Abd al-Aziz and Zubida really love each other. And they seem to be happy. I could not stand to live Zubida's life, but she probably could not stand to live mine. Abd al-Aziz never locks her up at home. But he doesn't have to. The lock is in her mind. She hardly ever leaves the apartment except to go shopping or to go to the steam bath (*al-hammam*). She has a maid to help her—usually a distant cousin from a hill village. And she spends most of her time looking after her three children.

She is very proud of their apartment, for which they paid 22,500 francs ($50) a month in 1977. This is a fortune in the eyes of my mother's family. It is furnished like a working-class American home except for one special room, which is furnished in traditional Moroccan style. She has a huge, shiny brown sofa that you sink into when you sit on it. And she has a thick rug with a gaudy peacock on a bright purple background. She keeps the rug covered with transparent plastic except when special guests come. There is flowery wallpaper on the walls, on which hang glossy copies of paintings by Brueghel. A huge glass chandelier hangs in the modern living room. (Everything was bought on credit.) The whole apartment induces awe on the part of my mother's family. However, Zubida hardly ever sees anyone from my mother's family anymore. Abd al-Aziz makes fun of them and says they are all stupid Jbala. So, except for my mother and my sisters, they only see *his* family and *his* friends.

Abd al-Aziz often brings his cousins and friends to the house to drink whiskey and watch soccer. This is shameful in Morocco. Many men drink with their friends, but not in front of their wives and their wives' sisters as Abd al-Aziz does. Personally, I see nothing wrong with drinking in moderation. But I don't like to see Abd al-Aziz and his friends become drunk and obnoxious in front of my sister. He does not respect her enough. But she does not complain. She seems to adore him. And she considers herself lucky that he took her back and that she lives in such a wonderful apartment with all that glossy furniture.

Zubida is by far the most traditional of my sisters. Although she usually wears western clothes like the rest of us, she still fasts during Ramadan and she would be shocked to know that my other sisters and I do not. She does not object to her husband's getting drunk in front of her with his friends, but she would be shocked to know that I always drink wine with my meals. Once, when Abd al-Aziz had a cold, she bought a chicken and had it sacrificed at the tomb of Sidi Bu Araqiyya, the patron saint of Tangier, in the hope that the saint would cure her husband. My sisters Rhimu and Nufissa thought this was hilarious and they told Zubida that she should have given the chicken to them. They love chicken roasted over a charcoal fire. Zubida is shocked because they smoke cigarettes. *They* are shocked that Zubida would sacrifice a chicken to cure her husband's cold.

5. *Fatima Zohra on her sister Rhimu (1954–),*
university student

RHIMU HAS A DIFFICULT CHARACTER. But she was never as mean as Zubida. And she and I have always been very close, although she never used to confide in me the way I confided in her. When we were little, and when we were together in Belgium and then in the States, I would tell her everything. But I often felt that there were many things that she was afraid to tell me.

Sometimes people are afraid. Rhimu is like that, I think. I don't know. She has always been very pretty and many, many men have wanted to marry her. But she always refuses. Maybe she is afraid to give herself wholly to a man. Maybe she is afraid that a man will control her. She likes to control people. And often she would choose men who were weak so that she could control them. And when she would meet a strong man who refused to let her control him, she was afraid. But that is what she needs: a strong man who would not tolerate any nonsense from her but who would also be gentle and understand her character.

Rhimu attended the American School in Tangier, as did my younger sister Nufissa. They both had scholarships and paid only 10,000 francs ($22.22) a month in tuition. But even this was a fortune in the eyes of most of the family. Everyone said my parents were crazy to waste their money on the education of their daughters. But my mother would simply answer that she had no sons. She and my father hoped that an American education would enable Rhimu and Nufissa to be rich some day and support them in their old age. All Moroccans who can afford to, and even some who cannot, send their children to foreign schools, usually French ones, because such schools are considered to be better than Moroccan ones. Everything from the West is considered to be better than what is from Morocco—except when it comes to religion of course.

The problem is that most of the American students at the American School were spoiled rich children who were more interested in smoking hashish and listening to wild rock music than they were in studying hard. And Rhimu and Nufissa were affected by these young Americans who would never have to support their parents in their old age. Year after year, Rhimu and Nufissa became more and more like these spoiled American children. They never stopped to think how hard my mother had to work to pay their tuition as my father's savings were gradually eaten up. And when they came to the States, they became even more like "hippies"— especially Rhimu. Neither of them knows how to cook or sew. And neither one of them is very sensible, although they have been getting better in recent years because they are beginning to understand what it means to be poor in Morocco.

Rhimu is never satisfied in one place or with one man for a long time. She always becomes restless and wants to change. When she was in the States, she wanted to be in Morocco. And whenever she is in Morocco, she wants to be in the States. Now she is studying at Muhammad V University in Rabat, where she has a government scholarship for about $100 a month. But she wants to finish college in the States.

Rhimu used to have a boy friend who is now a professor at Muhammad V University. Like dozens of other men, he was crazy about her. She says that he was too bossy and that he wanted her to live with his family. And she didn't want to be treated like a servant girl by his mother. I understand this. And she said that despite all his talk about overthrowing the king and creating a revolutionary new society in Morocco, he wanted to keep her cooped up at home just like a traditional Moroccan man. It is true that most of the professors and students at Muhammad V University are full of big talk about revolution, but when it comes to the role of women, they still think like their fathers before them. But, despite his flaws, this young man was really good, I think. And he loved Rhimu, but he was definitely not going to let her control him as she has controlled many of her boy friends in the past. And I think that is what she feared.

I do think that women should have much more freedom than they now have in Morocco. And I do believe that they should be paid the same as men when they do the same work. But when it comes to family, I believe that the man should be the head of the family. He should not be a dictator. He should consult with his wife. But in the end, he should be in charge. He should be the protector of his wife and children. I know many well-educated American women think this is ridiculous. But I don't.

I also think that every woman needs a man just as every man needs a woman. There is nothing sadder than a woman without a man or a man without a woman. And I do not want my sister to remain alone. She still has some very nice boy friends. She should choose the one she loves and marry him and have children. She is already twenty-six years old. She should not wait until she is no longer beautiful and young. It is true that there is more to a woman's life than marriage and motherhood. But I don't think any woman anywhere can really be happy without a husband and children any more than a man can be happy without a wife and children.

6. *Fatima Zohra on her sister Suad (1960–)*

MY SISTER SUAD IS RETARDED. My mother has taken her to many *fqihs*, to many saints, and to many doctors in the hope of curing her. But she cannot be cured. Some people say that her affliction is God's punishment for something bad that my mother did. And my mother is sometimes tormented by the fear that this is true.

Suad is really very sweet. She laughs and laughs at the slightest little thing. This can be annoying, especially if she is laughing at you in public and people start to stare at you. I remember once I was trying on an old skirt that I could no longer fit into. Try as I might, I could not clasp it shut around my waist. I was quite annoyed at myself for having gained weight. And then Suad laughed and laughed and I was annoyed at her. But then my other sisters and my mother started laughing too and I had to laugh with them.

But sometimes Suad really makes me angry. Once I told her to empty the garbage when she was visiting our apartment in Tangier. After twenty minutes, she still hadn't returned. She had met some boy in front of our building, and he thought he would take advantage of her simple-mindedness. He took her to a nearby field. I looked for her all over, as did my husband. Then hours later she came to the door with the empty garbage can in her hand as if nothing had happened. I was furious. And I told my mother not to leave her with me any more. I know it is not her fault. But as much as I love her, she infuriates me.

After that incident, I told my mother that we had to have Suad sterilized at a hospital. My mother was shocked. She said that that would be sinful. And she said that maybe someday God would cure Suad and she could have a husband and children like a normal woman. "Yes," I told my mother, "and maybe someday God will turn my brown eyes blue." Sometimes my mother makes almost as little sense as Suad. She even wanted to marry Suad to a young man in the hope that marriage would cure her. That is what many *fqihs* recommended. The poor girl cannot even dress or wash herself, let alone cook! And my mother wanted to find her a husband! Anyway, I insisted that she have Suad sterilized so that we would never have to worry about her becoming a mother. God forbid! And I paid for the operation.

In 1978, while my mother was in Belgium, Suad was staying with my aunt Suudiyya. And one day my aunt took her with her to a wedding at a village in al-Fahs. In the evening when the dancing girls were dancing, my aunt noticed that Suad was not with her. And she looked for her all over the village. Finally she remembered a deserted shack where the young men of the village would sometimes take the dancing girls. She rushed to it and forced open the door. And there she found Suad lying on the floor half-naked and half-conscious as four young men were hurriedly putting on their pants. She had the *muqaddim* call the police to arrest them. But when they were tried in court, the judge said that there was no proof that they had *forced* Suad to do anything. So he let them go. I was very angry when I heard about this. But I was thankful that I had insisted that Suad be sterilized.

My mother worries about what will happen to Suad when she dies. My sisters all love her as I do. But none of us has much patience with her. But I will always take care of her. I will never let anyone put her in an asylum in Morocco.

It is said that people like Suad are especially blessed by God. And there is a special quality about Suad that makes good people love her. Al-Hajj Muhammad has always been very good to her. And she adores him and his sense of humor. He does somersaults in my mother's living room sometimes and intentionally lands on my mother's lap. We all laugh when he does such things, but especially Suad.

My mother is very close to Suad, although she is sometimes mean to her. She complains that Suad doesn't listen to her. But in a way, Suad is the only one of us who really does listen to my mother and takes her seriously. We all adore my mother. But Rhimu, Nufissa, and I no longer live in her world of saints and spirits (*jnun*). And Zubida has always been distant from all of us. So it is really only with Suad that my mother can speak in her own words.

7. Fatima Zohra on her sister Nufissa (1961–), graduate of the American School in Tangier

MY LITTLE SISTER NUFISSA has always been sweet and gentle and funny. She is also shy. Since she is the youngest, I guess we all spoiled her a little bit. Like Rhimu, she is artistic. Whereas Rhimu paints, Nufissa writes poetry—in English. She writes in English because she attended

American schools all her life. She can hardly write a word of Arabic but she writes English flawlessly. This is common in Morocco. Many of the most famous Moroccan intellectuals speak and write French like Frenchmen because they studied in French schools and universities all their life. But few of them can write more than their name in Arabic. I myself do not write English flawlessly, but I write it much better than I do Arabic. And when my sisters and I write to each other, we always write in English. Zubida is the only one of us who knows how to write Arabic correctly. And Zubida and I hardly ever write each other.

Nufissa was always a very good student until the last years of high school. Then, in part because she had to change schools several times in several years, and in part because she became friendly with American hippies at the American School in Tangier, her grades were less good. She was accepted at an American university, but without a scholarship. So she couldn't go. She hopes to attend an American university next year.

Like Rhimu and me, she loves Morocco, but she finds it difficult to live there. My mother's family insults her because she wears sweaters and blue jeans and rides around Tangier on her motorbike. And she smokes cigarettes in public, even in front of my mother. In the eyes of my mother's relatives, this is like being a prostitute. Nufissa cannot stand this way of thinking.

And she does not like being poor. Since my husband and I returned to the States several years ago, my mother and my sisters (except Zubida) have been very poor. I send them money as often as I can, but I am not rich. I have been trying to arrange all the papers for them to come here to the States, but it takes a long time. I am doing what I can. Once Rhimu and Nufissa come here, they can complete their university educations and work part-time at the same time. That is natural here. But working in Morocco—when you are young and beautiful like Rhimu and Nufissa, and when your father is dead and you have no brothers—can be an unpleasant experience. A very unpleasant experience.

8. Al-Hajj Muhammad on the daughters of al-Hajja Khadduj

WHEN AL-HAJJ M.B. first decided to send his daughters Rhimu and Nufissa to the American School in Tangier, I told him that if he sent his daughters to a Christian school, they would become Christians. He and my aunt Khadduj said no. They said their daughters would meet rich Moroccan men at a Christian school because all rich Moroccans send their children to Christian schools. And they would marry these rich men and support my aunt and al-Hajj M.B. in their old age. Where are those rich husbands? It is true that Zubida is married to Abd al-Aziz, who is rich, and Fatima Zohra's husband in America is rich too. They both own automobiles! But Rhimu and Nufissa are still unmarried and Rhimu is already twenty-six! A woman should be married shortly after she starts to bleed and feel desire for a man. That way she will not get into trouble. A woman needs a man to control and guide her. That is why Rhimu and Nufissa are both crazy. They have no father and no husband to control them. And just as I warned al-Hajj M.B. many, many years ago, they have become like Christians. What Muslim girl would smoke cigarettes in front of her mother as they do?

We should shut all the Christian schools in Morocco and teach our young people only the way of Islam. Until we return to the path of Islam, the Christians will continue to control our stores, our factories, our hotels, our mines, and the minds of our young people.

Someday, God willing, we shall arise and cleanse the house of Islam of all Christian filth. And when we do, all those Muslims who have become like parrots mimicking their Christian masters in this world will have to return to the path of Islam or be punished according to the word of God.

May God guide my cousins, the daughters of my aunt Khadduj, especially Fatima Zohra who is like my own sister, back to the path of Islam. And may He remind Fatima Zohra that her poor cousin, al-Hajj Muhammad the peddler, has no son to provide for him in his old age.

Glossary

(Neither the letter *'ayn* nor the emphatics are distinguished.)

a'ila   Family. This term has the same multiple mean-
                 ings as the English word *family*. It usually refers,
                 however, to all of one's relatives—patrilateral,
                 matrilateral, and affinal. It can also refer to a
                 nuclear family or to all the descendants of one
                 man—through women as well as men. It is in the
                 latter sense that the House of Si Abd Allah is an
                 a'ila. The term derives from the verb *ala*, "to feed
                 and sustain" and "to provide for."

ar   Conditional curse. Generally, this conditional
                 curse is associated with a request. It only be-
                 comes activated when the request is refused.

baraka   Blessedness, holiness. The Prophet Muhammad
                 had more *baraka* than any other man, and his
                 patrilineal descendants (*shurfa*) are said to have
                 inherited his *baraka*. Saints are also believed to
                 possess great *baraka*. (Saints are also usually
                 believed to be descendants of the Prophet.) The
                 concept of *baraka* implies the idea of "purity"
                 (*tahara*).

barraka   Shack, usually built of tin. From Spanish *bar-
                 raca*.

baysar   Mashed fava beans or peas with olive oil, cumin,

	and paprika. *Baysar* is thought of as the food of the poor.
bulivar	Moroccan version of French "Boulevard." In Tangier, this refers to le Boulevard Pasteur, the main street of the new European city, as well as to the new European city as a whole.
Fassis	People from the city of Fez. The core of the Moroccan elite consists of a number of old families from Fez, so "the Fassis" is a term sometimes applied to rich Moroccans in general.
fqih	Teacher of the Quran. A *fqih* also chants the call to prayer and leads the congregational prayers in village and small urban mosques.
Ghmara	Arabic-speaking peasants in the highlands east of the Jbalan highlands.
hadith	Traditions concerning the actions and sayings of the Prophet Muhammad and his companions.
hammam	Public steam bath.
hayyik	Large piece of white cloth worn as an outer garment by women. It has been supplanted by the *jillaba* in cities.
hbus	Inalienable property used for religious and charitable purposes.
hjuba (sing. *hjab*)	Charms consisting of verses from the Quran. *Hjab* (*hijab*) also refers to a woman's veil, but it is not used in this sense in the colloquial Arabic of northern Morocco.
imara (pl. *imarat*)	Annual celebration at the tomb of a saint, known as a *musim* in most of Morocco. As in the case of the Christian "carnival," the religious facet of the *imarat* is sometimes submerged in the general revelry that occurs on such occasions.
irq	Clan (literally, "root" or "blood vessel"). An *irq* is composed of people who claim to have a common patrilineal ancestor, although they cannot demon-

strate such ancestry. An *irq* is, in effect, just a
large number of people with the same surname
but no common rights or obligations. It is thus a
dispersed, noncorporate clan. An *irq* is also referred to as a "circle of patrilineal kinsmen" (*darat
al-ummumiyya*).

Jbala (sing. *Jibli*)	Mountain people or "hillbillies." The Jbala are Arabic-speaking, sedentary agriculturalists in the highlands of northwest Morocco. According to the traditional ethnic stereotypes of Moroccan culture, the Jbala are stupid, ignorant, and generally incompetent.
jihad	Holy war, that is, war between Muslims and infidels. A Muslim who dies fighting in *jihad* is believed to be assured of admission to heaven.
jillaba	Hooded outer robe still worn by traditional Moroccan men and women.
jnun (sing. *jinn*)	Spirits dreaded by traditional Moroccans. (A female *jinn* is a *jinniyya*.)
khalifa (*khlifa*)	Literally, successor, deputy, representative. This is the source of the word *caliph*, the caliphs being the successors and representatives of the prophet Muhammad. This is also an administrative position in Moroccan government.
kif	Marijuana.
madina (*mdina*)	Literally, "city." It now refers to the "old" or "Arab" sections of cities in the Arab world, as opposed to the new, European sections.
mkhazniyya (sing. *mkhazni*)	At the present time, the *mkhazniyya* are uniform-clad employees in government offices. But during the Spanish Protectorate (1912–56) they were also policemen. And the Jbala still tend to refer to any uniformed and armed agents of the government as *mkhazniyya* (literally, "people of the government").

msid	School where the Quran is taught to little boys (and sometimes girls).
muqaddim (*mqaddim*)	From *qaddama*, to precede, to prepare, to tender or proffer. In this book, the word *muqaddim* is used to refer to two distinct categories of people. A *muqaddim*, in the context of the administrative apparatus of the Moroccan state, is a petty official who represents a city ward or a village (or several small villages). A *muqaddim*, in the context of saints' tombs, is a petty official in charge of the tomb and of offerings *to* the tomb. The term *muqaddim* is also used to refer to local leaders of lodges of Sufi brotherhoods.
mwaddaf	White-collar employee with a regular monthly income and a pension plan.
qasba	Citadel, fortress. (*Casbah* is derived from this word.)
qayyid	This is the colloquial form of classical *qa'id*. A *qayyid* is a rural administrator in charge of less important local officials such as *shaykhs* and *muqaddims*. The Jbala are terrified of their *qayyids*.
qbila	This is the classical Arabic word for "tribe" (*qabila*). But the Jbalan *qbila* is simply a territorially and administratively defined district, the inhabitants of which have no tradition of common ancestry.
Rif	Berber-speaking highlands and plains of northeast Morocco. The people of the Rif, or *Rifis*, are regarded as violent and dangerous by the Arabic-speaking Jbala.
sbaybi	Peddler, a poor merchant who buys small quantities of goods only to sell them at a marginal profit.
sdaq	Brideprice. Money given to the bride's father by the groom's father.

shaykh	Literally, "venerable old man." Like *muqaddim*, the word has both secular and religious meanings. In the secular, administrative sense, a *shaykh* is an official in charge of all the *muqaddims* in a rural commune (a commune consisting of a segment of a *qbila*.) In the religious sense, a *shaykh* is either a venerated Sufi mystic or a religious scholar (*alim*). (In bedouin societies a *shaykh* is a tribal chief.)
shurfa (sing. *sharif*)	Patrilineal descendants of the Prophet Muhammad by way of his daughter Fatima and his patrilateral cousin and son-in-law Ali. *Shurfa* are honored and regarded as pure and sinless—in theory at any rate.
siba	Anarchy, violence. Jbala sometimes refer to the time before the Spanish Protectorate as "the time of anarchy" (*waqt as-siba*). But this expression is also used to refer to the many years of resistance to the Spanish Protectorate (1913–26).
Susi (pl. *Swasa*)	A man from the Sus valley in southern Morocco. The Swasa are often grocers or other types of merchants in the cities of northern Morocco. They are regarded as being cunning and avaricious.
tajin	A brown earthenware serving dish with a lid. The word is also used to refer to any stew cooked and/or served in such a dish.
talib (pl. *tulba*)	A man who has memorized the entire Quran. Such men often earn money chanting the Quran at the "rites of passage" of Islam.
tarrah	A boy who carries bread to and from the public oven.
twaza (*twiza*)	A traditional system of labor whereby villagers would work for a fellow villager in return for a hearty meal.
ulama (*ulama'*)	Religious scholars. *Ulama* is the plural of *alim*, "one who knows."

Bibliography

The definite article *al* (*el*) is ignored in alphabetization.

al-Banna, Hasan
   1965   *Rasa'il al-Imam ash-Shahid Hasan al-Banna* (Epistles
             of the martyred leader Hasan al-Banna). Beirut: Dar
             al-Andalus.
Ben Barka, El-Mehdi
   1968   *The Political Thought of Ben Barka.* Havana: Tricon-
             tinental Publishers.
Bickerman, Elias
   1947   *The Maccabees: An Account of Their History from the
             Beginnings to the Fall of the House of the Hasmoneans.*
             Translated by Moses Hadas. New York: Schocken
             Books.
Boularès, Habib
   1981   Le Roi a toutes les cartes. *Jeune Afrique,* no. 1070
             (8 July 1981): 14–15.
Brown, Kenneth L.
   1976   *People of Salé: Tradition and Change in a Moroccan
             City 1830–1930.* Manchester: Manchester University
             Press.
al-Bu Ayyashi, Ahmad
   1976   *Harb ar-Rif at-Tahririyya wa Marahil an-Nidal: al-Juz'
             ath-thani* (The liberation war of the Rif and the stages
             of the struggle: part two). Tangier: Abd as-Slam Jasus
             (Guessous) and Sochepresse.

Chomsky, Noam
1974   *Peace in the Middle East? Reflections on Justice and Nationhood.* New York: Pantheon Books.
Chouraqui, André
1973   *Between East and West: A History of the Jews of North Africa.* Translated by Michel Bernet. New York: Atheneum.
Crapanzano, Vincent
1973   *The Hamadsha: A Study in Moroccan Ethnopsychiatry.* Berkeley and Los Angeles: University of California Press.
1980   *Tuhami: Portrait of a Moroccan.* Chicago: University of Chicago Press.
Daniel, Norman
1960   *Islam and the West: The Making of an Image.* Edinburgh: Edinburgh University Press.
Eickelman, Dale
1976   *Moroccan Islam: Tradition and Society in a Pilgrimage Center.* Austin: University of Texas Press.
1981   *The Middle East: An Anthropological Approach.* Englewood Cliffs, N.J.: Prentice-Hall.
Etienne, Bruno, and Mohamed Tozy
1980   Le Glissement des obligations islamiques vers le phénomène associatif à Casablanca. *L'Annuaire de l'Afrique du Nord* 18 (1979): 235–59.
Europa
1981   *The Middle East and North Africa 1981–82.* London: Europa Publications Limited.
Falwell, Jerry
1981   Future Word: An Agenda for the Eighties. In *The Fundamentalist Phenomenon: The Resurgence of Conservative Christianity,* edited by Jerry Falwell, pp. 186–223. Garden City, N.Y.: Doubleday.
Fanon, Frantz
1952   *Peau noire, masques blancs.* Paris: Editions du Seuil.
al-Faruqi, Ismail
1979   *Islam.* Allen, Texas: Argus Communications.